THE REAL THOMAS PAINE

THE REAL
THOMAS
PAINE

JOSEPH M. HENTZ

iUniverse, Inc.
New York   Bloomington

The Real Thomas Paine

iUniverse books may be ordered through booksellers or by contacting:

iUniverse
1663 Liberty Drive
Bloomington, IN 47403
www.iuniverse.com
1-800-Authors (1-800-288-4677)

ISBN: 978-1-4502-2644-8 (sc)
ISBN: 978-1-4502-2642-4 (dj)
ISBN: 978-1-4502-2643-1 (ebk)

Registered Copyright Number: txu 1-587-005

Printed in the United States of America

iUniverse rev. date: 04/30/2010

CONTENTS

PREFACE

The purpose of this study is to show that Thomas Paine is the Founder of the United States of America. By this, I mean that Thomas Paine should be credited with the recognition and gratitude as being the originator of the integrated idea and plan to create the United States.

Many colonists were persuaded to adopt Paine's ideas and they followed his lead. Among these converts, there were a courageous group of men, who have, by way of tradition been called "Founding Fathers." The most notable men in this group include: Benjamin Franklin, George Washington, John Adams, Thomas Jefferson, James Madison and James Monroe. These and other brave patriots of the American Revolution were converted to Paine's Plan to separate from Great Britain and establish the United States as a Free and Independent, Democratic Republic. As regards the, so called Founders Fathers, they were, really following fathers.

I fully agree that these wonderful men, and also, the self-sacrificing women who supported them, deserve "The love and thanks of men and women". But, it was Thomas Paine who was first, who lead the way; and who is the real Founder and creator in sole, of the United States of America.

Thomas Paine was an innovator and an inventor. "Every pamphlet of Paine's was in the nature of an invention, by which principles of liberty

- 1 -

and equality were framed in constructions adapted to emergencies of a republic." (Conway, p.91 & 92) The ideas and methods to create the United States are all contained in his immortal *Common Sense*. They were given in plain, explicit language. Taken together, they form an original integrated 'Blueprint' for a new Nation, designed to be governed by the people of that nation; without a King.

The component parts of Thomas Paine's integrated plan are as follows: Separation, Independence, Declaration, Unity, Eliminate Monarchic rule and succession, forge a Constitution to establish a Democratic Republic with Freedom, Liberty, Equality, and Security, in order to protect and preserve the Natural and Civil rights of all; Build a Navy; and wage a defensive war until victory is won in order to secure the Independence. Finally, do it now, "for the time hath found us."

GRATITUDE

Frances Theresa Sauter Hentz merits my first expression of thanks. Without her support, patience, advice, corrections, and flawless typing, I could not have completed this project. I acknowledge a special debt of gratitude to: my daughter Kathleen and my son Michael Max for their expert help in organizing the work; to my children Joseph, Jeanne, Chris, Michael Max and Kathleen for their encouragement, support and their forbearance of my obsessive talk about Thomas Paine for over fifteen years; to the multi-talented, intellectual Agnes Lou, for providing the color reproduction of the cover portrait of Thomas Paine, as taken from William Sharp's engraving after George Romney's 1792 portrait; to Major Johnson for his kind and scholarly assistance in locating key and hard to find supporting citations; to Penelope DeMeules for finding the *Tom's Words* article in the Los Angeles Times; to the genuine scholars such as Moncure Daniel Conway, Harvey J. Kay, Greg Nelson, William Woodward and the others as listed in the Bibliography who did the hardest parts, namely, digging out the basic biographical evidence used to describe the life of Thomas Paine.

Most of all, I owe a large debt of gratitude to Andrew J. Galambos. Without the knowledge and impetus gained from the lectures about Thomas Paine, given by Professor Galambos, founder of the Free Enterprise Institute, I would not have started to write about Thomas Paine.

CHAPTER 1
A SERIOUS THOUGHT

O ctober 18, 1775
"When I reflect on the horrid cruelties exercised by Britain in the East Indies – How thousands perished – How religion and every manly principle of honor and honesty were sacrificed to luxury and pride – When I reflect on these and a thousand instances of similar barbarity, I firmly believe that the Almighty, in compassion to mankind, will curtail the power of Britain" (Writings, V. 2, p. 195 & 196)

Paine continues his reflections. "She (Britain) hath basely tampered with the passions of the Indians. (She hath) imposed on their ignorance, and made them tools of treachery and murder. She hath employed herself in the most horrid of all traffics, that of human flesh, unknown to the most savage nations, (and) hath yearly – without provocation and in cold blood – ravaged the hapless shores of Africa, robbing it of its unoffending inhabitants to cultivate her stolen dominions in the West." "When I reflect on these, I hesitate not for a moment to believe that the Almighty will finally separate America from Britain."

"Call it INDEPENDENCE* or what you will, if it is the cause of God and humanity it will go on." (V.2, p.196) "And when the Almighty shall have blest us (with Independence), then may our first gratitude be shown by an act of continental legislation which shall put a stop to the

* caps mine

importation of negroes for sale, soften the hard fate of those already here, and in time procure their FREEDOM*." (V 2, p. 196)

It is noted that Thomas Paine used the term "The Almighty" three times while he scorned earthly kings. Damn the souls of those who call Thomas Paine an atheist. Paine never wavered in his fervent and worshipful belief in God.

"A Serious Thought" is a timeless masterpiece in only two pages. It should be taught and explained in schools. It is an early (October 18, 1775) and a powerful call for Separation, Independence, Emancipation and Mercy and Justice for native American Indians. It provides substantial PROOF that Thomas Paine is the true author of the Declaration of Independence and the original and independent founder of the United States of America.

---

* caps mine

CHAPTER 2
AN EARLY CALL
FOR INDEPENDENCE

In his *A Serious Thought* essay Thomas Paine wrote, "I hesitate not for a moment to believe that the Almighty will finally separate America from Britain. Call it Independency or what you will, if it is the cause of God and humanity it will go on." This article was published on October 18, 1775. Paine had finished the first part of *Common Sense* in October 1775. Both of these works leave no doubt that Paine's INTENT was to achieve independence; eliminate the king; and replace the monarchic form with a new system of government.

When we consider that the majority of the Colonists were loyalists, the creation of a Republic was no easy task. Centuries of regal tradition and unicultural schooling, coupled with volitional inertia and personal interests, worked against serious and open-minded consideration of any alternative to reconciliation. Paine: "their (the colonists) idea of grievance operated without resentment, and their single object was reconciliation...I had no thoughts of independence or arms. The world could not then have persuaded me that I should be either a soldier or an author. If I had any talents for either, they were buried in me, and might ever have continued so, had not the necessity of the times dragged and driven them into ACTION*. But when the country, into which I had

---

*   caps mine

just set my foot, was set on fire about my ears, it was time to stir. It was time for every man to stir." (Conway, p. 330)

It is understandable why the Colonists would be no more receptive to ending Royal Rule than present day Americans would be receptive to, and agree with the proposition that: We do not need a president. Paine had his work cut out for him. Resistance to change would be formidable. A proclamation of unconditional separation from Great Britain, though absolutely necessary, would be met with stiff opposition. Of course Paine was not deterred. One of the reasons why Paine was incontestably persuasive was that he was convinced that America would secede from Great Britain sooner or later. He knew, also, that Britain would escalate the war. More British troops were on the way. With unanswerable logic, Paine showed that to wage a murderous war, just to achieve the 'status quo', would be the height of folly. The Colonies were already at war with Britain. As Colonies, America was held in a step down or inferior position as a subordinate part of the British Empire. Reconciliation with Britain would mean that America, even if victorious, would go from the frying pan of subordination into the fire of war, and then back into the frying pan of submission. The word reconciliation appears nineteen times in *Common Sense*. Paine exploded the idea "as a fallacious dream".

We have an explicit written record of Thomas Paine's "blueprint" showing his intention to create the "Independent States of America". That record carries the title: Common Sense. No such comparable plan was forthcoming from Washington, Adams, Jefferson, or even, from Benjamin Franklin. Moreover, it was Thomas Paine's intention to consolidate the states into a constitutional union, governed by the people as a Democratic Republic.

Thank you, Doctor Paine for giving us a country!

On July 4th 1780, the University of Pennsylvania awarded Thomas Paine with an honorary Master of Arts degree. They should have awarded him an honorary Doctorate degree.

CHAPTER 3
REBELLION
TO REVOLUTION

B ecause various writers attribute a variety of causes for the American Revolution, my esteem for Dr. Moncure Daniel Conway urges me to single out his opinion on the matter as related to William Cobbett's view.

Conway wrote, "Paine's unique service in the work of independence may now be clearly defined. It was that he raised the Revolution into an evolution." (Conway, p.24) Thomas Paine's service also converted a rebellion into a revolution in order for the colonies to unite and separate from England and create a new, sovereign and independent country of their own. Conway also wrote, "After the 'Lexington massacre', separation was talked of by many." (p.24) However, "the members of congress were of the rich conservative 'gentry' and royalists". These men as well as Quakers and Tories were only thinking of reconciliation with England. All of them had to be converted because Thomas Paine was determined to create a new country to be governed, not by a king, but by the people themselves.

"MR. PAINE AND MR. PAINE ALONE"

From Moncure Daniel Conway's *The Life of Thomas Paine*, I learned about William Cobbett. Cobbett wrote a libelous biographical work about Thomas Paine which was published in Philadelphia in 1796. Years later, Cobbett, having learned that he was deceived into writing slanders about Paine, reversed his position and became a convert to Paine's ideas and extolled Thomas Paine's achievements.

Conway quoted a paragraph, taken from Cobbett's writings, in which Cobbett named three causes of the American Revolution. They are as follows. The first was the taxation problem. Secondly, "beastly insults' to Thomas Paine were a cause. Thirdly, the principles in the minds of the colonists were a cause. Cobbett then wrote, "Still it was Mr. Paine and Mr. Paine alone, who brought those principles into action." (Conway, p.24)

William Cobbett's statement is a powerful proof of Thomas Paine's priority in creating the United States.

CHAPTER 4
THE PLAN
TO CREATE THE
UNITED STATES

After the Battles of Lexington and Concord, April 19, 1775, Thomas Paine recognized that the American Colonies were at war with Great Britain and that a peaceful reconciliation with Her, with total independence for America, was impossible. Moreover, Paine correctly concluded that Britain's aim was nothing less than total conquest of the American Colonies. He foresaw that, if it were possible, Britain would pursue a course of action that would go beyond annexing the eastern seaboard of America. This would mean an attempt by the King for exploitative subjugation of, and imperial control over, the entire North American Continent.

It was at this time that Thomas Paine made up his mind and set his course. He wrote, "No man was a warmer wisher for a reconciliation than myself, before the fatal nineteenth of April, 1775, but the moment the event of that day was made known, I rejected the hardened, sullen-tempered Pharaoh of England forever; and disdain the wretch, that with the pretended title of Father of his people, can unfeelingly hear of their slaughter, and composedly sleep with their blood upon his soul." (*Common Sense*, Barnes & Noble, p.33)

Soon after April 19th, 1775 – and I assume no later than June, 1775 – Thomas Paine began collecting his thoughts, those incipient ideas which would form the innovative plan for a new nation. His exertions resulted in his immortal *Common Sense* which was published on January 10th, 1776. In this nonpareil production, Thomas Paine outlined his design specifications for the creation of a new country. The outline was no mere adumbration. It was an explicit blueprint integrated in order to achieve "something better". (*CS*, p.37)

The "something better" would not only be a new country, it would have a new form of government, which would be government by the people. Instead of government from the "top down", the government would be from the "bottom up", as repeated many times over, "government of, by and for the people". Such a system means "Democracy" and as practiced in the United States, Representative Democracy. Either way, there was a turning around from Autocracy to a form of Democracy. The creation of the United States of America was a Revolution.

Thomas Paine knew that the King along with the monarchic system had to be eliminated. Unfortunately, he knew that a defensive war was necessary. He wrote, "No going to law with nations; canon are the barristers of crown, and the sword not of justice, but of war, decides the suite." (*CS*, p.64)

For Thomas Paine, there was only one course of action to take. For him the only answer was the establishing of a new independent country. He wrote, "If there is any true cause of fear respecting independence, it is because no PLAN* is yet laid down." (*CS*, p.37) Because Thomas Paine did not think anyone else could do it – "no one was up to the mark" – he took it upon himself to devise a step by step plan to create the United States of America. The elements of Paine's plan are described as follows. (*Life & Writings*, Centenary edition, V. 8, p.69)

---

*   caps mine

SEPARATION: The colonies should unite and agree to secede from Great Britain because a new country was in the process of being formed.

INDEPENDENCE: Establish a totally free, independent and sovereign nation.

DECLARATION: "...nothing can settle our affairs so expeditiously as an open, and determined declaration for independence". (*CS*, p.51)

ELIMINATE ROYALTY: Thomas Paine devoted all of Chapter II, - "Of monarchy and Hereditary Succession", - to proving that America does not need a King. "Of more worth is one honest man to society, and in the sight of God, than all the crowned ruffians that ever lived." (*CS*, p.20)

DEMOCRACY: A Democratic Republic would replace monarchy and equal voting rights would insure that "...every man by natural right will have a seat." (in Congress) (*CS*, p.3)

EQUALITY: Laws and voting rights should apply to all, equally, without distinction. "Mankind being originally equals, in the order of creation, the equality could only be destroyed by some subsequent circumstance..." (*CS*, p.9)

SECURITY: Protection of people and property is a basic function of government. "Wherefore, security being the true design and end of government..." (*CS*, p.2) "...here too is the design and end of government, viz. freedom and security." (*CS*, p.4) "...let their business be to frame a Continental Charter...securing freedom and property to all men, and above all things, the free exercise of religion..." (*CS*, p.39)

FREEDOM: Freedom is necessary for life and the pursuit of happiness. "...the design and end of government, viz. freedom and security. (*CS*, p.4) "Freedom hath been haunted round the globe." (*CS*, p.42) "...and of the FREE AND INDEPENDENT STATES OF AMERICA*." (*CS*, p.67)

SIMPLICITY: "I draw my idea of the form of government from a principle in nature, which no art can overturn, viz. that the more simple any thing is, the less liable it is to be disordered; and the easier repaired when disordered..."(*CS*, p.4)

ECONOMY: Government "with the least expense and greatest benefit, is preferable to all others." (*CS*, p.2)

MOBILIZE: WAGE A DEFENSIVE WAR AGAINST England until the colonies achieve victory. "No going to law with nations; canon are the barristers of crown; and the sword, not of justice, but of war, decides the suit." (*CS*, p.64)

CONSTITUTION: "...let a Continental Conference be held..." (*CS*, p.38) "...let their business be to frame a continental Charter..." (*CS*, p.39) "In a former page (*CS*,p.38) I threw out a few thoughts on the propriety of a Continental Charter...as a bond of solemn obligation, which the whole enters into, to support the right of every separate part, whether of religion, personal freedom, or property." (*CS*, p.53)

RELIGION: "...Let their business be to frame a Continental Charter... securing freedom and property to all men, and above all things, the free exercise of religion..." (*CS*, p.39) A dozen pages later, Paine wrote, "As to religion, I hold it to b the indispensable duty of all governments,

---

*   caps mine

to protect all conscientious professors thereof, and I know of no other business which government hath to do therewith." (*CS*, p.52)

NAVY: "Let us build…" (*CS*, p.46) Thomas Paine devoted seven pages of *Common Sense* to urge the Colonists to build their own navy. This part was a compelling argument for unity and Independence. The reasons given, the logic, and the conclusion were indisputable.

REPUBLIC: To replace the British monarchic government in America, Paine opted to create a Representative Republic as the best way to achieve democracy at that time. He wrote that the new government: "being empowered by the people will have a truly legal authority". (*CS*, p.39) Because increases in population, public issues and distances would make it inconvenient for all voters to meet in one place, the legislative function would be managed by elected representatives, "who are supposed to have the same concerns at stake which those have who appointed them, and who will act in the same manner as the whole body would were they present." (*CS*, p.3)

As regards both elections and representatives of every rank, Thomas Paine proposed some explicit constraints. In the case of elections, frequency was advised, and he wrote, "Prudence will point out the propriety of having elections often." (*CS*, p.4) In the case of elected representatives, Paine wrote, "I have heretofore likewise mentioned the necessity of large and equal representation…." (*CS*, p.53)

Annual elections and broad and equal representation would have served to insure the elected official's fidelity to the people of his or her district; result in short terms; and obviate the need for career politicians.

TRADE and COMMERCE: Paine wrote, "Our PLAN* is commerce", and "…it is in the interest of all Europe to have America a free port." (*CS*, p.26) and "…peace with trade is preferable to war without it." (*CS*, p.60)

---

* caps mine

Thomas Paine integrated all of the elements described above into a cohesive plan to create a new country. In order to achieve the goal of a free, independent and sovereign country, Paine designed a step by step program, made up of a series of actions which resulted in the establishment of the United States of America. Moreover, the new country would employ a new system of governance which would unconditionally end monarchic rule. There would be no need for a King, or any other kind of autocrat, however described, however named. By hindsight, we know that the birth of America was something new, revolutionary, and indeed, an innovation. Also the integrated plan, as contained in Common Sense, to unite the thirteen British colonies in America, in order to form the Nation of the United States, was an innovation.

This is not to say that all of the targeted goals, as specified in *Common Sense*, were achieved as soon as Independence was declared. By way of examples, women's suffrage and emancipation would come later and short terms of office for elected politicians have yet to be implemented. In a letter to Jefferson, Richard Henry Lee expressed his disappointment in the approved copy of the Declaration. He wished that, "the Manuscript had not been mangled as it is. However the Thing, is in its nature so good, that no cookery can spoil the Dish for the palate of Freemen." (Lewis, p.164) In spite of the many corrections, additions and deletions in the adopted version of the Declaration of Independence, it, and the creation of America itself, were so powerful that they changed the world.

The basic elements, the building blocks, necessary to construct America are briefly restated here. They are: Unite and separate from England, Prepare a manifesto declaring the cession to the world, Cashier the King, Eliminate monarchic government, Wage a defensive war against England; Create a Democratic Republic; Prepare an amendable National constitution which would provide the rules which would secure and guarantee the natural and civil rights of all of the people without distinction, so long as the exercise of those rights did not interdict the rights of others.

Thomas Paine had included all of the above mentioned components in his *Common Sense* before the end of 1775. No one else had the requisite integrated PLAN. Accordingly, we must eliminate Washington, John Adams, Sam Adams, Jefferson, Benjamin Franklin, Patrick Henry, Robert Livingston, Roger Sherman, the signers of the Declaration of Independence, other than those listed above, and any other patriot, as an original Founder of the United States of America. Only Thomas Paine deserves the title: FOUNDER. It was his idea.

It was Thomas Paine's idea to turn historical political systems upside down. Instead of government administered by the political elite from the 'top down', government would be conducted and controlled by the people from the bottom up. That is, in other words, government of and by the people, within whom the natural power of governance resides. The plan for the formation of such a government came from the mind and heart of Thomas Paine.

The result, the construct, would be a country in which the "advance from that subordination" under a distant nation would allow for a level of societal Freedom and Liberty which was unique in the history of political nations and which would, by securing the natural and civil rights, of all of its citizens, provide an unprecedented opportunity for individuals to select the way they wanted to pursue their own happiness.

As we have seen, Thomas Paine created the complete plan in order to establish the United States; and he was the first person to do it. There is no evidence, prior to *Common Sense*, that Franklin, Washington, Adams or Jefferson, or any one else, designed a comprehensive plan in order to attain Independence or had the work published in pamphlet form and then worked to enhance the original composition in order to increase circulation and readership.

Common Sense is considered by many to be the most powerful and efficacious piece of persuasive rhetoric ever penned. I concur, and my opinion is that it has not been equaled. It changed the minds of many of the Colonists from reconciliation and subordination to separation and Independence. It produced a strong a consensus of those who were in favor of Independence. My opinion is that the Loyalists were in the majority. No matter, the delegates to congress believed or chose to believe that they were acting in harmony with the will of the people and unanimously voted for Independence.

No one credits Benjamin Franklin as the one who introduced a concrete step by step plan to establish the United States. The rejected "Albany Plan" of 1754 was an attempt to unite the BRITISH COLONIES in America under the rule of Great Britain, not as a separate, independent, and sovereign nation. In retrospect, Thomas Paine wrote, "In October, 1775...I had then formed the outlines of *Common Sense*, and finished nearly the first part; and as I supposed the doctor's (FRANKLIN) design in getting out a history was to open the new year with a new system, I expected to surprise him with a production on that subject much earlier than he thought." (Nelson, p.80)

By the end of 1775, Thomas Paine and Benjamin Franklin had become fast friends. Paine gave the first copy off the press of Common Sense to Franklin. My guess is that Benjamin Franklin was delightfully surprised, and I am not aware that he raised any objections or proposed any changes to Paine's immortal *Common Sense*. The following quote by Benjamin Franklin appears on page VIII of Joseph Lewis' book: "Others can rule, others can fight, but only Thomas Paine can write for us the English tongue." No citation was given and we can not assume authenticity. However, I trust Joseph Lewis.

George Washington did not provide a plan to establish the United States. He had his hands full trying to win a war with a part-time army, no navy, and lacking enough guns, ammunition, food and supplies to mount a sustained offensive. Americans owe to Washington a transport of credit and gratitude for what he was able to accomplish and for his perseverance.

Thomas Jefferson deserves credit and appreciation for his part in aiding the American Revolution. However he did not formulate a plan to secede from Great Britain.

John Adams failed to design a plan to create a Democratic Republic. After he had read Common sense, Adams became a convert in favor of total Independence; admitted that he could not have written it in "so manly and striking a style;" and then boasted that he would have made a better ARCHITECT of the work to construct an Independent Nation.

Of course John Adams was entitled to his opinion. Perhaps he could have been a better architect. Would Adams have devised a plan such that Slavery would be abolished when Independence was declared? This and many other questions could be asked because we view the events of 1776 from hindsight. In any case, Adams was too late. Thomas Paine's plan can be dated from April 19, 1775 – "The Lexington Massacre" – John Adams did not become a full convert to total Independence for over a year after that. In a letter to Abigail Adams on April 29, 1776, he wrote, "*Common Sense*...has come in seasonably to clear our doubts, and to FIX OUR CHOICE*." Adams was envious of Thomas Paine's achievement and he grew to hate him. Craig Nelson, in his excellent biography of Thomas Paine wrote, "Adams will in time have many terrible things to say about Paine, just as he had many dreadful things to say about nearly everyone he ever knew save Abigail..." (Nelson, p.95)

John Adams wanted to be remembered and credited as being the "stand alone", original and sole creator of the United States of America. He wasn't. Thomas Paine was.

---

*   caps mine

CHAPTER 5
CREATING A NATION
A BEGINNING

Freedom, Liberty and humanitarianism were part of Thomas Paine's make-up and part of his life. These qualities are indisputably manifested in his ageless essay, *African Slavery in America*. This essay was written a little over three months after Paine arrived in America on November 30, 1774. He began assisting Robert Aitkin with his new publication, *The Pennsylvania Magazine*, in January, 1775. At this time, Paine was well aware of the serious problems between Britain and America. Later, Paine would recall that the "single object (of the Colonists) was reconciliation". (Conway, p.330) Paine was busy writing and editing articles for *The Pennsylvania Magazine*. He did nothing about reconciliation or Independence until April 19, 1775. In retrospect he wrote, "I had no thoughts of Independence or arms. The world could not then have persuaded me that I should be either a soldier or an author." (p.330)

After April 19, 1775, Paine reversed his position. He would become an author and a soldier. He would do a lot more than that. He would create a new Country. He decided to establish a new independent, sovereign nation. It was an iron-clad resolution. The idea was a personal innovation. His decision was final and irreversible. Working alone, Thomas Paine originated a step by step blueprint in order to construct a country which would not have a king and which would be governed by the consent of its people. Paine's idea was to create a Democratic Republic.

Paine's first step was to formulate a design plan in order to achieve his goal. Then, he would consume himself in order to bring his creation to fruition. With indomitable will he would work until the complete establishment of the United States of America was accomplished.

Thomas Paine was already at work preparing the first step of his plan for separation from Great Britain and Independence when he published another essay. It was a very brief, but powerful article, entitled, *A Serious Thought*. It was published in the Pennsylvania Journal of October 18, 1775. In it Paine wrote, "...I hesitate not for a moment to believe that the Almighty will finally separate America from Britain. Call it independence or what you will, if it is the cause of God and humanity it will go on." (Foner, Vol 2, p.20)

I heartily agree with Doctor Philip S. Foner, who, in his admirable opus, *The Complete Writings of Thomas Paine*, stated that, "...it is definite evidence that Paine was thinking at this time (October 18, 1775) of separation of the Colonies from Great Britain."(p.20)

Thomas Paine was not the first one to use the words Separation and Independence. The ideas of separation and independence from Great Britain were not new. These subjects had been discussed, mainly in negative terms, for years before 1775. Historical evidence shows that most of the Colonists were against separation and independence. Prior to 1776, these subjects described something to disavow, or avoid, or oppose, or shun, or repudiate, or refrain from, or as hobgoblins. The subjects of Separation and Independence were considered treasonous and seditious. The Colonists were well aware of the penalty for such crimes; it was death by hanging. Thomas Paine, boldly, brought these subjects out in the open in his article, *A Serious Thought*.

It was no less dangerous to speak of dethroning the King. It is my opinion that talk of eliminating the King was scarce prior to January 10,

1776. If the subject were brought up, my guess is that it was discussed quietly, with discretion and, hopefully, in confidence.

In a few months, Thomas Paine would totally refute the need for a King. He went further. Paine debunked the idea of monarchic rule altogether and he disintegrated the idea of hereditary monarchy. This was done in *Common Sense.*

For now, it was enough to introduce the idea of Separation from England in a news vehicle that was available for public consumption. Paine considered the Press "the tongue of the word, and that which governs the sentiments of mankind more than anything else that ever did or can exist." The Press, the tongue of the world, citation is taken from a long and informative letter by Thomas Paine to Major-General Nathanael Greene, dated September 9, 1780. This is an amazing letter. It is a gem. For any student of Thomas Paine's works, it provides special insights into Paine's virtuous and valorous character. The extracted quote follows: "Now there is no other method to give this information a national currency but through the channel of the press, which I have ever considered the tongue of the world, and which governs the sentiments of mankind more than anything else that ever did or can exist" (Foner, p. 1189) [of course, today, one might use the word MEDIA instead of PRESS]

To my understanding, none of the so called Founding Fathers, including George Washington, Thomas Jefferson and John Adams, were writing articles advocating separation and independence in 1775; and then submitting these articles to the newspapers for general publication. *A Serious Thought* provides explicit evidence in support of proof that Thomas Paine was first and alone with the idea of creating America.

CHAPTER 6
CREATING A NATION
COMMON SENSE

C*ommon Sense* did it all; well almost. It changed the world. Historically, we know that for America there would be no turning back. The birth of a new nation was at hand. Ah! Hindsight, how wonderful it is. But it would be years before the United States achieved the status of an operationally secure and sovereign country.

Common Sense was published on January 10, 1776. From M. D. Conway, we learn that Dr. Benjamin Rush said, "*Common Sense* burst from the press with an effect which has rarely been produced by types and paper in any age or country." (p.25) Paine, himself, wrote, "Perhaps there never was a pamphlet, since the use of letters were known, about which so little pains were taken, and of which so great a number went off in so short a time. I am certain that I am within compass when I say one hundred and twenty thousand." (p.28) When I re-read the clause in the above quoted paragraph, "about which so little pains were taken", I have to chuckle. What a masterpiece *Common Sense* is. Paine's exertions during the fall season of 1775 seem monumental to me. I think it was a work of love. Perhaps the exhilaration of creating something new crowded out the discomforts of his labors. Thomas Paine had a peculiar habit of down-playing his achievements and productions, and, at times, he deflected credit due to himself, to others. Whatever value

Paine placed on *Common Sense*, his will specified that the head-stone of his grave should be engraved with his name and age and "author of *Common Sense*".

As to the number of copies of *Common Sense* that were printed, almost every biography of Thomas Paine provides estimates that run into hundreds of thousands. In *Crisis Thirteen*, April 19, 1783, Paine reflected, "It was the cause of America that made me an author," and "a Declaration of Independence made it impossible for me, feeling as I did, to be silent." (Conway, p.88) The colonists were not thinking of Independence; "their single object was reconciliation."

They wanted to reconcile with Great Britain. The thirteen colonies were not a constitutionally united nation. A constitution which was proposed and explicitly described in two separate instances in *Common Sense* would not be adopted until thirteen years later. The war was a problem. Most of the people were against that too. The war dragged on for five years after Independence was declared. Without French aid, the war would have lasted longer. France, that is to say King Louis XVI, provided aid in the form of an army, supplies, money, arms and generalship.

The Declaration itself would be no problem. Thomas Paine would compose that himself. He had written, "…but many strong and striking reasons may be given to shew (sic) that nothing can settle our affairs so expeditiously as an open and determined declaration for independence." (*Common Sense*)

The open and determined Declaration of Independence was composed by Thomas Paine. The component parts of the Declaration are contained in *Common Sense*. It was Paine who was determined to achieve independence and declare the fact to the world. It was Thomas Paine who was the only one who could compose the Declaration. No one else was up to the mark.

I refuse to believe that Thomas Paine would relegate such an epoch-making manifesto to a lawyer, or a staffer, or a clerk, or a political intern. After all, independence now was Paine's ideological innovation. He could not risk having an appointee obfuscate his humanitarian concepts of equality; natural and civil rights of all individuals; the basic and essential purpose of government and republican democracy, such that the government "being empowered by the people will have a truly legal authority." (*Common Sense*, Anchor Press, p.40) The clause, "Governments are instituted among men, deriving their just powers from the consent of the governed:" appears in both the John Adams and the Jefferson copies of Thomas Paine's original Declaration of Independence.

Some ten years later, February 18, 1786 in his *Dissertations on Government*, Paine wrote, "in republics, such as those established in

America, the sovereign power, or the power over which there is no control, and which controls all others, remains where nature placed it – in the people; for the people in America are the fountain of power." (Foner, Vol.2, p.369)

CONSTITUTION

A national constitution was proposed by Thomas Paine in *Common Sense*, two separate times. On page forty he wrote, "Let a continental conference be held…let their business be to frame a continental charter or Charter of the United Colonies." Ten pages later he wrote, "In page forty, I threw out a few thoughts on the propriety of a Continental Charter,…as a bond of solemn obligation, which the whole enters into, (in the case of America, all fifty states), to support the right of every separate part (each and every state), whether of religious freedom, or property." *(Common Sense*, p.40, 50)

Again, we see that Thomas Paine was first to propose a constitution. It was an essential component of his plan to create the United States. None of the so-called founding fathers were calling for a constitution which would effect the unification of the thirteen separate colonies.

George Washington did not offer such an idea. He was in the field. In a letter to Washington, dated July 30, 1796, Paine wrote, "But as to the point of consolidating the states into a Federal Government, it so happens, that the proposition for that purpose came ORIGINALLY FROM MYSELF.* I proposed it in a letter Chancellor Livingston in the spring of 1782, while that gentleman was Minister for Foreign Affairs". (Foner, Vol.2, p.692)

A DEMOCRATIC REPUBLIC

Unification of the colonies was at the top of the list of steps needed for creating America. He had written, "The Continental Belt is too loosely buckled". (*Common Sense*, p.57) Jefferson worked on constitutions for Virginia. There is scant evidence that he was interested in a National constitution or the establishment of the United States as a Democratic Republic. (Randall, p.250) In 1784, Jefferson wrote, "It is well known that, in July, 1775, a separation from Great Britain and ESTABLISHMENT OF REPUBLICAN GOVERNMENT*, had never yet entered into anyone's mind." (Randall, p.250)) This statement by Jefferson is strong proof that it was Thomas Paine's intention to create an independent country with a new system of government because those ideas had never entered anyone else's mind.

Paine, himself wrote, "the mere independence of America, were it to have been followed by a system of government modeled after the corrupt system of English government, would not have interested me with the unabated ardour that it did. It was to BRING FORWARD AND ESTABLISH THE REPRESENTATIVE*system of government that was the leading principle with me." (Lewis, p.184) To me this statement is conclusive proof that the creation, the very establishment of, the United States was Thomas Paine's innovation.

---

*   caps mine

We have seen that Thomas Paine preceded both George Washington and Thomas Jefferson in proposing a constitutional government, operated as a Democratic Republic. If anyone else originated this idea before Paine, he or she deserves credit. John Adams does not belong in that class. Paine wrote "But John Adams is a man of paradoxical heresies, and consequently of a bewildered mind. He wrote a book entitled, *A Defense of the American Constitutions*, and the principles of it are an attack upon them. But the book is descended to the tomb of forgetfulness, and the best fortune that can attend its author is quietly to follow its fate. John was not born for Immortality." (Foner, p. 913)

John Adams did not originate the idea of a representative republic or a constitution that would guarantee and preserve government by the people. Adams wanted government from the 'top down'. Thomas Paine wanted government from the 'bottom up'. Harvey J. Kaye wrote, "Adams was no democrat. And in years to come, he would grow to despise and envy Paine." (Kaye p.52,53)

CHAPTER 7
CREATING A NATION
AMENDABLE CONSTITUTION

Thomas Paine proposed a constitution which could BE AMENDED. This makes sense because it is unlikely that any constitution as first framed would be perfect. Defects would come to light over the course of time. "The best way of dealing with such defects is to provide a method of correcting them as they arise." The same thinking would apply due to substantial changes as a result of learning experiences, discoveries and innovation. Paine wrote, "No constitution which has not such a corrective can be permanent." The constitution of the United States specifies "the manner by which future additions, alterations, or amendments shall be made." Thomas Paine thought that in a constitutional, democratic Republic, there would be no need for insurrections or rebellions because the amendable constitution "provides and establishes a rightful means in its stead."

Without exception, I agree with Paine. The Civil War is history. It is my belief that America, that is to say Americans, now, can solve and correct any internal problem without resorting to the violence of riots, or insurrections, or civil war. This is so because Americans can amend the constitution. However, this seems to be a difficult and tedious process. In his thought-provoking book, *America Declares Independence*, the distinguished and scholarly Alan Dershowitz wrote, "The people themselves, the "governed", have decided to entrench, in our governing documents, certain fundamental liberties and limitations, which they designate as "rights", rather than mere preferences, and make these rights difficult to repeal, even by subsequent majorities. Our own Constitution requires a deliberately cumbersome amending process." (Dershowitz, p. 86)

Since I have made a citation from Alan Dershowitz' *American Declares Independence*, I ask pardon to digress for a moment to give an opinion. A great deal of commentary in Dershowitz' book is based on the general assumption that Thomas Jefferson is the author of the Declaration of Independence. Dershowitz himself would not claim that the Declaration is purely the work of Jefferson for the following reasons: In a thought comparing the Constitution with the Declaration, Dershowitz wrote, "Justice Arthur Goldberg was far wiser when he said that a living constitution must not be read 'as if it were a last will and testament – lest it become one'. The same can be said about the Declaration of Independence. Its ringing words should be read as its primary author intended..." The words 'primary author' indicate that Dershowitz was well aware that the adopted version of the Declaration contained contributions of others besides a number of changes, additions and deletions. If Jefferson is not the real, the original, author of the Declaration of Independence, it is my opinion that the conclusions reached by Dershowitz are subject to question and review. Also, Dershowitz wrote a lot about RIGHTS'. I wish he had given a clear definition of 'Rights'; or at least an explicit explanation of his understanding of the meaning of RIGHTS, in the form of definition.

I now return to the subject of creating a country. The United States separated from England, achieved independence, adopted an amendable constitution, and established a Representative Republic. Thomas Paine never said, all of this was my doing. He never said, "the credit for the accomplishments which resulted in the creation of the United States, belongs to me". He never said, I was responsible for the advances which were "necessary for a people to advance from that subordination in which they have hither to remained..." Paine wanted Emancipation and Women's suffrage. Both were attained, but not until after his death, June 8, 1809. Each step was a component part of Thomas Paine's integrated step by step plan to create the United States of America. However, if we infer that a democratic representative Republic was established, two very important specifications were verdantly by-passed. Paine was quite explicit about these two operational elements. One was "broad and equal representation"; the other was short terms of office. As regards the former, Paine wrote, "In a former page, I likewise mentioned the necessity of a large and equal representation..." and "Let the assemblies be annual, with a President only. The representation more equal. Their business wholly domestic, and subject to the authority of a Continental Congress. Let each colony be divided into six, eight or ten convenient districts, each district to send a proper number of delegates to congress, so that each colony send at least thirty. The whole number in congress will be at least 390." It is noted that when Paine suggested 390 representatives, the population of the colonies was about three million. Even if the U. S. population grew to only thirty million people, a proportional increase would add up to over three thousand representatives. This is the year 2008 and the population of the United States is three-hundred million. I do not think that the people of the United States ever had broad and equal representation in Congress.

As regards short terms of office, "Let the assemblies be annual, with a president only" was quoted in a preceding paragraph. Each year there would be a new congress, and each year there would be a new President of the United States. The President would be elected by Congress from a slate of delegates or representatives from one particular colony. The colony selected would be chosen by lot. In each of the following years a different colony would be chosen by lot, leaving out those previously selected. This method would continue until each colony would have a turn. Then, the process would start again. It is assumed that representatives and delegates from various districts, "who are supposed to have the same concerns at stake which those have who appointed them, and who will act in the same manner as the whole body would act, were they present," could be reelected.

It is clear, however, that with one year terms of office, the option of reelection or selection of a new representative would be up to the electorate of each district. Frequent elections would guard against the elected from forming interests separate from, or even, opposed to the general body of electors and prevent elected representative from "making a ROD for themselves". [ROD – a political career]

Would the history of America have been better with short terms and a "more equal" and broad representation? Would these constraints guarantee a better future for America? I don't know. Thomas Paine thought so. His exertions were directed to produce a better system in order to secure the "rights"...of Preservation of Life, and Liberty and the pursuit of Happiness for those living at the time and for all future generations. All of Paine's writings had this objective. He did not believe that the people of one generation had the right or authority to bind or control people of succeeding generations. In Common Sense, Paine exposed the evils of monarchy and hereditary monarchy, and exploded the rightness of both.

> "To the evil of monarchy we have added that of hereditary succession; and as the first is a degradation and lessening of ourselves, so the second, claimed as a matter of right is an insult and an imposition on posterity."

This brings up a touchy subject. The United States has laws enacted in former generations, which are binding today, and are likely to bind future generations. Paine wrote, "Every age and generation must be as free to act for itself, in all cases, as the ages and generation which preceded it. The vanity and presumption of governing beyond the grave is the most ridiculous and insolent of all tyrannies."

Here, in the United States, we have hereditary laws. Whether the laws "on the books" are good or bad laws is not part of this discussion. The case here is that the present generation did not vote for laws enacted in prior generations. Similar laws obligating future generations to make money payments, tend to make the matter more complex. Likewise, political debt incurred in prior generations, and left to be paid by future generations can cause problems even in those cases where the people in future generations benefit directly or indirectly from the original expenditures.

It seems, perhaps in a very limited way, that America has regressed to the times before 1776, when the King could say, "you shall make no laws but what I please" and, "There shall be no laws but such as I like" and the British parliament could, "...bind the Colonies in all cases whatsoever." The King's laws, dutifully 'rubber-stamped' by parliament became binding on all future generations. Federal laws have a similar permanency. Present day and future Americans may suffer for a time under laws that they did not vote for.

"...all Experience hath shewn, (sic) that Mankind are more disposed to suffer, while evils are sufferable..."

This idea, from the John Adams copy of Thomas Paine's original declaration of Independence, survives, intact, in the eviscerated, but adopted Declaration. But, thanks to Paine's idea of an amendable constitution, there is no need in America for riotous uprisings, or insurrections or armed rebellion. Americans can effect change by voting. There is no question but that Thomas Paine made the framing of a National Constitution a necessary component part of his plan to create the United States of America.

Thomas Paine set out to create a new country. From the start, his plan for the new nation was to create a REPUBLIC. This design plan called for a "new system" of government. Thomas Paine insisted that this "new system" of government would be conducted by the people of the new nation.

So, a monarchic form of government was out of the question. There would be no need for a king. Instead the people would elect their own political leaders. Accordingly, the new nation's government would be DEMOCRACY – demo-crat-, i.e. people-rule.

Therefore, Thomas Paine created a Representative Republic.

No one, but no one, was advocating, indeed insisting, that the independent colonies unite and establish a REPUBLIC. No one dared. They could be hung for treason. Thomas Paine stood alone. It was Thomas Paine who originated the idea, and presented a concrete plan in order to form the Republic of the United States. It is Thomas Paine who is the sole Founder of the United States.

All of the quotes in this chapter are from *Common Sense and the Crisis* by Thomas Paine. Anchor Books, 1973 Edition

CHAPTER 8
PROOF:
THE FORESTER LETTERS

In an attempt to scuttle Thomas Paine's integrated plan to create the United States, the Rev. Dr. William Smith published a series of letters attacking the fundamental ideas in *Common Sense*. These letters, signed "Cato", appeared in the Pennsylvania Gazette during April of 1776. Thomas Paine, in his famous *Forester Letters*, successfully refuted the arguments of Smith and those of like mind. This was no easy task, because most of the Colonists opted for reconciliation, not Independence from England.

But Paine, using the pen-name "Forester" repeated and reinforced his ideas that reconciliation with Britain was a "fallacious dream" and that Independence was the only way to eliminate a King and establish a Republic. Paine wrote that the *Cato Letters*, "are gorged with absurdity, confusion, contradiction and the most notorious and willful falsehoods." (Foner, *The Complete Writings of Thomas Paine*, p.61)

Paine also debunked "Cato's" contention that the Commissioners, sent from England, had the authority to negotiate a Peace Treaty. Thomas proved that the Commissioners had no such authority and he wrote, "No, Sir, they are not the ambassadors of peace, but the distributors of pardons, mischief and insult." (p. 64)

Paine wrote the second Letter in order to refute "Cato's" anti-independence ideas. What did "Cato" attack? Well, in addition to an attack on Thomas Paine himself, "Cato" tried to discredit all of the essential and fundamental reasons for separation and Independence given in *Common Sense*. "Cato" lacked Thomas Paine's vision. Besides, "Cato" weakened his own position by admitting that reconciliation still leaves open some probability that Great Britain will try again to subjugate America by force. The incontestable acuity of hindsight shows that "Cato's" arguments were in vain.

Paine's exertions proved successful, and at the same time, the magnificent *Forester Letters* provided a strong public notice that any attack on his passion to create the Free and Independent United States of America would be met with point by point rebuttal and searing rebuke.

The *Forester Letters* take up twenty-six pages of tight print in Philip S. Foner's meritorious opus *The Complete Writings of Thomas Paine*. In addition to exploding "Cato's" arguments against Independence, Thomas used these Letters to amplify and reinforce and reaffirm his intention to establish a new country without a King and also as a means to reach a wider audience. Paine had an unshakable belief that the transformation from Monarchy to Democracy must come from the will of the people.

Democracy was one of Thomas Paine's implacable principles. He knew that to achieve Independence, it must come from within, from the bottom up, not from the top down. In short, Democracy must come from the people. This is true because the people of a nation are the "natural" foundation of power. In the interest of operational efficiency, Paine's intention was to create a Representative Republic. The new Republic would be democratic because the representatives would be elected by the people. Paine was the FIRST to propose a Republic. Prior to *Common Sense*, there is no evidence that any one else was trying to create a Republic.

The third Letter addressed to "Cato" is dated May 8, 1776, less than sixty days before the Declaration of Independence. The last few pages of this monumental work provide a summary of the essential ideas contained in *Common Sense*, and a complete refutation of "Cato's" plea for reconciliation. History proves that Thomas Paine was successful. Here, it is important to note that Paine's efficacious and incontrovertible rebuttal was accomplished, "with a string of maxims and reflections, drawn from the nature of things, without borrowing from any one." This citation is followed by another: "...I scarcely ever quote; the reason is, I always think." (p.78)

These quotes prove, conclusively, that Thomas Paine was independent, and totally alone in his relentless pursuit to establish a new country, a Democratic Republic, which would eliminate, forever, monarchic rule on the North American Continent. No one, not Washington, not Adams, not Jefferson, not even Benjamin Franklin, was proposing that the Colonies unite and create a Representative Republic prior to *Common Sense*.

None of the above mentioned honored Patriots were writing anything in trenchant opposition to "Cato's" Loyalist appeal for reconciliation. Moreover, prior to *Common Sense*, none of those heroic and praiseworthy men published an explicit plan to secede from Great Britain, depose the King and establish an Independent Republic. Thomas Paine was the original formulator of the concrete and comprehensive plan to unite the Colonists and create the United States. All of the essential elements needed in order to do it are contained in *Common Sense*.

The original Patriots, having been inspired and converted to Thomas Paine's revolutionary ideas, followed his lead. To them, we owe a bountiful transport of gratitude. A select group, in the first rank of these great men, had come to be called "Founding Fathers". This is not quite accurate because Thomas Paine was the original "Founding Father".

Credit Paine as being first among peers, if you will, but when prejudice, bigotry and predilection are cast aside, I believe that Thomas

Paine will be recognized as the original, stand alone, founder and creator of the United States of America. In or out of context, John Adams was right when he said, "History is to ascribe the American Revolution to Thomas Paine." (Lewis, p.51) Adams was wrong if he meant that, that singular honor should go to John Adams. Priority belongs to Thomas Paine because he earned it and future American History books should say so.

"Cato" was offering "the false light of reconciliation." (Foner, p.81) Paine answered, "There is no such thing. 'Tis gone! 'Tis past! The grave has parted us – and death, in the persons of the slain, has cut the thread of life between Britain and America." (p.81) In addition to this Paine believed that the King would not agree to reconciliation. He wrote, "Conquest, and not reconciliation is the plan of Britain." (p.81)

This meant War. Because England was the invader, it was a war of defense on the part of the Americans. If Britain prevailed, the King would own the land, all of it. He would own "The Law" also. Is there any man or woman who would surrender such power to just one person? Comparing the history of creation and the history of Kings, Paine wrote, "God hath made a world and Kings have robbed Him of it." (p. 79)

Paine held fast to the principle that when a new country is being formed, the mode of government selected is strictly up to the people.

Since the war had already begun, there were only three possible outcomes for America: reconciliation, defeat or victory. The first meant continued subordination and subservience to the crown. The second meant that the Patriots would be hanged by the conquering British governors as traitors. The third would insure the creation of the United States of America.

Regarding Independence Paine believed that the "first and great question" came down to whether America could be happy under the government of Great Britain or under a government of its own.

As we know, Thomas chose the later and with indomitable will and unflagging zeal, he pursued his step by step plan. Eight weeks after the last *Forester Letter* was published, the first phase of his goal became a reality. The most sweeping and important political turn-around in history was achieved. It was accomplished by a unanimous manifesto proclaiming, "We do assert and declare these (American) Colonies to be free and independent States…"

CHAPTER 9
WORK IN PROGRESS
CRISIS: I, II, III, IV AND V

There were two persistent and exasperating problems with which Thomas Paine had to deal throughout the war. One was King George III himself, and the other was Toryism. Toryism describes the idea of remaining loyal to the King. Paine asked, "And what is a tory? Good God! What is he?...Every tory is a coward, for a servile, slavish, self-interested fear is the foundation of toryism; and a man under such influence, though he may be cruel, never can be brave".

As regards King George III, well Paine would never let up. He called the King "A common murderer, a highwayman (and) a house-breaker." A few pages later, Paine describes the King as a Sottish, stupid, stubborn, worthless, brutish man. Referring to the Tories, Paine wrote, "Let them call me a rebel, and welcome, I feel no concern from it; but I should suffer the misery of devils, were I to make a whore of my soul by swearing allegiance to one whose character is" – like King George III. Plainly, in this CRISIS paper Paine was warning Tories that their allegiance to the King would end in disaster. He wrote: The cunning of the fox is as murderous as the violence of the wolf." The British were making peace offers during the winter of 1776, in order to lull the Americans into complacency. These peace proposals were shown to be bogus. The peace offers included promises of mercy but not

Independence. Paine warned, "It is the madness of folly to expect mercy from those who have refused to do justice…" It is an old trick in warfare for an enemy to lull the opposition into a state of inactivity by tendering false peace proposals. In this case, these peace offers were not official and would not be binding. The British used the phony peace offers in order to seduce the Americans to lay down their arms, weaken their resolve and pander to the misguide hopes of the Tories. At the same time the British would reinforce their own offensive capabilities.

THE CRISIS I, December 19, 1776

A brief summary follows: This is the famous, "These are the times that try men's souls," *Crisis Paper*; and much more. In nine powerful pages, Thomas Paine provided a compendium of ideas and principles that he would repeat time and again throughout his writings. The main topics were: Tyranny, the King, Tories, Trade, Defense, Party Politics, Unity and Perseverance.

Britain wanted to enforce her tyranny, not only to tax, but to bind the Colonies in all cases whatever. Paine equated that with slavery.

In *Common Sense*, Paine wrote, "Our plan is commerce" and in his continuing effort to 'awaken every man to duty', Paine offered this incentive, "Not a place upon earth might be so happy as America. Her situation is remote from all the wrangling world, and she has nothing to do but TRADE with them. Then, in a preview of the Paine Doctrine, usually described as the Monroe Doctrine, Paine wrote, "I am as confident, as I am that God governs the world, that America will never be happy till she gets clear of foreign dominion."

The next point refers again to the irksome problem of the Tories.

"I wish with all the devotion of a Christian that the names of whig and tory may never more be mentioned."

In *Common Sense*, Paine had urged "Let the names of whig and Tory be extinct..." and in the last two pages of *Crisis One*, he made an impassioned plea for unity and support from all thirteen Colonies. He believed that with a force of thousands, a single successful battle would decide this world-changing contest in one year.

The date given for publishing *Crisis One* was December 23, 1776. Paine would write at least thirteen *Crisis Papers*. The first ten numbers were written through the first four years of a dismal war from 1776 to 1780. During this time, nothing like these amazing productions was published by Washington Adams, or Jefferson or anyone else, and during this time the United States was not victorious.

CRISIS II, January 13.1777

Crisis number two is addressed to Lord (General William) Howe, whom Paine calls an ingrate, an invader and a ridiculous character. Paine, again deprecates the King by calling him an insulting ruffian, a monster and a man of savage obstinacy.

It is in this *Crisis* that Paine introduces the designation, "The United States of America". Innovators originate things. After that, Paine exposed Britain's bogus peace offers. The phony peace offers rejected Independence. If official, which they were not, they would have been called "Articles of Surrender", along with a lame promise of mercy. In effect, the British proposed that if the Colonists would lay down their arms and surrender the continent, they would escape with their lives. Some trade off. America would give up Country, Continent and Freedom in exchange for an artificial amnesty under despotism. General William Howe was the one who introduced these impostures. No wonder why Paine tore into Howe saying, "Your avowed purpose here is to kill, conquer, plunder, pardon and enslave" ...Of course the 'peace offers' were unceremoniously rejected out of hand. Later, Paine would describe this episode, at length, in 'The Raynal Letter'.

Thomas Paine's bifurcated purpose of this CRISIS was to expose the folly of Great Britain and, also to rally the support of all of the colonies. The first object was to impugn the "pretended authority" of General Howe; and to show the wickedness of the British cause, and the impossibility of conquering America. The second object was to remove fear and encourage unity.

England could not CONQUER America at that time; and since the Declaration of Independence, England would never be able to CONQUER America. Thomas Paine knew it. It is my opinion that most of the Colonists were not so sure; and they were not providing the support that he was pleading for.

In the concluding thoughts of this comprehensive and illuminating work, Paine wrote, "I consider Independence as America's natural right and interest, and never could see any real dis-service it would be to England." He, again, expresses his belief that trade and commerce are activities that are separate from governments and politics. He added an autobiographical note: "If I have any where expressed myself overwarmly, 'tis from a fixt (sic) immovable hatred I have, and ever had, to cruel men and cruel measures. I have likewise an aversion to monarchy, as being too debasing to the dignity of man,...What I write is pure nature, and my pen and my soul have ever gone together...I never courted either fame or interest". (by "interest", Paine means money profits) These personal disclosures lend strong support to the opinion of many people that Thomas Paine was a great and a heroically virtuous humanitarian. In addition, Paine was an uncompromising pacifist; as the following quote, along with the historical evidence of his life's pursuits and actions will show. "My study is to be useful, and if your lordship (Howe) loves mankind as well as I do, you would, seeing as you cannot conquer us, cast about and lend your hand towards accomplishing a peace. Paine never stopped working for a negotiated peace during the war years. But the "hardened, sullen tempered Pharaoh" George III would have none of it. Paine would soldier on, nurturing his creation.

CRISIS III, April 19, 1777

The Third Crisis Paper is magnificent. Its thirty-four pages could serve as the basis of an ideological History of the American Revolution. The piece, by itself is a strong proof that Thomas Paine is the ideological founder, in sole, of the Free and Independent States of America.

In this number, Paine again attacks those opposed to Independence and unity. He is particularly hard on Quakers and Tories, whom he accuses of being hypocrites, traitors and cowards, because they are motivated by avarice. Ironically, if America were CONQUERED by Great Britain, "all property would fall to the conquerors and Britain could "bind the Colonies in all cases whatsoever"; and tax at will. In this case, Tories would end up as second-class citizens of a foreign power.

Crisis number three made three things perfectly clear. One, the King was determined to conquer America, "fully and absolutely". Two, Paine knew that Britain could not conquer America. Three, total Independence was not an accomplished fact. More work had to be done to achieve it, and, of course, the war had to be won. Paine needed more support. I am not convinced that at this time – Spring 1777 – that the Patriots were in the majority. In order to secure more followers, Paine reviewed the principle arguments in favor of Independence. He wrote that the natural right of the continent to be independent had never been called into question, and that America would benefit from Independence. Also, Independence was a necessity and moral advantages would be derived from it. Americans would benefit by making their own laws. Money profits from trade and commerce with all countries would help America grow and not be confiscated by the King to be squandered on oppressive wars, opulence, free land, pensions and other favors to the titled elite. The colonies had grown and had become prosperous. The greedy eyes of the King and his imperious sycophants wanted to control the production and trade of the Colonists. Slyly, the British leaders connived to foment rebellion in the Colonies so that Great Britain would have an excuse to invade and conquer the Colonies and thereby seize the whole Continent. Britain's aim was total conquest. The King and his ministry had no intention of ending the war by means of a Treaty of Peace. On the other hand, Thomas Paine never stopped working for peace. He was always ready to negotiate. However, I believe he would never agree to enter into peace negotiations with Great Britain unless there was, prior to opening negotiations, a confirmed, valid, formal, binding, and signed, unconditional agreement, that Great Britain recognized that the United States was participating as a free, totally Independent and sovereign Country. I have reason to believe that Benjamin Franklin was of the same mind. The same cannot be said for most of the Colonists. The Declaration was signed but enthusiastic acceptance of Independence in 1777 was almost as scarce as the doctrine of it in 1775. The Colonists were afraid of the British; and no wonder. They might be hung as rebels, or lose their homes. Then there is the fear of the unknown. Most Colonial Americans knew nothing about republican government. Centuries of Royal tradition made it difficult for the Colonists to embrace Independence. Generations of children were taught in their formative years to believe in the King, to honor him, to obey him, and to pray for him: "God Save The King".

Paine was trying to transform Tories into active patriots. He reverted to the theme that Great Britain's single and solitary goal was "conquest and confiscation". Britain had a "rage for conquest, and they had no doubt that they could conquer America with one stroke and prevail" by seizing the whole (continent) at once.

Paine's exertions in exposing Britain's aim for total conquest of America in order to win converts to the cause of Independence were generally unsuccessful. Quaker loyalists were, not only against independence, but they took sides with the enemy. Paine was extremely dissatisfied with their behavior. He considered them guilty of treason. His concerted attempts to reason with them proved to be of no avail. He admonished the Quakers, excluding those who supported independence and the war effort, that it was contrary to their pacific principles to bind America to Britain and thereby "dip her hands in the bloody" and ceaseless wars in Europe.

Paine was astonished that men and women would opt to live under and support a government that was continually and brutally waging war. I believe that Thomas Paine was deeply hurt by the treasonous opposition of the Quakers. I believe that Paine took umbrage at the actions of the Quakers to "subvert, overturn or bring reproach upon the independence of this continent as (unanimously) declared by congress" for two reasons. One was that an attack against independence was a personal attack on Paine himself because he initiated the idea of a separate and independent nation. The other was that the actions of the Quakers were impeding the step by step completion of Paine's revolutionary plan.

Again Paine returns to the CONQUEST theme. He gives quotes from three British Lords: Townsend, Talbot and Littleton. Each lord affirmed that the single goal of Britain was unconditional submission of America.

INFLATION:

Toward the end of this comprehensive Crisis essay (number 3) Thomas Paine provided an excellent explanation of Inflation. It is one of the best explanations of this subject that I have ever read. In one page Paine clearly explains that money inflation results in the decrease of an individual's savings, while increasing the individual's living costs. As a consequence, people suffer two injuries simultaneously. These remarks pertain to the effects of inflation. I have long held that the cause of inflation is printing paper money. After all, as I have heard, money is money and paper is paper.

Thomas Paine, then, returns to his unflagging exertions in order to secure support for the Independence from the ranks of Loyalists. He proposed a twofold plan. One part was a voluntary oath of allegiance to America, the other part was a tax of ten to twenty percent on all property. We know from hindsight that this scheme failed to provide the funds sufficient to carry on the Revolutionary War.

In the concluding pages of this classic Crisis number three, Paine again shows that he is willing to make peace with Great Britain, but only "As free and independent states". Also, with reconciliation and alliance with Britain, France and Spain would be our enemies. Alternately, with Independence, France and Spain would be our allies "therefore the only road to peace, honor and commerce is INDEPENDENCE".

CRISIS IV September 12, 1777

"Those who expect to reap the blessings of freedom, must, like men, undergo the fatigues of supporting it" is the famous first line of the fourth *Crisis*. It was written one day after Washington was routed at the battle of Brandywine Creek. To a person who is unacquainted with the writings of Thomas Paine, this *Crisis* could appear to be an improbable piece of propaganda. Paine says that the enemy's victories are really defeats. Alternately, with each loss, America wins by degrees. He warns General William Howe that it is only a matter of time before he is defeated. Then, Paine says that General Howe is just a "tool of a miserable tyrant".

I suppose that a loyalist reader would consider this Crisis a preposterous exercise of bravado. Paine's aim was to rally the troops during this dark period. He wrote, "We fight, not to enslave but to set a country free, and to make room upon the earth for honest men to live in. In such a cause, we are sure we are right."

CRISIS V March 21, 1778 [Lancaster]

Thomas Paine remained ever watchful of the progress of the Revolution. He stayed on the alert to detect any event, any problem, or any threat that could be harmful to the American Independence. He used the

Crisis Papers in order to counter negative events; solve problems, and quash threats. A serious problem arose in the spring of 1778.

A group in Congress conspired to remove George Washington from command of the army. John Adams, who held the elected position as the President of the Board of War and Ordnance, was a member of this group. Although Washington had not been victorious, his army had never been totally defeated. The cabal who wanted to depose Washington criticized his indecisiveness, his poor judgment and his sub-mediocre generalship.

Paine wrote *Crisis* number five in order to defend Washington and keep him from being fired. We know that Paine was dissatisfied with Washington's generalship. However, he thought that a change in leadership at this time would be disruptive and create additional problems.

Crisis number five was addressed to General Sir William Howe. In it Paine proceeded to censure, criticize, berate and ridicule Howe throughout this essay. Paine's propaganda pen went to work. Paine recommended that, upon Howe's death, he should be embalmed in tar and feathers. He described Howe as indolent, incompetent and a "hero of little villanies and unfinished adventures...the patron of low and vulgar frauds, (and) the encourager of Indian cruelties..."

Next, Paine devoted two pages to a salvo of vehement denunciation of Howe for his part in issuing counterfeit continental money. Paine was unsparing here and he accused Howe of meanness and of exhibiting "an inbred wretchedness of heart made up between the venomous malignity of a serpent and the spiteful imbecility of an inferior reptile." Paine viewed the counterfeiting tactic as an attack against humanity. Howe is reminded that counterfeiting is a felony which is punishable by death by hanging.

After making excuses for Washington's performance during 1776, Paine reveals his own expertise in military strategy and tactics. He does this in an oblique way, with a detailed critique of General Howe's operations during the same period. At the end of 1776, Paine concludes that Howe was no further ahead than at the beginning of it. By contrast, the Americans had two stunning victories at the end of December, 1776. One was the marvelous victory over the – paid to fight – Hessions at Trenton. The other was the victory over the British troops at Princeton which was "attended with such a scene of circumstance and superiority of generalship, as will ever give it a place on the first line in the history of great (tactical) actions."

This quote shows Paine's support for Washington. It was a calculated argument in favor of his retention as commander of the continental army.

Continuing to deprecate Howe, Paine asks, "What great exploits have you performed?" Paine describes Howe's movements as a military jig and like a puppy pursuing his tail. By way of contrast, Paine attempted to gloss over Washington's defeat at Germantown, Pennsylvania, in October, 1778, by saying that its' "success was not equal to the plan." Also, I believe that the happy news of the decisive American victory at Saratoga helped soften the negative impact of Washington's defeat at the battle of Germantown. Washington was saved and he persevered. Paine carries on the war with his pen and he is relentless. Again, he tears into Howe.

After Germantown and Saratoga, "you dreaded a second attack". Howe retreated to Philadelphia and hid himself "among the women and children." Paine insinuates that Howe is a coward and now he must forgo offensive strikes and protect his army against attack. Paine admonishes Howe that he is a stooge of England's "rage and lunacy" and the baseness of the King, his ministry and army; and is a party to forgery, perjury, treachery and theft. In an effort to gain more support, Paine wrote, "From such men and such masters may the gracious hand of Heaven preserve America!" Although she suffers now, she would suffer much more under the King… "The will of God hath parted us, and the deed is registered for eternity." Continuing, Paine cites British barbarity in India by tying men to the mouths of cannons and "blowing them away." Pressing home his case, Paine wrote, "America was young and virtuous. None but a Herod of uncommon malice would have made war upon infancy and innocence." ..."(This) country was the gift of Heaven, and God alone is their Lord and Sovereign." The "destruction of the goods of Providence...must be accounted for to him who made and governs (the world)".

These quotes re-echo Paine's question in *Common Sense* (p.41) "But where, says some, is the King of America? I'll tell you friend, he reigns above and doth not make havoc of Mankind like the Royal Brute of Britain." Indeed, *Crisis* number five is a detailed expansion of the ideas contained in *Common Sense*.

Accordingly, Paine repeats that America did not invade British lands, did not hire mercenaries, did not incite the Indians, and developed the country with its own settlers and "was indebted for nothing" to England. On the other hand England can look forward to nothing but a "waste of trade and credit and an increase of poverty and taxes." He tells Howe that he is no nearer to the conquest of America than when he started; he has lost twenty thousand men, and squandered "millions of treasure for which you have nothing in exchange". Paine concludes that England is nearly bankrupt and re-asserts that England cannot conquer America and he urges Howe, "Go home Sir". Neither Washington, Adams, nor Jefferson wrote, or could compose a work comparable to Paine's *Crisis* number 5. It is a brilliant exposition that could come only from the mind and heart of a man whose passion was to see his design through to completion.

CHAPTER 10
A PLAN NOT TAKEN

Thomas Paine added an appendix to his *Crisis* number five, probably in April, 1778, three years after the battles of Lexington and Concord on April 19, 1775. Paine described these three years as a "period which has given birth to a new world and erected a monument to the folly of the old." Of course, the period did not give birth to anything. Thomas Paine gave birth to a new nation. Then, comparing America with the ancient glories of Greece and Rome, Paine says, we are superior. This is so because we have better knowledge and sounder maxims of civil government. Paine claimed that, "Had it not been for America, there had been no such thing as freedom left throughout the whole universe"...The American Revolution was the most "Virtuous and illustrious revolution that ever graced the history of mankind." These are self-congratulatory sentiments because no one else was commending Paine.

After reminding the Americans what they are fighting for, he urges them to proceed with the war and become victorious. Again, Paine says that Britain cannot conquer America. They do not have a strategic plan to conquer. Even if they had a plan and the power to go about it, they would not be successful. Paine then, urges the Americans to assemble a formidable army and attack General Howe; "America, when collected is sufficient to swallow their present army."

Paine's plea: Finish the war and stop the bloodshed by attacking with a superior force. General Howe could have been defeated, just as

Burgoyne was. Paine was saying, if we hesitate now, we will "prolong the war and double both the calamities and the expenses of it." He continued his exhortation, saying in effect, we began the war with spirit, vigor and determination, let's end it the same way. "Here is the enemy; here is the army; here are the Tories; help us expel them". Whigs will welcome you, while the enemy dreads your assault. "What is there to hinder?" "Come on and help us." "America is her own mistress and (she) can do what she pleases." "Here are the laurels, come and share them."

Paine had said, "We can raise an army in a few weeks". It is typical of Thomas Paine that after he presents a plan, he provides a detailed, step by step, method in order to accomplish the objective of the plan. In this case, Paine's plan was designed to recruit 3,200 men from each state. It was brilliant. It was practicable, fair and orderly, and it would have resulted in a force in excess of 30,000 troops, recruited and supplied with a minimum of expense. In spite of Paine's prompting and urging his exertions were of no avail. John Adams, the titular head of the War and Ordnance Board, appears to have been a total failure in the mission of recruitment, arms and supplies procurement at this time. Washington's petitions to Congress were not much help. Jefferson remained a passive participant during the war years. However, he could have rendered some assistance, some relief by providing food supplies from his plantations. I do not know what John Jay was doing. Alexander Hamilton was assisting Washington. However, these patriot leaders were not entirely at fault. Congress was powerless to help because they were running out of funds. The main problem was that all of the states would not unite and mount a coordinated action against the enemy at "one principle point." Each state focused on its own interest and protection. Each state was loathe to unite and participate in Paine's plan. By the end of 1778, America was still mired in a dismal war.

Paine's aspirations as expressed in this memorable gem of persuasive rhetoric were not to be fulfilled. He would persevere and America would prevail. All of the victors would share in the laurels; all except one man.

CHAPTER 11
CRISIS VI THROUGH XIII

Crisis VI

A combination of amnesty and retribution was offered to the Americans by paid, sycophant commissioners, who were sent on a Kings errand. Their mission was a sinister attempt to get America to renege on their totally honorable Treaty of Alliance with France (February 6, 1778), undermine Independence, and thereby subjugate America to British royal tyranny. Total conquest was Great Britain's goal all along.

Thomas Paine was insulted and appalled by the blatant insolence and imposture of the nefarious scheme tendered by the uninformed and misguided Commissioners. Paine unsheathed his polemic pen. Poor Commissioners! He called them malicious, poisonous, foolish, devilish and dishonorable, for attempting to get America to break her treaty with France. Paine explained, "The treaty we have formed with France is open, noble and generous. It is true policy, founded on sound, philosophy, and neither a surrender or mortgage as you would scandalously insinuate. I have seen every article and speak from positive knowledge. In France, we have found an affectionate friend, a faithful ally; from Britain, nothing but tyranny, cruelty and Infidelity." (Did Paine write the Treaty and send it to Benjamin Franklin?)

Also, Paine used Crisis number six to answer British threats of further destruction. He wrote, "The mischief you threaten is not in your power to execute." He then lists several ways in which America could retaliate; such as espionage, sabotage and commando strikes. The example given here was selected because of its autobiographical significance. It recounts that Paine volunteered to participate in an incendiary strike.

> "While your – British – fleet lay last winter in the Delaware, I offered my service to the Pennsylvania navy-board then at Trenton, as one who would make a party with them, or any four or five gentlemen on an expedition down the river to set fire to it…"

This tactical plan was novel, hazardous, and required the elements of surprise, stamina, daring, judgment, timing and leadership. I believe Thomas Paine could have brought it off; however, the plan was rejected.

Paine had written, "There is no evil which cannot be returned when you come to incendiary mischief…and as you do, so shall you be done by."

Taking another approach, the commissioners attempted to entice American soldiers to fight for the King, "their rightful sovereign", against the French, "our late mutual and 'natural' enemies." Paine, who rarely misses a chance to censure and ridicule George III, (Mr. Guelph) calls him "a man of humble capacities", and worthless. Paine cautions, "unless you wish to see him exposed," you ought "to keep him out of sight." After this laughable remark, Paine rejects the idea that France is the 'natural' enemy of both England and America and he proceeded to explode the very concept. "I deny that she ever was the natural enemy of either, and that there does not exist in nature such a principle. The expression is an unmeaning barbarism, and wholly unphilosophical, when applied to beings of the same species."

Thomas Paine was unsparing in his condemnation of the King, his ministers and commissioners. In effect, he accused them of moral turpitude. He considered their subversive schemes to be detestable and devilish. The British proposal to have the American Patriots break their sacred trust with themselves, and also break their solemn treaties was unthinkable. Compliance with such corrupt proposals was termed "horrid and infernal" by Paine.

The Alliance with France prevailed, and with a bonanza of French aid America was victorious and the war came to an end at Yorktown, Virginia in October, 1781.

The commissioners spent a lot of time, energy and money trying to get America to stab France in the back. They failed. Fourteen years later, George Washington succeeded where the commissioners had failed. With just a stroke of a pen, he signed the "Jay Treaty".

Crisis VII

Philadelphia, November 21, 1778

After three years of war, England had not conquered America. She assumed that she would be victorious. No plans were made in the event of defeat. Unopposed at sea, she had invaded with a large, trained, well equipped army. She had every advantage. On the other hand, America had to raise, train and supply a new army. Yet, the triumph that Britain had taken for granted was not achieved, and as Thomas Paine knew, could never be achieved. At this time, the King would consider the possibility of defeat, nothing less than seditious heresy. The war continued; and as Paine described it, the King's army conducted it in a "low, cruel, indolent and profligate" manner. Paine wanted the people of England to know about the barbarous operations of their armies in America. The King and his ministers managed the news and kept the British subjects in the dark about the actual events of the Revolutionary War.

Governments love secrecy. A key part of Crisis Seven was the disclosure that it was the intention of the King and his cabinet to conquer America. If they could annex America as a conquered country, the King would own all of the land. Then the King could distribute huge parcels of land to his governors and favorites. The British people would not reap any benefits from the added territory, but they would have to pay the taxes in order to pay off the costs of the war. Reconciliation was out of the question. The goal of King and cabinet was total conquest. Their plan was to goad the Americans into armed rebellion, then defeat them and thereby gain a continent; "and silence them forever."

Paine continues, "In a general view there are few conquests that repay the charge of making them." Except in cases of defense, Paine considered war to be "inglorious and detestable". In general, wars of conquest are waged to extend commerce and dominion, and Paine declared that Britain controlled both before they "BEGAN to conquer". Paine then asked, "What then, in the name of Heaven, could you go to war for?" He followed with, "War can never be the interest of a trading nation, any more than quarrelling can be profitable to a man in business. But to make war with those who trade with us, is like setting a bull-dog upon a customer at the shop door." Accordingly, it is not in the interest of the people of England to support the war on commercial principles. Paine also claimed that the war should not be supported by the people of England on the basis of "falsely understood" National Honor. He defined national honor as "the best character of an individual is the best character for a nation." Paine concluded that the invasion of America and "laying the country desolate with fire and sword," destroyed England's National Honor. Turning to financial matters, Paine informs the English people that the interest on Great Britain's debt is "at least equal to one half of her yearly revenue." If the war is continued, England could go bankrupt. By contrast, America has zero debt. Paine was convinced that Britain's failure was as certain as fate. He had shown that America could not be conquered and that Britain could not conquer America.

"Most of the arguments made use of by the Ministry for supporting the war, are the very arguments that ought to have been used against it; and the plans, by which they thought to conquer are the very plans in which they were sure to be defeated."

"I know what England is, and what America is, and from the compound of knowledge, am better enabled to judge of the issue, than what the King or any of his ministers can be."

Paine summed up his remarks to the English people by stating that American Independence will stand; and England can't prevent it by force of arms. Even if you had conquered America, any trade advantages gained would be off-set by years of burdensome taxes levied to pay off the costs of the war. What would the People of England get in return for the tax money paid out? Nothing. Paine repeats that the lands of a conquered America "might have been parceled out in grants to the favorites at court, but no share of it would have fallen to you."

Pointing his pen at the members of Parliament, Paine says, the same fate awaits you. You won't share in the booty either, because conquered or ceded lands belong to the King. Tax money collected in those lands would go directly into the Kings coffers.

Analogously, mercantile and manufacturing trade would suffer, if America were conquered. Businessmen would lose the rich potential profits derived by supplying manufactured items needed due to the inevitable increase of immigrants who will flock to a free, Independent and peaceful country.

History shows that everything in this amazing Crisis paper was true. England lost a war and a continent. The dreams of the elite, the lords, the ministers and the members of parliament, vaporized along with the cannon smoke at Yorktown. King Guelph the Obstinate (George III) will be remembered as the monarch during whose reign, Thomas Paine created a new world. As usual, the unhappy task of paying off the cost of a war which ended in ignominious defeat fell to the English working people.

Paine concluded this Crisis with the advice that England should follow America's, that is Thomas Paine's, lead and establish a Republic and make peace with both America and France. Paine never stopped working for peace, but he knew that the probability of a quick negotiated peace with Independence, had no other foundation than hope. I believe that Paine wrote Crisis Seven out of a sense of duty and presented it to the people of England as a gift. I believe, also that it was an undeclared address aimed at Washington, Adams, Jay and Jefferson. I am not sure they read it.

Crisis VIII

March 1780

The eighth *Crisis* paper was published on March 17, 1780. At this time the United States was nearing the lowest ebb of the Revolutionary War. Washington's army at Morristown, New Jersey was suffering through a harsh winter. Officers and men were subsisting on short rations. There were mutinies and desertions and there was talk of capitulation. America was virtually bankrupt. The continental dollar was worth about one penny.

During this dark period, Thomas Paine was willing to try anything in order to preserve the Independence. Again Paine wrote to the English people in order to convince them that an Independent America was in their interest. He repeated his arguments that America can't be conquered; the European powers are opposed to Britain's war against the Americans; your trade is going to ruin; and your only prospects are continued misfortune and devastating debt. Paine even went so far as to threaten England with invasion. I suppose that would somehow be a joint war effort with France, Spain and perhaps Holland siding with the United States as allies. Considering the weak financial condition of America, at this time, the idea of invading Britain seems far fetched. However, Paine used this possibility to stress that, since the war was not waged on British soil, the people of Britain did not have to endure the horrors of it. Then, Paine made an appeal from the heart. He spoke of the miseries of the war; the homes destroyed; furniture chopped up for firewood; homeless women and children, suffering from the cold, and wandering in the street; and the "carnage and slaughter, the miseries of a military hospital, or a town in flames."

What if the shoe were on the other foot? If Britain were invaded, the English people would be the ones who would suffer; and they could reflect that they brought the evils of war upon themselves. With the Americans, the case was just the opposite. It was Great Britain that invaded America with thousands of troops. The Americans had not brought it on themselves. "On the contrary, they had by every proceeding endeavored to avoid it, and had descended even below the mark of congressional character to prevent a war." I believe that the "Olive Branch Petition" of July 8, 1775, over two months after the breaking out of hostilities, qualifies as an example of a proceeding taken in order to avoid the Revolutionary War. Reconciliation and nothing but reconciliation with Great Britain was goal of the Colonists in 1775. The members of the Second Continental Congress were of the same mind in 1775; that was that reconciliation was the only option. The servile, groveling petitions to the King prove the fact.

In this part of his *Crisis VIII*, Paine made a significant disclosure. He wrote, "The national honor or the advantages of Independence were matters, which at the commencement of the dispute, they had never studied, and it was only at the last moment that the measure was resolved on."

To me, this quote proves Thomas Paine's priority in originating the idea of total Independence. To the exclusion of any other option,

Thomas Paine had decided on Independence in April, 1775. He began his outline for *Common Sense* at that time and had it completed by October 1775. *Common Sense* was Paine's blueprint for the construction and establishment of the United States of America. The term The United States of America appears on page 79 in *Crisis II*, of *Common Sense and the Crisis*, Anchor Press. In *Common Sense*, Paine totally exploded the idea of reconciliation and totally refuted any other option save Independence.

No one antedated Thomas Paine with a total concept for the creation of a new nation. No one composed an integrated plan to form the British Colonies in America into a new, independent and sovereign country before Thomas Paine. No one presented a step by step plan in order to establish a new system of government without a King, and constitutionally operated by the people as a Democratic Republic.

It is for these reasons, that I believe that Thomas Paine is the real creator and founder of the United States of America.

Crisis IX

June 9, 1780

After five years of war, such as it was, America was not conquered, and Britain was not victorious; just as Thomas Paine predicted. As a military leader, Washington was a dud. He was at fault also, for neglecting to provide for his troops. The first duty of a commander is to supply provisions for his men. Instead of writing those doleful letters to Congress for food and supplies, Washington should have done the job himself. Besides, Congress had no money. John Adams, as President of the War and Materials Board and in spite of all of his self-declared abilities, was no help.

It was Thomas Paine who found a way to provide relief for Washington and his army. He had initiated a "subscription" with a generous contribution from his own meager savings. This fund raising campaign was successful enough to carry Washington through until the end of 1780.

In *Crisis IX*, Paine made a valiant attempt to rally the spirits and determination of the patriots. This was no easy task. Morale was low and the loss of Charleston, South Carolina on May 12, 1780 was a disaster. Paine wrote that America was "lulled in the lap of soft tranquility (and) she rested on her hopes, and adversity only has convulsed her into action." He described war-time America as "brave in distress; serene in conquest; drowsey while at rest; and in every situation generously disposed to peace." Paine added that the British victory at Charleston, "threw a drowsiness over America; and he attempted to show that America could reap an advantage if the Charleston defeat could "rouse us from the slumber" of the last twelve months.

It was Thomas Paine who was brave and effective during the dark days of the Revolution and it was Washington who was "drowsey" when Paine wrote, "rouse us from slumber", I believe that this was an indirect way of urging Washington to act. Later, in a published Letter to George Washington, Paine wrote, "you slept away your time in the field".

As regards America's generous disposition for peace, Paine would agree to open negotiations only after Britain removed her armies from the continent and made a formal agreement to officially recognize the total Independence of the United States. He would reject any offer in which total Independence, the innovative offspring of his mind and heart, would be compromised.

In the last part of this Crisis Paper, Paine urged, "It is now full time to put an end to a war of aggravations..." Again he called for "unanimity and exertion", and yet again he made a plea for new recruits. Thomas Paine's perseverance was amazing. However, his pleas were not answered and by the end of the year, 1780, America would be on the verge of capitulation. In the mean time Paine would try again. This time he would make a determined plea for something he hated; that is taxes. He would give this offering the title of *The Crisis Extraordinary*. (on the Subject of Taxation)

The Crisis Extraordinary

October 6, 1780

This superlative and timeless Crisis is truly extraordinary. It was composed when the war was all but lost and Washington's poor army was shrinking due to desertions. Congress was powerless to help. The thirteen states refused to provide united support with recruits and funds. Thomas Paine took it upon himself to devise a plan to raise taxes in order to continue the war. He appealed to the financial interest of the Americans. Paine attempted to convince the Americans that if the British were victorious, their taxes would be ELEVEN times greater.

The work merits our attention. It could have come only from the prodigious mind of Thomas Paine. I do not believe that George Washington, John Adams, Jefferson or Jay or any other of the so called founding fathers could or would have produced a composition like it. At first reading the piece seems complex and overly detailed and the math might put some people off. But, with a piece-meal approach and a little time and a few pencil calculations, the interested reader will be well rewarded.

Paine effectively explained that, if Britain conquered America, she would tax each American FORTY shillings per year. But, if America emerged victorious, the per capita tax would only be FIVE shillings per year. He emphasized that the tax burden imposed by a vengeful and avaricious King would be EIGHT times greater unless America prevailed. Paine based his calculations on the present tax rate of the English people plus the additional tax money needed to pay off the cost of their war.

However, the yearly tax to fund the war for each American would be about THIRTEEN shillings. This amount is only ONE THIRD of the British per capita tax each year. In order to buttress his case, Paine contrasted the costs of war damages in Philadelphia with a projected tax. He wrote, "Look at the destruction done in this city. The many houses totally destroyed, and others damaged; the waste of fences in the country round it, besides the plunder of furniture, forage and provision." The value of property destroyed or plundered would amount, on average, to TWO-HUNDRED shillings per head. This loss dwarfs the THIRTEEN and a- fraction shillings needed from each person to carry on the war against Britain.

For four years the United States lacked sufficient money, men, and supplies. A unified will of the thirteen separate and independent states was absent. In some degree or other, most of the Americans were loyalists. Congress was out of funds; the Revolutionary war was at a stalemate;

Washington was dormant; and the infant Republic was on the verge of collapse. Two million pounds were needed to continue the war against the enemy. This was a huge sum, especially when one considers the sorry state of America's financial condition. Who could find a solution to this grave crisis? From Washington, Adams, Jefferson and John Jay, we heard nothing. Acting alone, Thomas Paine stepped up to the challenge. His behavior here, is purely consistent with his exertions at Trenton; in exposing Silas Deane; in defending Washington; in rejecting a bogus peace treaty; and in contributing personal funds to aid the "cause". Without exception, Paine would always move with alacrity to attack and crush any threat to the preservation of the Independence of the United States.

This time, Paine shouldered the unpopular burden of proposing a tax plan. In order to make the odious measure palatable, Paine came up with an ingenious method of softening the impact of a new tax. Paine wrote:

"The annual sum wanted is two millions, and the average rate in which it falls is thirteen shillings and four pence per head. Suppose then that we raise   half the sum and sixty over. The average rate thereof will be seven shillings per head."

Paine, then, proposed to borrow the second million. If successful, the plan would have a double effect. First, America would be able to continue military operations; and second, the per capita tax would be only about seven shillings per year on the second million. (At that time, according to Paine, the cost of a pound of coffee was between five and six shillings.) Think of it! If Washington were victorious, the United States of America could have been "purchased" with a contribution of a few pounds from each adult.

As usual, once Paine offers a plan, he then outlines a method to put it into effect. In this case he suggested that the Congress and the separate states raise the needed two million in taxes by means of duties on imports and property taxes. The total tax burden for the following year would have been no more than fourteen shillings "per head". This would have been a slight increase over the present tax of thirteen shillings and four pence per head and a bargain price indeed for a country. Alas, Paine's brilliant plan was never put into effect. The start of the new year of 1781 found the United States no further ahead than she was when she first started on that fateful day of April 19, 1775, the battles of Lexington and Concord. This was the darkest period of the Revolutionary War since Christmas eve, December 24, 1776, one day before the historic assault on the Hessians at Trenton, New Jersey began.

Again in January, 1781, Washington's army was on the verge of collapse and defeat. But, Thomas Paine would never give up. At this time, Congress decided to send an envoy to France in order to request financial aid from King Louis XVI. Colonel John Laurens was appointed to be the envoy, after both Adams and Hamilton declined. Laurens requested that Paine go with him as his official secretary, but Congress refused to grant Paine an official title or pay for his expenses on this critical mission. Paine seized the opportunity and agreed to accompany Laurens as his companion. Major William Jackson was appointed as Laurens official and paid secretary. Paine paid his own expenses.

Thomas Paine, Colonel Laurens and Major Jackson sailed for France on February 11, 1781. They landed at Boston, Massachusetts 195 days later on August 25, 1781 with over two million silver livres and supplies.

According to Aldridge, The United States obtained six million livres as a present and ten millions as a loan. (*Man of Reason*, page 88) Craig Nelson wrote that France gave the United States twelve million livres and loaned it eighteen million more during the Revolution. The mission was a huge success. France merits the credit and gratitude of Americans because it was France who provided the money, the troops, the arms and supplies which enabled the United States to be victorious at Yorktown on October 19, 1781. France, that is, King Louis XVI was persuaded to provide the means for the one large decisive battle that Paine was aching for five years. The battle of Yorktown ended the war.

Crisis X

March 5, 1782

In the opening sentence of the introduction to Paine's *The American Crisis X*, Doctor Foner gave an admirably concise summary of the American victory at Yorktown.

> "On October 19, 1781, Lord Cornwallis, outnumbered three to one on land and cut off from fresh supplies by sea, surrendered his army of 7,000 men at Yorktown." (*The Complete Writings of Thomas Paine*, Collected and Edited by Philip S. Foner, PH.D., Vol. l, P. 189)

One month later, November 27, 1781, King George III appeared before parliament with his royal hat in his hand in order to beg Parliament to continue the war. Paine reviewed the King's address in the first part of Crisis X. He called the King's speech a curiosity that was "read with a laugh and dismissed with disdain". (Foner, Vol. l, p. 189) Then, Paine reviewed the speech in detail, as only he could.

The King accused the Americans of starting the war. Paine answered that the King rejected the humblest petitions with sullen insolence;

practiced savage cruelties and the most scandalous plundering and incited the Indians and Negroes against the colonists. The King wanted the Americans back as subjects "attached to my person". In the following page, Paine described George III as being perverse and barbarous, and accused him of being a sycophant and a hypocrite. Paine's rebuttal recalls what he wrote, six years before, on January 10, 1776, in answer to another speech by the King which appeared in Philadelphia on that very same day. At that time, Paine described the Kings speech as bloody-minded, base, wicked, and "a piece of finished villainy", which deserves a "general execration". "The Speech...is nothing better than a willful audacious libel against the truth, the common good, and the existence of mankind..." (Common Sense, Anchor Press, p. 53)

George the third's post Yorktown speech was no different. Poor king. He was a loser and he was reduced to the level of a beggar. His real purpose was to plead for more tax money from the already oppressed people of England so that instead of being a King of an island, he would be a King of a continent. Even though the obstinate desires of the King were hopeless, Paine urged the Americans not to relax. He stressed the necessity of working to prepare to defend and to secure what had been won.

In the next part of this *Crisis*, Paine, again, brought up the unpopular subject of taxes which were necessary to conclude the war and secure the Independence. He approached this in an unusual way by contrasting an event which was right, but unpopular with an event which was wrong, but popular. Paine gave two examples. The first was his proposed Tax plan as detailed in The Crisis Extraordinary, and the second example was The Silas Deane Affair. In both cases, Paine had a dual purpose, in my view.

Paine used both examples to provide additional information. I believe, also, that Paine used both examples as an indirect way of scolding Congress and those who were not contributing financial support of the Revolution. It is my opinion that the examples were given as a way of getting back at certain members of Congress who opposed him for exposing Deane, and as a recondite rebuke for not implementing his tax plan.

The Deane disgrace has been well researched and recorded. Deane conspired to use Paine's grand idea of the revolution as a means to get rich. His scheme was detected and he became a traitor. Paine wrote, "He endeavored to effect by treason what he had failed to accomplish by fraud". (Foner, Vol. 1, p. 197) Paine continued, "His character has been that of a plodding, plotting, cringing mercenary, capable of any disguise that suited his purpose. His final detection has very happily cleared up those mistakes…" (Foner, vol.1, p. 198)

Henry Laurens, father of John Laurens, did not side with the mistaken, envious, wrongheaded, elitist clique, - Adams, Jay, G Morris, and others, - who were at least, partially responsible for Thomas Paine's decision to resign as the secretary of the committee of foreign affairs. As indicated, this, perhaps awkward, digression concerning Silas Deane's betrayal and attempted fraud, was an oblique – "See, it told you so" – requital, aimed at Paine's detractors. Paine thought that the "digression was necessary to give". I concur.

The second part of Crisis X is a detailed discussion about taxes. Neither the States nor Congress did enough to provide sufficient funds to conduct the Revolutionary War. Finally Thomas Paine had to raise the money himself. In a footnote in volume number one, page number 197, of his monumental opus – *The Complete Writings of Thomas Paine* – Doctor Philip S. Foner wrote, "Paine sailed for France early in 1781, to ask the French Government for financial assistance for the American Republic…Paine went with (colonel John) Laurens, arriving in France in March, 1781. They returned to America in August with two and a half livres (sic) (perhaps two and a half million livres), and a boatload of stores and clothing. These funds and supplies enabled Washington to prosecute the campaign which resulted in the defeat of Cornwallis at Yorktown."

Craig Nelson reported that King Louis XVI "loaded Paine with favors" and gave the Americans "4.8 million livres in money and materials". (Nelson's *Thomas Paine*, p. 153) Alfred Owen Aldridge wrote that the amount obtained was "six million livres". (Aldridge, p. 88) Moncure Daniel Conway wrote, "The gift of six millions was confided into the hands of Franklin and Paine". Paine sailed from France on June 1, 1781, and arrived in Boston on August 25, 1781 "with 2,500,000 livres in silver, and in convoy a ship laden with clothing and military stores". (Conway, P. 70)

Thomas Paine deserves a large share of the credit for obtaining the huge amount of aid from King Louis. Benjamin Franklin deserves a transport of credit as well. The aid could not have come at a better time. Because the timing was perfect, it gives rise to a haunting question. Why was King Louis XVI disposed to be so generous at this critical time? After all, we know that Franklin had been laying the ground-work for obtaining financial aid from France for four years. Indeed he had, already been successful. Franklin had "arranged the transfer of substantial sums both before and after the arrival of Laurens and Thomas Paine." (Aldridge, p. 88) We know, also, from Lamartine* that King Louis "Loaded Paine with favors. Why was there such a dramatic and bountiful out-pouring of aid within a few weeks after Paine arrived in France? I wish we were able to learn more about what transpired during those critical weeks. Alfred Owen Aldridge wrote, "Very little can be discovered abut Paine's activities during this brief visit to France apart from a few references by members of Benjamin Franklin's entourage in Paris." (Aldridge, p. 88) Craig Nelson wrote, "This episode is one of many where the lack of Paine documents is especially regrettable." (p. 154)

---

* Alphonse-Marie-Louis Lamartine. 1790-1869; French poet; Historian, Author of the *Histoire des Girondins*. Webster's new *Biographical Dictionary*, Merriam-Webster, Inc., 1988, p. 578.

I hope the scholars will do more research on this critical episode in the future. Lamartine was born in 1790, nine years after this event. How could he know that King Louis XVI loaded Paine with favors? What source did Lamartine use? Surely, the discovery of any secondary or tertiary material, which would corroborate Thomas Paine's phenomenal success, would be of great historical significance. Of course, I believe that it was Thomas Paine's incontrovertible influence on King Louis that won the day. The King moved without delay. He backed up his decision with all of the money and military supplies needed to end the war with a glorious allied victory at Yorktown, Virginia on October 19, 1781.

Without the massive aid from France, the war would have been prolonged; and without Thomas Paine's successful exertions in France there would have been no aid. Once again we see that Paine was doing everything in his power to protect and preserve his innovative creation, the free and independent Republic of the United States of America.

Crisis XI

May 22, 1782

Britain had lost the war. The single aim of King George III was to subjugate America by conquest. After six years of invasive, aggressive, destructive and murderous warfare, he failed. After Britain's war ending defeat at Yorktown, the King and his ministers continued their attempt to gain what was never theirs. Instead of using the force of arms, this time the British resorted to a policy of deception and fraud. No wonder why Paine called the King a "hardened sullen tempered Pharaoh". The scheme of the British was to break the honorable treaty of Alliance between America and France. If this deception was successful, it would have set the stage for another armed assault on America.

Paine was unsparing in his condemnation of Britain's base, conspiratorial tactics. He used the words perfidious, dishonor, disgrace, insidious and corrupt in his description of Britain's attempt to seduce the United States into breaking faith with their best and most generous ally. Paine wrote that Britain was "beaten, but not humble; condemned but not penitent; they (King, ministers and parliament) act like men trembling at fate and catching at a straw". (Foner, Vol. l, p. 214) In Crisis number six, Paine described the Treaty of Alliance with France in 1778, as "open, noble and generous." There is no doubt that the Treaty helped America to persevere during the bleak period of 1779 and 1780; and laid the diplomatic ground-work for the amazing Franco-American victory at Yorktown in 1781.

Both France and the United States remained true to their pact through seventeen difficult years when, in 1795, Washington dishonored himself and the United States, by signing the "Jay Treaty". Thomas Paine had written that if Britain proposed that America should break her Alliance with France, such a proposition would be an example of "perfidiousness, and such disregard of honor and morals, as would add the finishing vice to national corruption". (Foner, Vol. l, p. 270) Paine hoped that the Franco-American Alliance would be maintained indefinitely. He wrote, "There is nothing which sets the character of a nation in a higher or lower light with others, than the faithfully fulfilling, or perfidiously breaking, of treaties:. (Foner, Vol. l, p. 215) Washington managed to do, with a stroke of a quill, what Great Britain could not accomplish in seventeen years. As we shall see later, Paine will have a few choice words to say about Washington's pusillanimous decision.

A Supernumerary Crisis

May 31, 1782

Thomas Paine declared his moral code several times in his writings. It was: Loving mercy, Doing justice and helping my fellow man. On the first page of his immortal *Age of Reason,* Paine wrote, "I believe in the equality of man; ("Mankind being originally equals in the order of Creation..." *Common Sense*. p. 18) and I believe that religious duties consist in doing justice, loving mercy, and endeavoring to make our fellow creatures happy."

The Supernumerary Crisis is a beautiful example of Thomas Paine putting into practice what he believed. It was address to Sir Guy Carlton, commander of British forces in New York. Here, in brief, is the story. One, Captain Huddy, of the (New) Jersey militia was murdered by a party of refugees in the British pay and service. The name of the refugee officer who ordered the murder was Lippencott. George Washington demanded that Lippencott be turned over as a murderer. The British refused to deliver up Lippencott. In stead, the British surrendered an innocent British officer to suffer death for the crime of Lippencott. The name of that British officer was Captain Asgill.

In four pages of masterful rhetoric Thomas Paine tried to persuade Guy Carlton to give up the guilty murderer and save the innocent Asgill. Paine followed up with a Letter to Washington urging the release of Asgill. This act of mercy by Paine, no doubt, influenced Washington to communicate to Congress his desire to set Asgill free. Congress complied with Washington's wishes and Asgill was released.

Crisis XII
To The Earl of Shelburne

October 29, 1782

In September, 1782, Lord Shelburne gave a speech in which he declared his opposition to American Independence. Shelburne went so far as to say that American Independence would result in the ruin of England. I think that both Shelburne and the King were hoping for some kind of 'eleventh hour' reconciliation; or failing that, they would try to continue the war. Of course, while Thomas Paine was alive, any variety of reconciliation without complete Independence was totally out of the question. With Paine, there were only two options. The choice was either the total unfettered, sovereign, free and Independent United

States of America, or war. One might wonder if Shelburne ever read *Common Sense*, in which the word reconciliation appears no less than nineteen times. With incontrovertible logic, Paine disintegrated the idea of reconciliation.

However, Shelburne did have a point. He said, "There were numbers, great numbers there (in America), who were of the same way of thinking, in respect to that country being dependent on this (England), and who, with his lordship, perceived ruin and independence linked together." There were many die hard loyalists; many pacifists; people who were apathetic; conservative adherents of various religious sects; those who would not contribute financial support to the Revolutionary war; those whose money profits from trade would be secure under monarchic rule as well as any other; numbers of people opposed to the idea of a constitutional Democratic government over all of the states; those who never gave a thought to the idea of a unified federal government.

I firmly believe that the Americans as described above constituted a clear majority; and I believe, as well, that those patriots who were committed to Independence and victory over the British were in the minority. In spite of this, Paine said that Shelburne was deluded and that he was a stranger to the mind and sentiments of America. This is not accurate. Shelburne was a stranger to the mind and sentiments of Thomas Paine. The sentiments of most Americans, a majority of the inhabitants of America, were not the sentiments of Thomas Paine. I believe, as I have said before, that Thomas Paine projected his ideas of Freedom, Liberty, Independence and Republican Democracy into the minds of the inhabitants of America. Paine was speaking for the Americans on the basis that they would embrace his ideas if they knew about them and could understand them and if they willing act in accordance with them. But, few Americans understood what Paine was creating.

When we recall that women could not vote, minors could not vote, men without property could not vote, loyalists would not vote, and an estimated thirty percent of the people were illiterate, one might well question whether a "new system"; a "new era" of government mattered. It mattered to Thomas Paine. He was consumed with the work of creating a new Nation, a Democratic Republic, governed at the pleasure of the people, where the power of governing resides.

Thomas Paine's innovative dream was almost complete. The war was won and all that remained was a formal Treaty of peace between Great Britain and the United States which would give formal recognition and unconditional acceptance of American Independence. Britain was trying every stratagem they could in order to circumvent acknowledging that the United States of America was a separate, free, independent and sovereign country. They even attempted to make a separate peace with France. I believe that the Shelburne speech was a ploy in the maneuvers to relegate American Independence as a subject for deliberation during the peace negotiations but not as a pre-condition for negations to begin. There was no chance that Thomas Paine would entertain any peace proposals unless Independence was recognized first. "Are not the repeated declarations of congress, and which all America supports, that they will not even hear any proposals whatever, until the unconditional and unequivocal independence of America is recognized; are not, I say, these declarations answer enough?"

Paine reinforced his position by saying, "The prosecution of the war by the former ministry was savage and horrid; since which it has been mean, trickish and delusive." Paine had recalled those years when America's petitions were rejected and unconditional submission was demanded. He reviewed that America was the "seat of war", not England, and the Americans were the sufferers of the "wanton destruction" and "insolent barbarity" at the hands of Britain; and as a result, thousands of innocent people were murdered.

Paine repeated that Britain had been treacherous during the war and she was not to be trusted after it. He asked, why throw good money after bad? "By arms there is no hope. The experience of nearly eight years, with the expense of an hundred million pounds sterling, and the loss of two armies, must positively decide the point." Shelburne had no hand in the American cession and his spurious efforts to compromise the American Independence were futile. Paine's conclusion was, "As America is gone, the only act of manhood is to LET HER GO."

Although this "Letter" was addressed to the Earl of Shelburne, I believe that Paine hoped that it would be read by all in England and France as well as in America. I earnestly believe that Paine intended his ideas to be read and understood by the members of Congress in order to warn them about Britain's schemes and to deter any last minute back-sliding. It may be recalled that, in a similar way, Paine wrote the *Montgomery Dialogue* in June, 1776, a few days before Congress voted on the resolution to declare Independence, in order to deter any opposition to it. Paine was ever watchful.

Crisis XIII

April 19, 1783

"The times that tried men's souls' are over and the greatest and completest revolution the world ever knew, gloriously and happily accomplished."

The Treaty of Paris would not be completed until September 3, 1783. But, Thomas had achieved his goal, the creation of the United States of America. The terms of the Treaty, among others, included the formal recognition of America as an independent nation and securing fishing rights in the North Atlantic. Independence gave birth to a new country unlike any other. Paine wrote, "To see it in our power to make a world happy – to teach mankind the art of being so – to exhibit on the theatre of the universe, a character hitherto unknown – and to have, as it were, a NEW CREATION* entrusted to our hands, are honors that command reflection, and can neither be too highly estimated nor too

---

* caps mine

gratefully received. America [The United States of America] was a new creation, and America had an originator. The idea of creating the United States of America came from the mind of Thomas Paine. The thought that a group of men – women would be excluded – sat down together and at a specific moment, had the simultaneous brain storm of creating a new nation, without a king, along a part of the coast of a sparsely inhabited continent, defies even the boundless limits of mysticism.

George Washington was a convert. John Adams admitted that Paine changed his mind and his course. Jefferson procrastinated. After *Common Sense*, Benjamin Franklin became an esteemed and honored patriot and a loyal and supportive friend of Thomas Paine. I am truly grateful for the accomplishments of Washington, Adams, Jefferson and many other patriots who are traditionally described as "Founding Fathers". I readily join with all who give credit to these men where the credit is due. However, I refuse to praise them either for deeds that they did not do, or for ideas that they did not originate. Paine, then, proceeded to give a description of what was achieved. "Never, I say had a country so many openings to happiness as this."

"Her setting out into life, like the rising of a fair morning, was unclouded and promising. Her cause was good. Her principles just and liberal. Her temper (was) serene and firm. Her conduct (was) regulated by the nicest steps, and everything about her wore the mark of honor." It may be that this metaphorical assessment of the birth of the United States expresses ideals aimed at by Paine but may not be accepted as being historically accurate. What other country "can boast so fair an origin"?

Who else was writing descriptions of the creation of the United States in such utopian terms in 1783(?); certainly not Washington, Adams, Jefferson and Jay. I continue to believe that the above quotes of Thomas Paine are recondite biographical statements.

Paine proceeded by recalling that America never faltered during adversity, overcame all obstacles, and emerged victorious. Accordingly,

America justly earned the reputation as a country having an excellent character. He urges, "Let then the world see that she can bear prosperity: and that her honest virtue in time of peace, is equal to the bravest virtue in time of war." America was entering a period of peace and Paine wrote, "In this situation, may she never forget that a fair reputation is of as much importance as independence." It gives a country dignity and "commands a reverence where pomp and splendor fail." He cautioned that the honor of the Revolution should never be besmirched. Then in one of the most comprehensive compliments to himself and to the American Revolution that I have ever seen, Paine wrote that the Revolution "has contributed more to enlighten the world, and diffuse a spirit of freedom and liberality among mankind, than any human event (if this may be called one) that ever preceded it."

Thomas Paine was the American Revolution. Of course, we can't say that. We must say something like: Thomas Paine embodied the principles of the American Revolution. If we think of the American Revolution as an innovation, all of the pieces come together. In the last chapter of his excellent biography of Thomas Paine, the esteemed scholar Craig Nelson refers to Independence as something that needed to be invented. The United States of America was something new. It was an innovation, and I was happy to read that Craig Nelson referred to the adoption of Paine's ideas and INNOVATIONS. Paine's major innovation was the integration of ideas such that the monarchic form of government was replaced by a Democratic Republic in which the natural rights of each individual are secured and protected equally. This is not to say that there is no room for improvement. The Constitution provides for that.

I now return to *Crisis XIII*. Paine wrote that the struggle was over, and "with the blessings of peace, independence and universal commerce," America could do as she pleases. Now it was time to focus on strengthening the union of the States; and each step taken to achieve a greater unity must bear the mark of honor. In *Common Sense* he had written "It is not in numbers, but in a union that our great strength lies". Paine stressed that the great national character of America depends on the strong union of the separate states. Thomas Paine was creating a new country. A sovereign nation was absolutely necessary. His words, "The whole country is called to unanimity and exertion" – given as an example from *Crisis IX* – echo the theme of unity which runs through all of the pages of *Common Sense* and the *Crisis Papers*.

Paine was pleading for a central government with the unified states as its component parts. A united Nation was necessary in order to take equal rank with the other sovereign countries of the world. It would provide an army for security at home, and a navy for the protection of our ships at sea, and international commerce. In the future treaties of alliance or peace or commerce would be forged under the Flag of the United States of America.

Thomas Paine invented the United States of America. In effect, he said that as a united entity, "wisely regulated", America had the prospect of being the happiest INVENTION* in government which the circumstances of America can allow. A small service, harmlessly rendered by each state would form an "aggregate" which would devolve to the benefit of the entire nation.

Paine's visionary objective was the establishment of a constitutional UNION OF THE states. (According to Foner's reference work and also the Anchor Press edition, Paine used capital letters for emphasis). His vision transcended the jealously guarded autonomy of the individual states and the self-importance of their leaders. The Articles of Confederation of 1777 were ineffective. Finally, in 1787, a national convention met in Philadelphia in order to draft a constitution. This was eleven years after a national charter was publicly proposed by Paine in *Common Sense*. The constitution was not completely adopted until 1790; and then, only because the Bill of Rights was tacked on to it. The resulting product of the constitutional convention was a document that had all of the marks of a

---

*   caps mine

work put together by a committee. If a person imagined that the framers of the constitution had the intention of providing perpetual work for lawyers, that person must conclude that the framers succeeded.

Paine concluded this timeless *Crisis Paper* by furnishing some autobiographical comments which I believe are incontrovertible indications that he independently and willfully had the intention of creating a new nation, totally separate from Great Britain and at the same time establishing a new governmental system without a King.

He wrote, "It was the cause of America that made me an AUTHOR*." He considered reconciliation with Britain "impossible and unnatural". He realized that the only way to save America was a "Declaration of Independence". This recognition "made it impossible for me, feeling as I did to be silent". In the course of more than seven years, Thomas Paine exhausted all of his energies in order to "conciliate the affections" of the Americans and to unite their interests in order to ASSIST in the FOUNDATION – WORK of the REVOLUTION. He wrote, "Independence always appeared to me practicable and probable..."

Paine's ASSISTANCE had a unique character, namely: FIRSTNESS. He converted George Washington to the idea of Independence, and Washington said so. He converted John Adams to the idea of total independence, and Adams admitted it. Jefferson was a "Johnny-Come-Lately" convert. In addition, Paine's ASSSISTANCE in the foundation – work of the Revolution exhibited a special characteristic of leadership when he was the first to propose continental unity by means of a national Constitution, as detailed twice in *Common Sense.*

"Let a Continental Conference be held...let their business be to frame a Continental Charter. Always remembering that our strength is continental, not provincial; securing freedom and property to all men, and above all things, the free exercise of religion..."

"In page forty, I threw out a few thoughts on the propriety of a Continental Charter...a charter is to be understood as a bond of solemn

---

*   caps mine

obligation, which the whole enters into, to support the right of every separate part, whether of religion, personal freedom, or property."

Paine knew that Independence could be achieved on the condition that "the sentiments of the country (people) could be FORMED* and held to the object." The sentiments, of enough people, to establish Independence, were FORMED by Thomas Paine in *Common Sense*; and it was Thomas Paine who held enough people to the object by means of the *Crisis Papers*.

"The scenes of war are closed" and Paine persisted in giving credit to the American people for their support of Independence throughout the war "till they (the people) crowned it with success." What support? The enlistments, the money, the arms, the supplies and provisions that Paine was pleading for, were not forthcoming from "they", the people in a unified effort by all thirteen states. Full credit and gratitude is owed to those who contributed what they could.

As regards the "crowning success" of the decisive and war-ending victory at Yorktown, the French army and navy, the generalship of Rochambeau and money, supplies and arms from France, provided more support than the American people, including, in my opinion, Washington and those members of Congress who knew what Paine accomplished, and yet failed to extend the credit and gratitude that was due to him.

Paine ended Crisis XIII by saying that he followed the war from beginning to end. He did a lot more than that. He created a new country and he knew it. I believe that Paine wanted to be thanked for establishing the Republic of the United States. Expressions of gratitude and appreciation for his writings were forthcoming; but total recognition, acknowledgment and gratefulness as the original founder of the United States of America were absent. So, Paine complimented himself: "I shall always feel an honest pride in the part I have taken and acted and a gratitude to Nature and Providence for putting it in my power to be of some use to mankind."

---

* caps mine

CHAPTER 12
VIGILANCE AND ACTION

I n a long letter to Benjamin Franklin dated May 16, 1778, Thomas Paine expressed his optimism about the War and independence. "I think (the) fighting is nearly over, for Britain, mad, wicked and foolish, has done her utmost"... "The Affairs of England are approaching either to ruin or redemption."... "For my own part, I thought it very hard to have the country set on fire about my ears almost the moment I got into it; and among other pleasures I feel in having uniformly done my duty, I feel that of not having discredited your friendship and patronage."

When Paine wrote "For my own part" and "having uniformly done my duty", I believe that he was making a veiled disclosure that he intended to create the United States and that he had been acting to make it a reality. His optimism may have been premature, but it did not deter him from devoting all of his time and talents from striking down every objection to independence and overcoming every barrier to the recognition and security of Independence.

ACTION

Paine supported Washington when in 1778, a group in Congress, including John Adams, were plotting to replace him. Paine's *Crisis* number five, dated March 21, 1778, gives evidence of his support, even though he was not entirely happy with Washington's generalship.

ACTION

Again, Paine was alert and acted in another case. He learned that the British were attempting to subvert the financial stability of the states by printing and circulating counterfeit money. In a letter, dated April 11, 1778, to Henry Laurens, Paine pointed out that counterfeiting is a felony. It is forgery and "operates to the injustice and injury of the whole continent". (Conway, p. 43) Again, Paine repeated the word CONTINENT, which brings to mind what he wrote proposing a Continental Charter in *Common Sense*, "always remembering that our strength is continental, not provincial."

ACTION

A salient case of Thomas Paine's continuing vigilance, is the "Silas Deane Affair". Deane's attempted fraud could have been costly to the Revolution. Paine discovered Deane's scheme to enrich himself with the blood money of fallen, wounded and suffering patriots. Paine exposed Deane. Klobbe's commentary in *Saint Thomas Paine* (chapter ten), along with most of the biographies of Thomas Paine provide accounts of this regrettable episode. Paine used this conspiracy to put the members of Congress, and others, on notice that the Revolution, undertaken to create the United States, was not to be traduced for the purpose of 'wind-fall', money profits. Deane became a traitor. Later, both Robert Morris and Gouverneur Morris admitted that they were deceived about Deane's treachery. I think that Congress owes Thomas Paine an apology. It can be done posthumously. "Better late than never."

ACTION

Here is another example of Paine's vigilance and action. Paine watched Congress like a hawk. He was in constant touch with a number of his friends in Congress who respected him and who kept him informed of what Congress was doing. When Paine learned that some members of Congress were thinking of using and possibly ceding America's fishing rights off the coast of Newfoundland, as a bargaining piece in future peace negotiations with Britain, he stepped right up with his formidable pen. Paine's brilliant article in 1779, on "Peace and the Newfoundland Fisheries" exploded the disabling and contradictory idea of ceding the natural and sovereign maritime rights to Britain or any other Nation. America's rights were recognized in the Paris Peace Treaty in 1783.

ACTION

Paine was elected to the post of Clerk of the Pennsylvania Assembly on November 2, 1779. According to Conway, he introduced an act to abolish Slavery in that State, on the same day he was elected. The Pennsylvania Act Abolishing Slavery was passed into Law on March 1, 1780. Thomas Paine's Preamble to this Act is a timeless, humanitarian, and literary Masterpiece. Paine's construct was total Independence and total, not partial, Freedom and Liberty for all without distinction including women and slaves.

In a letter to Washington, dated June 5, 1778, Paine wrote, "She (Britain) must see the necessity of acknowledging, sometime or other, the Independence of America"...Soon after this letter Congress returned to Philadelphia. According to M. D. Conway (page 47), "In Philadelphia Congress was still surrounded by a hostile population"; and, "Even so late as November 24, 1778, the French Minister (Gerard) wrote to his Government: "Scarcely one quarter of the ordinary inhabitants of Philadelphia now here favor the cause (of independence)." This is strange because Independence had been declared over two years ago. Although Paine was famous, he lacked both the support and the gratitude of the majority. The unity he passionately worked for was absent, and he was living on the edge of poverty.

In a letter to Henry Laurens, dated September 14, 1779, Paine indicated his poor financial circumstances. In the same letter, he made an indirect admission regarding his idea of creating the Democratic Republic of the United States.

"I need not repeat to you the part I have acted or the principle I have acted upon…it was neither the place nor the people but the Cause itself that irresistibly engaged me in its support; for I should have acted the same part in any other Country could the same circumstances have arisen there which have happened here."

"I find myself so curiously circumstanced that I have both too many friends and too few, the generality of them thinking that from the public part I have so long acted, I cannot have less than a mine to draw from. What they have had from me, they have got for nothing, and they consequently suppose I must be able to afford it." (Conway, page 60)

The phrase, "What they have had from me" constitutes what I believe to be an affirmation and indirect testimony that Thomas Paine set out, with indomitable will, to create the United States of America.

CHAPTER 13
THOMAS JEFFERSON:
THE RELUCTANT PATRIOT

There is no evidence that Thomas Jefferson had any intention of composing a Declaration of Independence prior to June 11, 1776. At this time he was appointed by Congress to a five-man committee to frame a "Declaration". The other members were: Benjamin Franklin, John Adams, Robert Livingston, and Roger Sherman. It is noted that the directive of Congress was to prepare a Declaration of Independence and nothing else. No order was given by Congress to draw up a bill of articles proposing reconciliation and peace with Great Britain.

Since Thomas Jefferson has been given credit as the author of the Declaration of Independence, (hereafter referred to as the "Declaration") and also, since he is included, in general, as one of the "Founding Fathers" of the United States, a review of his activities starting in 1774 is pertinent. In my opinion, such a reexamination is in order because continuing scholarly research has brought to light new information that has proved that some early assumptions about American History, which have been carried forward year after year, were wrong. Also, many scholars and students of American History do not believe that Jefferson was the real author of the Declaration; nor do they believe that he was the original "founding father" of the United States. It is my belief that he was a following founder. Let's take a look at the record.

IN JULY OF 1774, Jefferson drafted a declaration of rights for the Virginia Convention. Randall tells us that it was written under the working title, "Instructions to the Virginia Delegates in the Continental Congress."(Randall, p.210)

Randall further informs us that Jefferson "wrote quickly and surely", but, "He did not stop to check every detail"; "He left blanks for dates", because he did not intend it for publication. (Randall, p.209) Jefferson's own words were, "They were drawn in haste, with a number of blanks, with some uncertainties and inaccuracies of historical facts." (Heritage Press, p. 244)

Jefferson intended to present these incomplete instructions, in person to the Virginia Convention for consideration as Resolutions. However, on his way to Williamsburg, he got sick and returned home. He sent his "instructions", by messenger to Peyton Randolph who was the moderator of the Virginia Convention. He sent another copy to Patrick Henry. Payton Randolph received the "Resolutions" which were read and voted on. They were voted down and set aside. Since Jefferson's Resolutions were not adopted, they were not included in the official printed resolutions of the convention. I have little hope that the original draft will be found. However, according to Randall, some of Jefferson's admirers gave a new title to his "instructions". They named it a *SUMMARY VIEW OF THE RIGHTS OF* <u>BRITISH</u> *AMERICA* "and put two hundred copies through the press of the Virginia Gazette before the end of 1774." A *Summary View* was reprinted in Philadelphia, and twice in London. (Randall, p.216) I would love to see a copy of each because the title change indicates that other alterations may have been made. The scholars should conduct an investigative inquiry into this matter because what has come down to us is suspect.

Here is the gist of what Jefferson was proposing in his *Summary View*. It consists of two main ideas. The first was, we will keep the King; and second we will eliminate the British Parliament. His position was, "It is neither our wish nor our interest to separate from her..." (Heritage

Press, p.260) Jefferson was willing to retain the King and to acknowledge him as the executive head of the British empire. This meant a union with Great Britain, a weaker union perhaps, but still union. He wrote, "...on their part, let them be ready to establish UNION on a generous plan..." (Heritage Press, p.260)

Contrast this with Thomas Paine's, "We...reject and renounce all Allegiance and subjection to the Kings of Great Britain..." Jefferson referred to the American colonists as your subjects in British America. At this time Jefferson's goal was nothing more than redress and reconciliation and the establishment of "fraternal love and harmony through the whole empire," of which British America would be a part. (Heritage Press, p.261))Compare the above with Paine's "We utterly dissolve and break off all political connection..."

Clearly, "Jefferson's call for an Empire of Colonies under the rule of a king but not Parliament was far afield from total separation from Great Britain, and unconditional Independence. I am not aware of any evidence that Jefferson, during the year of 1774, would disavow the monarchic system, and at the same time, totally renounce his loyalty to the crown, and reject and break off all political connection with Great Britain; and publicly propose and work for the creation of the United States as a new sovereign country without a King. Willard Sterne Randall summarized the years events in one line when he wrote, "In late 1774 no one, not even Jefferson, was ready to sever allegiance to the King or to separate the American colonies from the British Empire." (Randall, p.215)

At the start of the new year of 1775, Thomas Jefferson remained a Loyalist. There is no evidence that he was proposing a new system of government without a King. There is no evidence, up to this time that Jefferson had any intention of composing a Declaration of Independence. His firm and determined position, far from being an argument for Independence was an unyielding and resolute plea for the American Colonies to remain a part of the British Empire.

CHAPTER 14
THE SIXTH MAN

Thomas Jefferson was not chosen as one of the five delegates elected to represent Virginia in the Second Continental Congress. Instead, he was chosen as the DEPUTY of Peyton Randolph, in case the ailing Randolph could not attend. In effect Randall says that Jefferson was the sixth man on Virginia's list of respected leaders.(Randall, p.228) Since the Second Continental Congress would not reconvene until May of 1775, Jefferson had a lot of time to devote to Monticello. Most of his time was spent in breeding horses and, along with his other duties, stocking his wine cellar.

However, during the first part of this historic year, two events will unanswerably show what Jefferson's position was. The first event was the introduction by Lord Chatham of a conciliatory bill in the House of Lords on February 1, 1775. The measure called for an IMPERIAL union with the Colonies. It was a plan for reconciliation, not total Independence. The proposed plan was" noisily voted down by an overwhelming and bellicose ministerial majority", according to Randall (p.233).

Jefferson was disappointed. In a letter to William Small, one of Jefferson's former teachers, he wrote, "When I saw Lord Chatham's (conciliatory) bill, I entertained high hope that a reconciliation could have been brought about."(Randall, p.234) The letter to William Small (3) was dated May 7, 1775. By this time, Jefferson had received the news of the Lexington and Concord battles on April 29, 1775. Clearly, Jefferson continued to hold out for reconciliation with Great Britain.

He was not ready to propose unconditional separation and sovereign Independence at this time; nor was he ready to propose or even assist in the establishment of a new country with a new non-monarchic, non-autocratic government system. The second event is another example of Jefferson's unwillingness to sever all ties with the crown. This is described in the next paragraph.

Around May 7, 1775, Patrick Henry, with a force of six-hundred men, marched in armed rebellion against Williamsburg and the royal governor of Virginia, Lord John Murray Dunmore. Jefferson took the side of the British against Patrick Henry and the American patriots. Can you imagine!

As the commander of the Albemarle Country British militia, Jefferson joined his troops with the British Regulars under Lord Dunmore's command. Whether the action of Patrick Henry was right or wrong is not in question here. The fact is that Jefferson sided with the British. Acting in his official capacity as a colonel and commander of a county militia, in concert with other principal Loyalists, Jefferson was successful in stopping Henry's defiant uprising. If Henry's revolutionary insurgents had prevailed, Lord Dunmore might have been killed.

This incident occurred when America was already at war with Great Britain. Jefferson knew it. At least, he was well aware of the armed conflict of April 19, 1775, the battles of Lexington and Concord. However, it is not my purpose, here, to speculate on the pros and cons of what might have been. Nor is it my purpose to condemn Jefferson.

My point is that, at the time of Patrick Henry's incursion, Jefferson acted as a Loyalist and gave no indication that he was ready to reject and renounce all allegiance and subordination to the King of Great Britain and the King's royal governors, ministers and administrators. Up until May 7, 1775, there is no evidence that Jefferson intended to compose a Declaration of Independence.

The second Continental Congress convened in May, 1775. John Hancock was elected president, replacing Peyton Randolph who returned to Virginia in order to resume his duties as Speaker of the House of Burgesses. He pressed Jefferson to write an address to Governor Dunmore and the people in agreement with the sentiments of congress. Jefferson's address was a strong plea for self-government and free trade. It was not a clear and concrete repudiation of the King. It was not a manifesto calling for the utter dissolution of all political connection with Parliament and Great Britain. It was not a rejection of the monarchic form of government and not a proposal for a new governmental system to replace the monarchy.

According to Randall, Jefferson's address was voted on and passed, but Jefferson was absent when the final vote was taken. Again, Peyton Randolph pressed Jefferson to represent Virginia in the Second Continental Congress. Jefferson complied, "almost hesitantly". (Randall, p.239) Willard Stern Randall did not say reluctantly. Traveling in his own "coach and four" with two slaves, Jefferson took almost two weeks to get to Philadelphia. Along the way, he stopped to buy a retired race horse. As a late arrival on June 21, 1775, he was able to participate during the last half of the May to August 1775 Congress, by doing some committee work. He did not like disputes and he avoided participating in debates on the floor in Congress. He described himself as a "passive auditor" and was aptly named a silent member of Congress.(Lewis, p.161) John Adams said that while Jefferson was in Congress he "never heard him utter three sentences together". (Hazelton, p.120) During this time there is no evidence that Jefferson intended to compose a Declaration of Independence. He returned to Virginia on August 1, 1775. Early in August Jefferson wrote a letter to his loyalist cousin, John Randolph. The letter clearly reflects Jefferson's mind set. He expressed his wish for "a restoration of our just rights" and his desire to withdraw "totally from the public stage" in order to live in "domestic ease and tranquility." (Randall, p.247)

At the end of 1775, there was no change in Jefferson's position. When he wrote, "a restoration of our just rights", he meant the rights of British America from British Americans. In another letter to John Randolph, Jefferson wrote, "Believe me, dear sir, there is not in the British empire a man who more cordially loves a union with Great Britain than I do" (November 29, 1775) (Randall, p.250) He said nothing about renouncing and eliminating the king and royal rule. But he did allow that he would "yield" to a connection with Britain on terms acceptable to the Americans. In effect, Jefferson wanted "Home Rule" and having the United States remain a part of the British empire. At the end of 1775, Thomas Jefferson was a LOYALIST.

Later, in his Notes on Virginia, he wrote, "It is well known that in July, 1775, a separation from Great Britain and establishment of republican government had never yet entered into anyone's mind." (Randall, p.250)

When Jefferson left Congress in December, 1775, he was unaware that the question of separation and the establishment of a Republic would be addressed and answered in a few weeks in a thin pamphlet of some 55 pages. The work "burst from the press" on January 10, 1776. (Dr. Benjamin Rush, Lewis, p.44) In it, its author wrote, "nothing can settle our affairs so expeditiously as an open and determined declaration of independence," and "But it is the independence of this country of Britain, or any other, which is now the main and only object worthy of contention..." and, "We have it in our power to begin the world over again," and, "The birthday of a new world is at hand,..." – *Common Sense*.

During the years of 1774 and 1775 Jefferson never called for the creation of a Republic; never called for a Declaration of Independence, never argued against reconciliation with Great Britain; never renounced allegiance to King George III. At the close of 1775 Thomas Jefferson remained a loyal British Virginian and a loyal British American. He was 32 years old.

CHAPTER 15
JEFFERSON IN 1776

We have seen that at the start of 1776, Jefferson had written nothing about dethroning the King; declaring the United Colonies an independent and sovereign country and framing an amendable constitution for it. Also, I am unaware of any evidence that Jefferson intended to be the author of a Declaration of Independence and be the first one to propose that the united colonies establish a Republican form of government prior to this time. Randall wrote, "Like most Virginia leaders, Jefferson had been unwilling to face the idea of a total break with England when he wrote his *Summary View* in July, 1774," and "In all that long winter and spring of 1775, at home in Monticello, Jefferson apparently wrote almost nothing." (Randall, p.258)

However, he did research and write a long historical piece after January 19, 1776, according to Randall – which confirmed Thomas Paine's earlier assertion in *Common Sense*, that the American Colonies were established by American sweat, toil, risk, money and blood and not exclusively at the expense of the British Nation. (Randall, p.258)

After the burning of Norfolk, Virginia, during the first week of January, 1776, Jefferson returned to Monticello. From Randall we learn that, "For the next four months Jefferson tried to live the life of a country squire, among other things, concerning himself with stocking his deer park;" and helping to foal a new mare. (Randall, p.257) Then, on March 31, 1776, Jefferson's mother died. "Her death added to all (of) his other anxieties over the war and his wife's health and apparently triggered a five week bout of migraine headaches that left him bedridden and unable to write about her death on anything else."

So, March 31, 1776 plus five weeks takes us up to the first week of May 1776, when Jefferson was about to rejoin Congress in Philadelphia. Here again, I say, there is no evidence up to this time that Jefferson had a concrete, explicit, step by step plan for the total amputation of America from England, along with a total breaking off of all political, governmental, administrative and commercial control by Great Britain.

Jefferson did not publish a design plan to create the Republic of the United States of America, nor did he indicate in any way that he had any intention of composing a Declaration of Independence up to the first week of May, 1776. He did not have to do either. Thomas Paine did both.

In the first case, all of the elements necessary to create the United States were integrated into a concrete plan to establish America as an independent, sovereign, Democratic Republic. The components of Paine's plan are explicitly described in his *Common Sense*. As to a Democratic Republic, Paine wrote, "Let a continental conference be held," "...let their business be to frame a Continental Charter," and "the whole being impowered (sic) by the people..." I understand this to mean government of, by, and for the people. This is Democracy. If we assume that no two people are alike, political democracy is difficult to explain and attain. So, I shall pass over that subject for now.

In the second case, which concerns the absence of any evidence that Jefferson intended to be the author of the Declaration of Independence, the following quotes are presented. They are taken from the Barnes & Noble edition of *Common Sense*:

"...Nothing can settle our affairs so expeditiously as an open and determined Declaration for independence."

"Should a Manifesto be published, and despatched (sic) to foreign courts, setting forth the miseries we have endured, and the peaceful methods which we have ineffectually used for redress; declaring at the same time, that not being able, any longer, to live happily or safely under the cruel disposition of the British court, we had been driven to the Necessity of breaking off all connection with her."

"But the most powerful of all arguments is that nothing but independence, i.e. a continental form of government, can keep the peace of the continent and preserve it inviolate from civil wars."

"..until, by an independence we take rank with other nations."

"and, until an independence is declared, the continent will feel itself like a man who continues putting off some unpleasant business from day to day..."

These quotes show the pure sentiments of Thomas Paine's mind and heart. They also reflect the driving commitment of his will to create a new country. Buy contrast, Jefferson never wrote anything like the ideas contained in the above quotes prior to the publication of *Common Sense*.

Also, we have seen that there is no evidence that Jefferson had any intention of composing a Declaration of Independence up until the last week in May, 1776. On the other hand, Thomas Paine must have intended to compose the Declaration because he had already written it. Paine made that disclosure in his brilliant *A Dialogue Between the Ghost of General Montgomery just arrived from the Elysian Fields; and an American Delegate in the wood near Philadelphia*. In this Dialogue, Paine, speaking through the Ghost of General Montgomery declares, "The decree is finally gone forth. Britain and America are now distinct empires."

This important Dialogue was probably published during the crucial period between June 1, 1776 and June 10, 1776 because Congress approved a bill to nominate a committee to draft the Declaration on June 10, 1776. Benjamin Franklin, John Adams, Robert Livingston, Roger Sherman and Thomas Jefferson were the members selected to draft the Declaration. As regards Paine's *General Montgomery Dialogue*, it is certain that it was published before Friday, June 28, 1776.

Here "at the eleventh hour", less than four weeks before July 2, 1776, we have no indication that Jefferson intended to write an original Declaration of Independence. We do know that Jefferson was appointed and as such, his work, as well as the work of the committee selected to formulate a Declaration of Independence, was an assigned task. Whether Jefferson was chosen as a substitute for Richard Henry Lee because Lee had to return to Virginia at that time, I do not know. However, we do know the following for sure:

An original Declaration existed prior to Jefferson's first draft because "The Decree is finally gone fourth," was proclaimed in Paine's *General Montgomery Dialogue*. (Regarding the *Montgomery Dialogue:* William M. Van Der Weyde wrote that Thomas Paine "had the dialogue printed in pamphlet form in Philadelphia just before Congress appointed its committee to draft the Declaration of Independence.")

Paine wrote this dialogue to combat delaying the Declaration: "you have no time to lose" and also to heat up the cold feet of those members of Congress who were opposed to Independence, and who still held out with hope for reconciliation with Great Britain.

Thomas Paine was totally conversant with the activities and discussions in Congress.

Richard Henry Lee's (Virginia's) resolution for total separation and independence was proposed on June 7, 1776. Congress voted to postpone the vote for independence until July 1, 1776. Deliberations on the subject of Independence – not on the Declaration - were held in Congress on this day and on the next day, Tuesday, July 2, 1776.

Congress voted in favor of R. H. Lee's resolution and on July 2, 1776 the United States became a free sovereign, and Independent Nation.

Jefferson did not "draw" the Declaration before June 11, 1776, the date when he was appointed to the committee to provide a prospective Declaration which would be subject to inspection, review, change and approval by the members of Congress. Also, there is no evidence that Jefferson wrote anything in favor in Independence or establishing a Republic before June 11, 1776.

Willard Sterne Randall re-enforced this assertion, when he wrote, "In his Summary View, he (Jefferson) had not gone so far as to recommend independence; nothing he had written since then for public consumption had gone any further. In Congress, he had coauthored key documents with the conservative John Dickinson. When instructions to vote for independence had arrived in Philadelphia, Jefferson had been among those opposed to introducing them for a vote until there was stronger support from the more timid states."

None of the other four members (Franklin, Adams, Livingston, Sherman and Jefferson) of the committee appointed to draft the Declaration ever claimed to be its author.

CHAPTER 16
JEFFERSON IN CONGRESS
MAY 15, 1776 TO
SEPTEMBER 3, 1776

Jefferson left Monticello on May 6, 1776; and arrived in Philadelphia on May 14, 1776, and entered Congress on May 15, 1776. This was the same day that the Virginia Convention unanimously approved the resolution that Virginia's delegate to the Continental Congress be instructed to propose that Congress "Declare the United Colonies free and independent states absolved from all allegiance to or dependence upon the crown or Parliament of Great Britain, and to give Virginia's assent to whatever measures may be thought proper and necessary by the Congress for forming foreign alliances and a confederation of the colonies". (Randall, p.263)

In my mind and in my heart I feel a large and respectful sense of admiration and gratitude for those honorable and courageous Virginians for their leading role in achieving Independence. It is noted without further comment, that Jefferson was not present in the Virginia Convention when their unconditional Declaration was adopted. So, he was not in Williamsburg on May 15, 1776, when "all 112 delegates shouted aye." (Randall, p.262)

-On May 15, 1776, Jefferson entered Congress

-On May 15, 1776, Virginia voted for Independence

-On May 16, 1776, Jefferson wrote to his friend Thomas Nelson. (A)

-On May 27, 1776, Jefferson dutifully presented Virginias proposal for Independence to Congress; John Hancock, presiding.

-On June 7, 1776, Richard H. Lee delivered Virginias momentous resolution that, "These United Colonies are, and of right ought to be, free and independent states."

(A) This is the letter in which Jefferson wrote, "I suppose they will tell us what to say on the subject of independence".

-On June 8, 1776, Members of Congress debated on whether to vote for Independence.

-On June 10, 1776, Congress voted to postpone the vote for Independence until July1, 1776.

-On June 10, 1776, Congress voted to create a committee to prepare a Declaration of Independence.

-On June 11, 1776, Congress appointed five members to the committee to prepare the 'Declaration'.

The committee members were: Benjamin Franklin, John Adams, Robert Livingston, Roger Sherman and Thomas Jefferson.

We have seen that from May 6, 1776, to June 11, 1776, Jefferson did not write the Declaration. If Jefferson had any intention of preparing a Declaration, he could have informed John Hancock that he would do it and save the time and trouble of another committee. What was Jefferson doing during this period?

From W. S. Randall we learn: "Here in late May and early June of 1776 he finished writing a series of bleak reports and recommendations that resulted from the failed American invasion of Canada…"(Randall, p.263)

Randall also wrote, "As soon as Jefferson learned that the Virginia Convention had declared Independence from Great Britain and was creating a commonwealth, he set about writing the first of three drafts of a new constitution for his home country."(Randall, p.267) Jefferson was working on these drafts between May 26, 1776, and June 13, 1776; on that date "Jefferson sent his third draft south (to Virginia) with George Wythe." (Randall, p.269)

Prior to starting work on the Virginia Constitutions, Jefferson had written a letter dated May 17, 1776, by Hazelton and dated May 16, 1776, by Lewis, to his friend Thomas Nelson, Jr. In this letter, Jefferson betrayed his thinking at that time. He wrote, "…should our convention propose to establish now a form of government perhaps it might be agreeable to recall for a short time their delegates." (Hazelton, p457) Clearly, Jefferson was willing to be recalled to Virginia. He continued, "It is a work of the most interesting nature and such as every individual would wish to have his voice in. In truth it is the whole object of the present controversy; for should a bad government be instituted for us in future it had been as well to have accepted at first the bad one offered to us from beyond the water without the risk & (sic) expense of contest." (Hazelton, p.457) It occurs to me that if Jefferson responded to a recall to Virginia, he would be placing a higher priority on Virginia than the creation of the United States. Also, if the members of the Virginia Convention wanted the assistance of Jefferson, they could have recalled him at any time, seeing that he was an assigned delegate.

Since Virginia's Declaration for Independence was adopted unanimously by "all 112 delegates", (Randall, p.262) I believe that it is safe to say that Jefferson's counsel was not needed, and since he had been dispatched to Congress in Philadelphia, he could neither vote on nor delay the triumphant proceedings in Williamsburg on May 15, 1776.

That part of the "Nelson Letter", "…for should a bad government be instituted, for us… from beyond the water…without risk and expense…" shows that Jefferson was still a Loyalist in May, 1776, and not a 'true blue' unalloyed patriot. In this same letter, he wrote, "I suppose they will tell us what to say on the subject of Independence...", and "...but this I mention to you in confidence..." (Hazelton, p.457)

Is it any wonder why Jefferson wanted Thomas Nelson, Jr., to keep the contents of this letter confidential? [Thomas Nelson was a staunch, self-sacrificing patriot, a Virginia delegate to the second continental Congress and a signer of the Declaration of Independence.]

The part in the above quote, viz, "should a bad government be instituted for us..." is mystifying. Who would do the instituting, "beyond the water"? Of course the answer would be Great Britain. Such an event would mean a continuation of a tie with Great Britain. It would require some form of reconciliation with Britain which, in turn, implies some form of British control. A little bit of control is control.

Anyone who reads *Common Sense* with attention and understanding knows that Thomas Paine totally obliterated the prospect of 'reconciliation' as a "fallacious dream." Why would the Americans fight a 'hot' war for no other reason than to achieve the status quo? That would be like going from the frying pan into the frying pan. Jefferson should have learned from *Common Sense*. In *Common Sense* Thomas Paine wrote, "Volumes have been written on the subject of the struggle between England and America...and the period of debate is closed. Arms, as the last resource, decide the contest..." (Anchor Books, p.27) On page 58, Paine rephrases, "Where is our redress? - No going to law with nations; cannon are the barristers of Crowns; and the sword, not of justice, but of war, decides the suit." We know with apodictic hindsight that Great Britain, that is, the King and parliament would never have agreed to any form of reconciliation on terms such that they would be agreeable to and accepted by the Americans. Britain's aim was total conquest, period. Thomas Paine knew it. "It is our delaying that encourages her (Britain) to hope for CONQUEST;" and, "The policy of Britain has ever been to divide America...well knowing that could she once get them to stand singly, she could conquer them unconditionally."

(Anchor Books, p.216) Britain wanted to divide and conquer. Her goal was absolute imperial domination of the Colonies. No American history scholar can dispute this fact. Paine knew that any peace or reconciliation overture would fail. If the offer came from England, it would be a mere expedient and, in effect, a ruse. If the offer came from the Colonists, it would be rejected. Paine wrote, "Every quiet method for peace hath been ineffectual. Our prayers have been rejected with disdain." From Thomas Paine we have the impassioned response: "For God's sake let us come to a final separation." (*Common Sense*)

We now come to the time when Jefferson would 'draft' a Declaration of Independence and present it to Congress. As said, he was appointed to the committee to prepare it on June 11, 1776. According to Randall, Jefferson worked "for two weeks, between June 13 and June 28, 1776," in order to prepare the Declaration. In a letter to Will Flemming on July 1, 1776, Jefferson admitted that he was directed to "draw" it. When he described writing the Declaration, Jefferson usually used the words 'draw', 'drew', 'draft', and 'frame'. He never said that he was the author of the Declaration. He never said that the Declaration of Independence was an original composition, formulated by me alone. Jefferson never claimed authorship of the Declaration of Independence during his lifetime.

In a letter to James Madison dated August 30, 1823, Jefferson wrote, "...whether I had gathered my ideas from reading or reflection I do not know. I know only that I turned to neither book nor pamphlet while writing it. I did not consider it as any part of my charge to invent new ideas altogether and to offer no sentiment which had ever been expressed before." (Hazelton, p. 144) That's right. Jefferson did not go beyond the bounds of his assigned charge by inventing new ideas. He did not have to because the new ideas were already invented by Thomas Paine. All of the new ideas were contained in *Common Sense.*

As to: "I turned to neither book nor pamphlet while writing it", Joseph Lewis' commendable book *Thomas Paine Author of the Declaration of Independence,* provides strong, and as I believe, conclusive proof that

Thomas Jefferson copied the Declaration from Thomas Paine's original composition. Lewis wrote, "In view of the fact that Jefferson and Adams both copied the Declaration from the original manuscript…" (Lewis, p.303)

Jefferson's words, "I did not consider it as any part of my charge…" goes to show that drafting a Declaration was an assigned task. He was a lawyer. He used the term "transaction" to describe one of the greatest events in political history. He considered himself to be a "passive auditor". (Hazelton, p.145) John Adams tells us: "Mr. Jefferson had… attended his duty in the house a very small part of the time, and when there, had never spoken in public." And, "During the whole time I sat with him in Congress, I never heard him utter three sentences together." (Hazelton, p.120) It appears that Jefferson was not happy in congress. He wanted to go home. He did not wish to stay in Congress and provide a measure of leadership or contribute to the war effort and stabilizing and strengthening the baby Republic. In my opinion Willard Sterne Randall gave a very accurate description of Thomas Jefferson during this epoch – making period of time. It is worth quoting here "Jefferson was determined to quit Congress and return to Virginia Politics. He could not see into the future. To him the continental Congress was but a temporary meeting in convention of delegates from the new states, of little importance in the long run. Even if there were a permanent confederacy of states, it would be of far less importance than the reshaping of the weak old English colonies into strong independent countries. Jefferson wanted to join his friends in Virginia in an effort that mattered far more to him than writing of declarations and resolutions in Philadelphia. He wanted to carry out a revolution that would last, a revolution in the laws of his native country, Virginia, a sweeping legislative reform movement that would transform the old semi feudal tidewater aristocracy into a democratic Republic." (Randall, p.279)

Jefferson was a Virginian. His focus was on the sovereign country of Virginia.

By way of contrast, we see a sharp contrast between Thomas Paine's thinking and that of Jefferson, "…'tis not the affair of a city, a country, a province or a kingdom, but of a continent…", and, "Let a continental conference be held…" and "By an Independence we take rank with other nations." These quotes, along with others in *Common Sense* provide proof that Thomas Paine's thinking was global and that his goal was not just to create independent States but to create the United States.

The first step in Paine's innovative, step by step, plan to establish the United States as a sovereign country was Independence. This first step was accomplished when Congress unanimously adopted Richard Henry Lee's Resolution of June 7, 1776, that "These united colonies are, and of right ought to be free and independent states", on July 2, 1776.

The second step was a Declaration: "…nothing can settle our affairs so expeditiously as an open and determined declaration for Independence…" (*Common Sense*) This step was initiated on Friday, June 28, 1776, when Jefferson presented his Declaration paper to Congress, John Hancock presiding. This is the only evidence that Jefferson was the author of the composition which is called "The Declaration of Independence."

Because so much has been written about the content and language of the Declaration, only <u>five</u> items are selected for consideration. The first is, "That all men are created equal". I am not aware of any evidence that Jefferson believed that "all men are created equal."

The second item is the last sentence of the second paragraph of both of Jefferson's and Adams' drafts. It is, "To prove this, let facts be submitted to a candid World, for the truth of which We pledge a Faith, as yet unsullied by Falsehood." Perhaps Jefferson could write such a line. I don't know. But, I do not believe that lawyer Jefferson would use it in an international manifesto. Thomas Paine could write such a line and he did. In chapter fifteen of his book, *Thomas Paine, Author of the Declaration of Independence,* Joseph Lewis provides an excellent explanation, and as I believe, proof that Thomas Paine was the author of this sentence.

Thirdly, Jefferson was not the author of the "anti-slavery clause" in the Declaration. The ideas and the explicit language of this condemnation of the trade and practice of slavery came from Paine's vitriolic denunciation of it in his, *An Essay on African Slavery in America*. In chapters ten and eleven, (pages 138 to 169), Joseph Lewis provides an excellent analysis of the "Slavery Clause". I think it should be taught in schools. Also, see the "slavery section" in the *Source* chapter.

The fourth item is the last part of the sentence in the "Slavery Clause" which is as follows: "He has prostituted his Negative for Suppressing every legislative Attempt to prohibit on to restrain an execrable Commerce, determined to keep open a Markett where men should be bought and Sold, and that this ASSEMBLAGE OF HORRORS MIGHT WANT NO FACT OF DISTINGUISHED DIE*". This unusual clause is in both John Adams' copy and Jefferson's copy of the original Declaration of Independence (1) I do not believe that Jefferson was the author of this line, and I do not believe that he was the author of "anti-slavery clause", and I do not believe that Jefferson was the author of the Declaration of Independence.

Five: Thomas, Mister "Passive Auditor", Jefferson did not defend the copy of the Declaration that he submitted to Congress. According to Jefferson, John Adams did defend it. "This however I will say for Mr. Adams, that he supported the Declaration with zeal and ability, fighting fearlessly for every word of it." (Hazelton, p.145) There is no evidence that Jefferson mounted any defense of the Declaration while some parts of it were being eliminated and other parts altered. He remained a "silent Witness" from Friday, June 28, 1776 to July 4, 1776. I can understand why Jefferson did not see fit to defend the Declaration. Independence was already achieved on July 2, 1776. John Adams was doing his best to defend the draft. Also, Jefferson knew that some form of a Declaration would be adopted because there were enough votes in favor of it to assure a majority. Besides, the draft submitted by Jefferson

---

*   caps mine

was not an original composition by him. He copied it from the original written by Thomas Paine. John Adams wrote, "I have long wondered that the original draft has not been published. I suppose the reason is the vehement Phillipic against Negro Slavery". (Hazelton, p.180)

Much has been written about the many changes made to the draft submitted by Jefferson to Congress on June 28, 1776. These changes included alterations, additions and deletions. On July 8, 1776, Jefferson sent to Richard Henry Lee "a copy of the Declaration of Independence as agreed to by the house & (sic) also originally framed." Jefferson wrote "framed", he did not say composed. R. H. Lee wrote back, "I thank you…, and I wish sincerely…, that the Manuscript had not been mangled as it is…" (Hazelton, p.344) Also, when Abigail Adams compared her husband's hand-written copy of the original Declaration to the approved and printed version, she wrote, "I cannot but be sorry that some of the most manly sentiments in the Declaration are expunged from the printed copy." (Hazelton, p.349)

In a letter to John W. Campbell dated September 3, 1809, Jefferson wrote: "In answer to your proposition for publishing a complete edition of my different writings, I must observe that no writings of mine, other than those merely official have been published, except the Notes of Virginia and a small pamphlet under the title *A Summary View of the Rights of British America* …I do not know whether your view extends to official papers of mine which have been published…I say nothing of numerous draughts of reports, resolutions, DECLARATIONS*, etc. drawn as a member of Congress or of the Legislature of Virginia, such as the Declaration of Independence, Report on the Money Unit of the United States, the Act of Religious Freedom, etc, etc; these having become the acts of public bodies, there can be no personal claim to them…" (Lewis, p.288)

When the sun rose on Friday, July 5, 1776, the first two steps – Independence and Declaration – of Thomas Paine's plan to create the

---

*   caps mine

United States, were accomplished. America was now a free, independent and sovereign country. According to Randall, Jefferson's "strongest reaction was to let it be known that he did not want a second term in Congress; and he "was determined to quit Congress and return to Virginia politics." (Randall, p.279) He made repeated requests to be relieved. "By July 29, 1776, his pleas to go home were shrill. To Richard Henry Lee, he wrote "For Gods sake… I pray you to come. I am under a sacred obligation to go home." (Randall, p.282)

On September 3, 1776, Thomas Jefferson was relieved by R. H. Lee. He went home.

CHAPTER 17
AFRICAN SLAVERY
IN AMERICA

Thomas Paine was an idea man, and more. He was an inventor, and more. He was an ideological innovator and a tireless worker. When these attributes are considered in the light of Thomas Paine's acknowledged humanitarianism and accredited achievements, a picture of a man pure of mind and heart emerges. A close and comprehensive study of Thomas Paine's life and works reveals that he led a life of heroic virtue. As a matter of personal integrity, Paine never compromised his political motives or his Religious Principles.

"As in my political works my motive and object have to give man an elevated sense of his own character, and free him from the slavish and superstitious absurdity of monarchy and hereditary government; so, in my publications on religious subjects, my endeavors have been directed to bring man to a right use of the reason that God has given him; to impress on him the great principles of divine morality, justice, and mercy, and a benevolent disposition to all men and to all creatures..." (Conway, p. 241)

An example of Thomas Paine's faithful adherence to his principles of Justice, Mercy, and a benevolent disposition to all men (and women), is his early essay on *African Slavery in America*. This memorable essay is also positive PROOF that Thomas Paine is the author of the Declaration of Independence because the 'anti slave" clause in the Declaration has the same language, thrust, passion and thought-prints as the *African Slavery in America* essay.

Less than three months after Thomas Paine arrived in America, he became a contributing editor on Robert Aitkin's Pennsylvania Magazine. Paine's *African Slavery in America* essay was published in this magazine on March 8, 1775. In this article, Paine called the Slave Trade a savage practice in which "Christianized" people participate. He called the Slave Trade an: "execrable commerce." He wrote, "To go to nations purely to catch unoffensive people, like wild beasts, for slaves, is an outrage against Humanity and Justice…"

The same accusatory condemnation of slavery was an important part of the original Declaration of Independence, and is referred to as the "Slavery Clause". In it, Thomas Paine accused King George Guelph III of waging cruel war against Nature itself. He wrote, "This piratical Warfare, the opprobrium of infidel Powers, is the Warfare of the Christian King of Great Britain." "He has prostituted his Negative for Suppressing every legislative attempt to prohibit or to restrain an execrable Commerce, determined to keep open a Markett where men should be bought and sold, and that this Assemblage of Horrors might want no Fact of distinguished Die…" Only Thomas Paine could have composed such a line.

In his chapter eleven on Jefferson and Slavery, in the enduring opus, *Thomas Paine Author of the Declaration of Independence*, Joseph Lewis provides convincing, and I think incontrovertible evidence that Thomas Paine is the real author of the Declaration of Independence. For a number of reasons, Joseph Lewis thought that Jefferson must bear the onus for expunging the Slavery Clause from the Declaration. Lewis wrote, "The Slavery Clause in the Declaration of Independence could not have been written by an owner of slaves nor could an owner of slaves have written the Declaration of Independence." (Lewis, p.166)

I agree with Joseph Lewis' conclusion and I believe that the Declaration of Independence itself is a powerful PROOF that Thomas Paine was the creative architect of the United States.

FREEDOM FOR ALL

Thomas Paine was elected as clerk of the Pennsylvania assembly on November 2, 1779. The Pennsylvania Act Abolishing Slavery was introduced on the same day. The preamble to this act is pure Thomas Paine. Its lofty humanitarian, intellectual, and spiritual expressions are truly uplifting. I join with all others who consider this piece a literary work of art and a timeless master-piece. This preamble shows Paine's perseverance. It proves that Paine was inveterately determined to eradicate the "execrable" practice of slavery.

The Pennsylvania Act Abolishing Slavery: "The first proclamation of emancipation in America" was passed (Lewis, p. 169) on March 1, 1780. It was a grand achievement. One might speculate that its adoption gave Paine a modicum of satisfaction, as a partial offset, against the hurt and disappointment that he sustained by the elimination of the "Anti-Slavery Clause" in his Declaration of Independence. The Preamble to the Pennsylvania Act Abolishing Slavery provides strong evidence in support of Paine's plan to achieve freedom for all.

CHAPTER 18
THE FAIL SAFE DIALOGUE PROOF

Thomas Paine wrote, *A Dialogue Between the Ghost of General Montgomery Just Arrived from the Elysian Fields and an American Delegate, in a Wood near Philadelphia.* It was published around the second week of June, 1776. Lewis says shortly after June 10, 1776. (Neither Conway or Foner provide an exact date.) The timing was providential because the pamphlet appeared during the most important period of political history. It came at the crucial time when the members of the Second Continental Congress were deliberating on the subject of Independence.

Virginia had passed a resolution (May 15, 1776) instructing its delegates in Congress to vote for Independence. The instructions arrived in Philadelphia on May 26, 1776, and on June 7, 1776, Richard Henry Lee proposed the resolution that "These united Colonies are…Free and Independent States." The vote on this famous Resolution was delayed due to the opposition by some of the members of Congress. It is noteworthy that Thomas Jefferson was among those who were opposed. It appears that Jefferson welcomed the deferment.

It is certain that Jefferson did not prevent the postponement. On June 9, 1776, Congress voted to postpone the vote on R. H. Lee's Independence Resolution until July 1, 1776. Two days later, (June 11,

1776) Congress appointed a committee to prepare a formal Declaration of Independence. It is noted that Congress did not appoint a committee to prepare a proposal for reconciliation and peace with Great Britain.

It is well documented that the five men appointed as a committee to compose the "Declaration" were, Benjamin Franklin, John Adams, Robert Livingston, Roger Sherman and Thomas Jefferson.

Paine worked assiduously in order to have the *Dialogue* in the hands of the Congressional delegates during this historic period. Clearly it was intended to counter and rule out any back-sliding or hesitation in his drive for independence. In question and answer form, and in only six pages, this timeless work provided a concentrated and passionate synopsis of all of the salient and compelling arguments contained in *Common Sense*. Moncure Daniel Conway thought that Paine's *A Dialogue Between the Ghost of General Montgomery Just Arrived From the Elysian Fields and an American Delegate in a Wood near Philadelphia* was one of his most effective pamphlets. (Conway, p.33) I concur.

There remains three extremely important points to be made. The first can be dismissed with a question. Who else was writing anything like the *Montgomery Dialogue*? Neither George Washington nor John Adams, nor Benjamin Franklin, nor Alexander Hamilton, nor Thomas Jefferson, nor any one else wrote anything on this subject with such single-minded and unanswerable persuasion. Why? The answer is that the first step in Paine's goal was Independence. Without Independence, Thomas Paine would not be able to proceed with his revolutionary vision. And, of course, that vision, that dream, that innovation was nothing less than the step by step creation of a new country without a King, the governmental operations of which would be controlled by the electorate.

For the second point, the following quote is given. "But I forbear to reason any further with you. The decree is finally gone forth. Britain and America are now distinct empires". (Foner, p.92)

After assuring the Delegates – by the ingenious method of speaking through Montgomery's ghost – that they have nothing to fear from either their enemies or their friends, and that France is anxiously waiting for the American Colonies to declare Independence, Paine urges his imaginary delegate, "Go, then, and awaken the Congress to a sense of their importance; you have no time to lose." (Foner, p.92)

Then, (again, through the ghost) Thomas makes a momentous statement. It is both an historic pronouncement and startling disclosure. Here it is: "THE DECREE IS FINALLY GONE FORTH. BRITAIN AND AMERICA ARE NOW DISTINCT EMPIRES."* To me, this breathtaking revelation is proof positive that the "DECREE" was the real and original Declaration of Independence as composed by its author Thomas Paine. Moreover it is proof that the Declaration of Independence was a completed production at or before the time when the *Montgomery Dialogue* was published.

The first two points provide strong proof that Thomas Paine had a step by step plan to create the United States and also that he was the real author of the Declaration of Independence. Both the *Montgomery Dialogue* and the Declaration prove that Thomas was hard at work on his plan. The third point is about the *importance* of the Delegates.

In the Dialogue, Paine wrote, "Go, then, and awaken the Congress to a sense of their importance; you have not time to lose." And "your country teems with patriots – heroes – and legislators, who are impatient to burst forth into light and importance." (Foner, p.92)

It is my firm opinion that this exhortation was not lost on those delegates and patriots who were willing to assume the seats of power. After all, with Independence, new American governors would be called for in order to fill the vacant seats of the deposed royal governors. In street parlance, this was a case of "move out little doggie, because a new dog is moving in". Also, other positions of "light and importance became open. These posts can be described in terms equivalent to Secretaries of War,

---

*   caps mine

Defense, Treasury and Foreign Affairs. Of course, Paine's psychological inducement "to burst forth into light and importance" (Thomas did not say fame and fortune) must have been more appealing to some more than others. We, all of us, have egos. But who can be the judge of the motives of others? All we can do is refer to accomplishments and actions proved by history. We can say, for example, that Washington and Adams accepted positions of distinction and prestige. On the other hand, Jefferson declined to serve in Congress and went home to Virginia and became its governor from 1779 to 1781.

It is not my purpose to dwell on the motives of those wonderful men and women who followed Thomas Paine's lead. My focus is on the contributions that each of those Revolutionary Patriots made in order to achieve Independence, which was the critical first step in Paine's plan to create a new country. It is for their contributions and achievements that I profess my heartfelt thanks and appreciation. In addition, I profess a special gratitude to those unsung and largely forgotten patriots whose contributions and sacrifices were made without a thought of tangible recompense or reward or public esteem, but purely out of personal honor. I intend to do more research on those unsung patriots as described above. Those, who like Haym Salomon, for example merit our remembrance and unalloyed and enduring gratitude.

The Montgomery Dialogue is a superlative piece of rhetorical persuasion. It is a "classic". I believe it was a material factor in inducing the delegates to the Second Continental Congress to lay aside all other questions except separation from England and focus only on Independence. It was written to convince Congress that the time to act was now. Now was the time to secure the benefits of freedom for the Colonists as well as themselves, and, indeed for all future Americans, because this might be the last chance to do so.

I believe, also, that Paine's emotional outburst, "the DECREE* is finally gone forth…" besides being a veiled disclosure that he, Thomas

---

*   caps mine

Paine is the true author of the Declaration of Independence, carried some weight in helping Congress fix their choice. How much weight? I don't know. We do know that Congress declared Independence and approved its Declaration unanimously. Thomas had achieved the first part of his goal to establish a new country without a King.

CHAPTER 19
TRENTON

I believe the surprise assault on the Hessian base at Trenton was Thomas Paine's idea. In a letter to Lund Washington on December 17, 1776, George Washington rote, "Our only dependence now is the speedy enlistment of a new army. If this fails, I think the game will be pretty well up..." "The losses he had sustained in New York strengthened his sense that he had to dodge large scale confrontations..." (Chernow, p.83) Washington told Congress "We should on all occasions avoid a general action or put anything to the risk..." (p.83) Alexander Hamilton was of the same mind.

Thomas Paine's idea was: attack. Paine knew as well, and perhaps better than anyone else, that there was no alternative save war in order to bring Britain to terms. He was not about to stand by and see his creation die on the vine.

Hamilton was sick in bed when the decision to surprise the Hessians was made; but he got up and served bravely in the victorious attack. That Paine planned the Trenton attack, including when to do it – Christmas Night – and how to do it – by surprise – has neither been corroborated nor authenticated. Although there is no evidence that Washington was conversant or interested in strategic military operations, he did have tactical experience from the "French and Indian" war and justly deserved the credit and honor he received from those victories for which he was responsible. The triumph at Trenton was not one of those victories for which Washington was responsible.

From all of the accounts that I have read about the abysmal condition of Washington's troops after the retreat from New York, they were in no condition to mount an offensive. Washington believed that General William Howe's next move would be to seize Philadelphia. He wrote a letter to Congress informing them that, "it will be impossible for our small force to give them any considerable opposition…" (McCullough, *1776*, p.263) In another letter to John Hancock, he wrote, "Philadelphia … is the object of the enemy's movements," and nothing less than our utmost exertions" could stop Howe, and that his own force was too thin and weak to count on. (p.264)

From his letters and "doom and gloom" dispatches, I get the feeling that Washington might have been considering the option of retreating to Philadelphia and assuming a defensive position there. I don't know. However, I do not believe that Washington was ready and willing to lead his bedraggled army, into a direct, force against force, confrontation with the British. Washington told Congress that, "We should on all occasions avoid a general action or put anything to the risk, unless compelled by a necessity into which we ought never to be drawn." (Chernow, p.83) Alexander Hamilton and Washington were in perfect agreement. Both preferred to rely on restricted skirmishes, such as raids and "hit and run" tactics.

The morale of the troops was as low as the temperature which was freezing. Shelter was scarce and the army was short of winter clothing, uniforms, boots, blankets and food. The most important thing was morale. Spirits were so low that deserters went skulking off into the night. Adding to Washington's woes was the fact that a large number of short term contract enlistments would expire on January 1, 1777. He wrote to Congress, "Ten days more will put an end to the existence of our army." (p.84) David McCullough described the situation well and in a few words. "…men were dreadfully dispirited. Many had given up…Hundreds had deserted. Many of those left were sick, hungry… miserable…" (*1776*, p.263)

When we consider the sorry condition of the army and Washington's fear of a direct assault and most important of all, the total lack of morale, we are moved to ask: why the sudden reversal? What changed George Washington's mind? Of course, I believe that it was Thomas Paine who came up with the idea and plan to attack. I believe that Paine, personally or through a third party convinced Washington to strike. McCullough informs us that Washington had received "a remarkable letter, written by Joseph Reed, on December 22, 1776" (p.271) According to McCullough, Reed wrote, "It was time something was done, something and aggressive and surprising" and "Even failure would be preferable to doing nothing." Reed suggested Trenton and continued, "I will not disguise my own sentiments that our cause is desperate and hopeless if we do not take the opportunity of the collection of troops at present to strike some stroke. Our affairs are hastening fast to ruin if we do not retrieve them by some happy event. Delay with us is now equal to total defeat." (p.271)

At that time Joseph Reed was the Adjutant General of the Continental army. His letter, although not a direct order to attack, strongly suggested that aggressive action must be taken now. This reminds me of Paine's urging in *Common Sense* that "if something is not done in time, it will be too late to do anything…" (*Common Sense*, p.63) In a diplomatic way, Reed advised Washington to consider the element of surprise in his next move and even allowed that a failed engagement would be better than nothing. I suppose Reed's thinking was that another loss would not preclude final victory. In any event, the cause of America would go on. The last line of Reed's letter translates into a stark: delay is defeat. This also reminds me of a line from *Common Sense*, "Why is it we hesitate? From Britain we can expect nothing but ruin." (p.50) This quote referred to the question of Independence or subjugation prior to

July 4, 1776. In this case the choice for Washington was either "strike some stroke" now or suffer defeat and disgrace.

Joseph Reed's letter was the closest thing to a mandate to a commander in the field, without an explicit "or else", that I have ever seen. Clearly, Reed is urging Washington to "take the opportunity of the COLLECTION* of troops at present and strike some stroke". This makes sense to me because, according to McCullough, all enlistments would expire on New Years day, 1777, (*1776*, p.69) just eight days away. It is noted here that Paine, in his first *Crisis Paper*, employed the word COLLECTED* when he wrote, "A summer's experience has now taught us better; yet with those troops, while they were COLLECTED*, we were able to set bounds to the progress of the enemy, and, thank God? They are again assembling." (Foner,Vol.1,p.54)

Washington got the message. He would spend the next three days vigorously preparing for the assault on the Hession encampment in Trenton, New Jersey. He would begin the operation on Christmas night, December 25, 1776. Now, Washington could proceed with a confidence that totally displaced the defeatism expressed in his woebegone letter to his cousin, Lund Washington, only five days ago. Now, he and his poorly equipped, rag-tag army were armed with that all important element which was absent only a few hours ago. The missing element was MORALE. It was supplied by Thomas Paine's immortal "These are the times that try men's souls" – *Crisis Paper* number one. It was published in the Pennsylvania Journal on December 19, 1776. (p. XVI) Based only on suppositions, it is my opinion that the timing of the "These are the times that try men's soul", *Crisis Paper*, was part of a deliberate plan to get Washington to take action. What I write now is pure conjecture and speculation and I am not aware of any historical evidence that would support my assumptions.

It is my considered opinion, that Joseph Reed's letter, dated December 22, 1776, to Washington, was a joint effort by Reed and Thomas

---

*   caps mine

Paine. I believe that Paine and Reed devised a plan aimed to convince Washington that his best course of action was to engage. It was a two step plan. Paine's famous *Crisis I* would appear first, on December 19, 1776. A copy of it would be delivered into George Washington's hands. Then, Joseph Reed's signed letter would be presented to Washington a few days later. I assume Washington weighed the contents carefully. But enough of gratuitous assumptions. Washington had the Crisis read to the troops, prepared for battle, descended on Trenton, achieved a glorious victory there and followed it up with another at Princeton. Washington was praised to the skies. Both David McCullough and Craig Nelson gave detailed and informative accounts of the battle of Trenton. I thank them for their excellent work. If McCullough made an implicit connection with Thomas Paine and the victory at Trenton, Craig Nelson's account was more direct. Describing the action of the American troops in the heat of battle, Nelson wrote, "Firing with musket and cannon and striking with bayonet, they screamed, 'These are the times that try men's souls!'"

I continue to believe that the surprise attack on Trenton was Thomas Paine's idea. I believe he planned the entire operation. I believe Paine's battle plan was adopted by Washington. I believe that lieutenant James Monroe either knew or found out later that Paine deserved credit for the Trenton victory. I hope the scholars will discover more evidence to support these views.

CHAPTER 20
EASTON AND ONWARD

An unusual event occurred on January 21, 1777. Thomas Paine was appointed by Congress to serve as secretary to a commission to negotiate with the Indians in Easton Pennsylvania. It may be asked why Paine was selected for this post. After all, he was not a member of Congress. He couldn't vote. He was poor and he had never held a public office in America.

Paine had arrived in Philadelphia on November 30, 1774. At the time of his above mentioned appointment, he had been in America just one week short of twenty-six months. During this time he did some editing and wrote a few articles for a local newspaper. He also wrote a small, seditious and controversial, booklet which he had published pseudonymously. After America declared Independence, Thomas Paine joined the Revolutionary army, and in December, 1776, he wrote a stirring essay which he labeled *The Crisis*. Evidently, the Council of Safety in Philadelphia considered Paine's record sufficient to warrant his selection as Secretary to the Commission. Paine did go to Easton and I assume the negotiations with the Indians were successful. Conway assumed that the report of the meeting was written by Paine, who was paid for his services. Conway also said that the money paid to Thomas Paine was refunded. (Conway, p. 37)

Less than three months after Thomas Paine's appointment as secretary to the Council of Safety, he was elected as Secretary of the

Committee of Foreign Affairs. On April 17 1777, Congress transformed the "Committee of Secret Correspondence" into the "Committee of Foreign Affairs". (p. 37) Conway wrote, "Paine was really the Secretary of Foreign Affairs". In effect, Thomas Paine became the first Secretary of State of the infant "Democratic" Republic of the United States of America. In my opinion, a better qualified man for this position did not exist on planet earth. I believe that the selection of Thomas Paine for this all-important office was a singular honor bestowed on him. It reflected Congress' growing recognition of Paine's contributions and achievements.

When we recall that our impecunious immigrant "Needleman" had landed in Philadelphia less than two and one-half years ago, his appointment to such a prestigious position must be considered a very special event. The members of Congress were well aware of Thomas Paine's powerful pen. His *Common Sense* "had dictated the Declaration of Independence". (p. 38) [This is a powerful testimony by M. D. Conway that Thomas Paine is the author of the Declaration.] His first *Crisis* pamphlet "had largely won its first victory." The Declaration had opened the door for the members of Congress to rise to the occasion, and "to burst forth into light and importance," and to advance from mere Colonial "Locals" to historical players on the world stage. Prior to the amazing victory at Trenton, the Americans were militarily winless. Craig Nelson wrote, "In twenty-one months of fighting, the rebels had not achieved one notable victory". (Nelson, p. 108)

The triumph at Trenton was a major reversal. It gave the military component of the Revolution a new lease on life at the darkest hour of the revolution. Hope and confidence replaced the gloom of despair. Also, as Craig Nelson astutely recorded, the fear of the formidable empire of Great Britain was mitigated. (p. 107)

There might have been another reason why Congress would award such a critical office to Paine. Perhaps word got around that Thomas Paine helped to devise the plan for the Trenton operation. Did Paine originate the idea? Did he dream up a battle plan to deploy the troops that remained in a maneuver that was totally unexpected, and then sell the idea to Washington? I don't know. David McCullough made a forthright admission when he was describing George Washington: "He (Washington) was not a brilliant strategist or tactician, nor a gifted orator, nor an intellectual. At several crucial moments he had shown marked indecisiveness. He had made serious mistakes in judgment." (McCullough, *1776*, p. 293)

It is not unlikely that some members of Congress knew that a serious effort was made in order to induce Washington to act. It is just as likely that there were some members of Congress whose opinion of Washington was the same as described by McCullough, above. Whatever credit was given to Paine by Congress for the first *Crisis* paper and for the success at Trenton, the vote was in Paine's favor and he became the first Secretary of the Committee of Foreign Affairs.

There is one more thing to say about Paine's appointment. In Chapter four of Craig Nelson's excellent biography of Thomas Paine, Nelson wrote, "On April 17, (1777) after being nominated by John Adams, Paine won congressional appointment, at a monthly salary of seventy pounds, to be Secretary of the Committee of Foreign Affairs (previously the Committee of Secret Correspondence). This federal assignment set him at the very nexus of power between the two men he most admired, George Washington and Ben Franklin." (Nelson, p. 113)

The thought expressed in this quote has haunted me ever since I first read it. Why would John Adams offer the name of Thomas Paine as a candidate for such an important office? It is well documented that John Adams hated Thomas Paine. Could it be that Adams was requested, perhaps urged, by Benjamin Franklin to secure Paine's services as the New Foreign Secretary? I don't know. It is known, however, that Franklin had been in France since December 21, 1776. As the highest ranking ambassador of the new Republic his contributions were of great value to the American Revolution. Benjamin Franklin admired Thomas

Paine and trusted him as much, and perhaps more, that any other man in Congress. A request by Franklin to have Paine nominated by John Adams could hardly be refused. The canny Ben Franklin knew that his critical dispatches would be received by the Foreign Affairs Office. That meant that, if Paine was the Secretary of the Committee of Foreign Affairs, his (Franklin's) dispatches and all other foreign correspondence would come into the hands of Thomas Paine first.

With or without Franklin's help, Paine won the election and assumed the duties of the acting Secretary of State of the United States of America.

Two days later, April 19, 1776, on the second anniversary of the Battle of Lexington and Concord, Crisis number three was published. This production focused on Paine's top priority which was winning the war. It will be seen that Thomas Paine's added responsibilities as Secretary of the Committee of foreign Affairs would be a harmonic and an efficacious compliment to his unabated exertions in order to secure and perpetuate the Country that he had established.

CHAPTER 21
WORKING THE PLAN

Because of the great victory at Trenton on December 26, 1776, the new year started out on a high note for the Americans. It was not known at the time that this high mark would not be reached again for five years. The conduct of the Revolution began to go down hill and the war was almost lost at the start of 1781. There were a few bright spots such as: Saratoga, General Greene's operations in the south, and the exploits of John Paul Jones, and, of course, Yorktown. As regards all of the battles of the Revolutionary War, I leave their accounts to those historians who are experts in military operations.

However, regarding the victory at Saratoga in October of 1777, with due credit to Benedict Arnold, some History texts call this the turning point of the Revolutionary War. They are wrong. The turning point of the Revolution came when Thomas Paine put pen to paper and wrote *Common Sense*. The prologue to the turning point occurred on April 19, 1775. Thomas Paine called the event the "Massacre at Lexington". It was then that Paine came to the unalloyed realization that the King of Great Britain would settle for nothing less than the total CONQUEST of America. In July of 1775, Thomas was the only one who understood this. He recognized that America must become a separate and Independent country. He saw clearly that reconciliation with England was impossible. He saw that any alternative to "A country of our own" was false. Nothing would do but complete Independence.

The Knowledge that Britain's design was total CONQUEST provided Paine with a unique advantage over the, so called, "founding fathers". Since CONQUEST was out of the question, Paine's understanding gave him the power to predict the future of America if reconciled with Britain. His prediction was crystal clear. With reconciliation the result would be ruin. With Independence, the result would be The United States of America.

Was Thomas Paine's perception correct that Britain's aim was CONQUEST? Was it a fact? Was it a quantum of real knowledge? I don't know. Paine thought so, and that is what mattered. That is what was important. Moreover, he projected this "Knowledge of Britain's intent" into the minds of the American Colonists. Paine had to think for the Colonists because an estimated eighty percent (perhaps more) of them did not have either an intelligent or an informed understanding of what was happening. Paine wrote, "I happened to come to America a few months before the breaking out of hostilities. I found the disposition of the people such that they might have been led by a thread and governed by a reed. Their suspicion was quick and penetrating, but their attachment to Britain was obstinate, and it was at that time a kind of treason to speak against it. They disliked the Ministry, but they esteemed the Nation. Their idea of grievance operated without resentment, and their single object was reconciliation."…."I had formed my plan of life, and conceiving myself happy and wished everybody else so. But when the country, into which I had just set my foot, was set on fire about my ears, it was time to stir. It was time for everyman to stir." (This quote was copied from M. D. Conway's *The Life of Thomas Paine*, page 330. It also appears in the *Crisis number seven, Common Sense and the Crisis,* Anchor Press, Doubleday, 1973, page 167.)

Common Sense had done its work. Independence was declared. The darkest days were over. Now, at the beginning of 1777, Thomas Paine would commence addressing and overcoming every problem and every obstacle to final Victory. To this end, Paine directed his energy and talent with "unabated ardour" for seven years, in order to establish the representative system of government…" (Lewis, p. 184) In retrospect, Paine wrote, "It has been my fate to have borne a share in the commencement and complete establishment of one Revolution (I mean the Revolution of America)." (p. 260) Others followed and others shared, but it was Thomas Paine who originated the idea to establish the representative system of government, which he named, "The United States".

CHAPTER 22
TESTIMONY

On page four of his *Thomas Paine and the Promise of America*, Harvey J. Kaye wrote, "he (Thomas Paine) dedicated himself to the American cause". This is true. It is no less true that Thomas Paine initiated the *cause*. In *Common Sense*, Paine originated the idea of creating an "American nation-state". Paine then proceeded with an iron will and rock-ribbed perseverance to make his innovation a reality. His *Crisis Papers*, his advice on military tactics, his work as acting Secretary of State (1777-1778), his enlistment in the Revolutionary Army, and his unflinching readiness to perform hazardous duty, his unfailing support for Benjamin Franklin, his work to prevent the Silas Deane fraud, his personal money contributions to aid Washington's army, taken all together, these things prove that Paine would settle for nothing less than Unity and INDEPENDENCE.

Adams, Jay, Gouverneur Morris, were not doing what Thomas Paine was doing. Because of the elitist and envious attitude of these self-serving men – especially John Adams – they did not always support Thomas Paine's exertions and in some cases, they worked against them. Harvey J. Kaye expressed these thoughts far better than I ever could: "And yet as great as his contributions were, they were not always appreciated, and his affections were not always reciprocated. Paine's democratic arguments, style and appeal – as well as his social background, confidence, and single-mindedness – antagonized many among the powerful, propertied, prestigious and pious, and made him enemies even within the ranks of his fellow patriots. Elites and aspiring elites feared the power of Paine's pen and the radical implications of his arguments."(Kaye, pages 5,6)

Kaye mentions, on page seven, one J. G. A .Pocock's observation that Paine is "difficult to fit into any kind of category." I don't think it's so difficult. Think of Thomas Paine as an innovator, and confusion vaporizes. Paine wanted government of and by the people, true democracy. Paine's "fellow patriots" did not understand his design; or did not want to understand what Paine was trying to create. I doubt that it is understood today. (2009)

Kaye wrote, "...we find no FOUNDER more committed to the progress of freedom, equality and democracy than Paine."(p.13). Here, Kaye, not only, affirms that Paine is a FOUNDER but he is included in the first rank of founders. The idea comes first. This makes Thomas Paine first among peers. Washington, Adams, Jefferson, Hamilton and even Benjamin Franklin followed Paine's lead. They were great Patriots. They deserve full credit for their contributions; but they were not originators.

As provided by Kaye, the quotations on page sixteen of James Otis, Francis Hopkinson, Joseph Warren, Jefferson and Washington go to prove that these Patriots were Loyalists prior to January tenth, 1776. Kaye wrote, "*Common Sense* changed all that". (p.16) I concur. Kaye continued on page seventeen: "In spite of how the pamphlet differed fundamentally in content, language, and tone from all hitherto published pieces, almost everyone assumed a leading figure of the American political elite had written it." To the qualities of *Common Sense*, as described by Kaye, I would add rhythm, flow, rationality, masterful logic, adherence to principle, compelling persuasion, universality in scope, riveting decisiveness, and heart.

Common Sense is the original blueprint, the design plan, for the creation of the United States as a Democratic Republic. The DECLARATION itself is *Common Sense* in brief outline form. When

Harvey J. Kaye wrote, "The Declaration of Independence, though drafted by a Virginia aristocrat and edited by a committee of colonial gentlemen, issued from the force of *Common Sense*, authored by an immigrant workingman who would proudly describe himself as a "farmer of thoughts",(p39) he came close to ascribing authorship of the Declaration to Thomas Paine. Jefferson copied the Declaration from Paine's original manuscript, or from John Adam's copy of it. The final version of the Declaration was mangled and weakened as attested to by both Abigail Adams and Richard Henry Lee. Even Alan Dershowitz, in referring to the Declaration of Independence employed the words, "its primary author". (*America Declares Independence*, p.166, 167) If I understand correctly, Dershowitz believes that Thomas Jefferson is the primary author of the Declaration of Independence. I have total respect for the honored, accomplished and distinguished Alan Dershowitz and his opinions. However, I believe that Thomas Paine is the primary author of the Declaration. Along with Joseph Lewis, I do not believe that Jefferson composed the "Slave Clause' in the Declaration. I do not believe that Jefferson believed that that all men and women were created equal, "in the order of creation". Prior to June tenth, 1776, when Jefferson was assigned to serve as a member of the committee to prepare the Declaration, there is no authentic, verifiable evidence that Jefferson had any INTENTION of composing a Declaration of Independence. Jefferson himself, in a letter to William Fleming, around July first, 1776, wrote that he was directed to "draw" a Declaration; "a Declaration...which I was lately directed to draw."(Hazelton, *The Declaration of Independence, Its History*, p.464)

Independence was declared, but it would take five more dismal and frustrating years before Paine made it a reality at Yorktown; and another year and one half before England recognized it with the Treaty of Paris, April 1783.

The Constitution of the United States would be forged six years later in 1789. Prior to January 10, 1776, *Common Sense*, no one was advocating a Constitution of the United States. At that time the United States did not exist. In an extremely rare instance of Paine giving himself credit for any of his original ideas, he wrote, "I ought to stand first on the list of federalists, for the proposition for establishing a general government over the Union came ORIGINALLY* from me." (Foner, p.913) The same thought was expressed by Thomas Paine in a letter to George Washington, dated Paris, July 30, 1796.

I wish to conclude this chapter by expressing my thanks and appreciation to Doctor Harvey J. Kaye for his excellent Thomas Paine and the Promise of America. It should be the basis of a college course. In my opinion, Kaye's book is much better than those popular Biographies which seem to contribute to the temporal apotheosis of the so-called 'founding fathers'. Kaye managed to pack a huge quantity of facts and information in only 260 pages. Yet, the telling flows briskly, cogently, and with more effect than some much larger history volumes. Also, Kaye is a master at writing brief summaries of pivotal historical periods. His recap of events leading up to "1776" and his account of the war ending victory at Yorktown are splendid examples of his art.

In the last five chapters, Kaye seems to have in mind some agenda for ideological change in what Thomas Paine might call the science of governance. I am not qualified to speak to this. However, I am fully confident that whatever change is desired by the people, it will be accomplished constitutionally.

Perhaps the future will bring the "broad and equal representation" and short terms and Constitutional Review every seven years, and frugality in the cost of governance, all of which Paine proposed. I don't know if these things would solve the problems OF America. They might buy us some time.

---

*   caps mine

WHO SAYS ORIGINAL? TWO TESTIMONIES

In his *Dialogue Between the Ghost of General Montgomery Just Arrived from the Elysian Fields; and an American Delegate in a Wood Near Philadelphia*, Thomas Paine has General Montgomery say, "And as for your enemies, they have done their worst. They have called upon Russians – Hanoverians – Hessians – Canadians – SAVAGES and NEGROES to assist them in burning your towns – desolating your country – and in butchering your wives and children."* (Foner, p.92)

Moncure Daniel Conway, in his commentary on the *Montgomery Dialogue* wrote, "The allusion to the arming of NEGROES and INDIANS against America, and other passages, resemble clauses in one of the paragraphs eliminated from the ORIGINAL Declaration of Independence."*

Conway continued: "...and there can be little doubt that the antislavery clause struck out of the Declaration was written by Paine, or by someone who had Paine's antislavery essay before him." In the following passages it will be observed that the antitheses are nearly the same – "infidel and Christian", "heathen and Christian". (Conway, p.33) Both passages are provided, in small print on the same page.

From the Declaration of Independence: "This piratical warfare, the opprobrium of INFIDEL powers, is the warfare of the CHRISTIAN King of Great Britain."*

From Paine's essay on "African Slavery in America: "...purely to catch inoffensive people, like wild beasts for slaves, is an height of outrage against humanity and justice, that seems left by HEATHEN, nations to be practiced by pretended CHRISTIANS."* (Foner, Vol 2, p.18)

Of course, I do not believe that Jefferson composed the "Anti-Slavery clause" in the Declaration. I concur with Conway, who thought, along with Joseph Lewis, that it was Jefferson himself who struck it out.

*   caps mine

If Jefferson did not put it in the Declaration who did? Surely Thomas Paine is the logical choice. But this leads to questions of dual authorship and further complications. As a discussion of such digressions is not a part of this chapter, I return to the two testimonies of originality.

We saw that Moncure Conway attributed the authorship of the "Slavery clause" to Thomas Paine. Conway went on to say, "Paine had no reason to suppose that the Declaration of human freedom and equality, passed July 4th (sic) could fail eventually to include the African slaves. The Declaration embodied every principle that Paine had been asserting, and indeed Cobbett is correct in saying that whoever may have written the Declaration, Paine was its author." (Conway, p 34) An example of the principles that Paine had been asserting can be found in the introduction to *Common Sense*. "The cause of America is in great measure the cause of all mankind."

For me, these two testimonies provide powerful evidence of Thomas Paine's plan to create the United States.

SUPPORTING EVIDENCE FROM MONCURE DANIEL CONWAY

The following brief paragraphs provide supporting evidence that Thomas Paine is the FOUNDER of the United States of America.

"As one amongst thousands who had borne a share in that memorable revolution…" (p.99)

"The portion of the Jefferson Papers at Washington written by Paine would fill a good volume." (p.99)

"Our very good friend the Marquis de la Fayette has entrusted to my care the Key of the Bastille…as a present to (Washington)." Paine considered the key as an "early trophy of the Spoils of despotism; and the first ripe fruits of American Principles transplanted into Europe…" (p.111)

"That the principles of America opened the Bastille is not to be doubted…" (p.111) The principles came from Thomas Paine.

"I wish most anxiously to see my much loved America. It is the country from whence all reformation originally must spring." The very next sentence shows Paine's continuing interest in abolishing slavery. "I despair of seeing an abolition of that infernal traffic in negroes." (Letter, March 16, 1790. P.111) Obviously, Paine thought that his America was the original well-spring of Republican Democracy.

In a letter to Washington dated, July 21, 1791, Paine acknowledged his support for the French Revolution. "After the establishment of the American Revolution, it did not appear to me that any object could arise great enough to engage me a second time…principle is not confined to time and place, and that the ardour of seventy-six is capable of renewing itself." (p.123)

Moncure Daniel Conway did not hesitate to record his recognition of Paine's leadership: "In America, while writing as with his heart's blood the FIRST plea for its independence," and in France…when he was FOUNDING the FIRST republican society, and writing its declaration."* (p.126)

Thomas Paine stuck to his principles. In his address and Declaration of the Friends of Universal Peace and Liberty – August 1791 – he wrote, "If we are asked what government is, we hold it to be nothing more than a national association; and we hold that to be the best which secures to every man his rights and promotes the greatest quantity of happiness with the least expence. We live to improve, or we live in vain; and therefore we admit of no maxims of government or policy on the mere score of antiquity or other men's authority, the old whigs or the new." (p. 130)

Again, Conway reinforced his assertion and our confidence when he wrote that Paine "carried to success his anti-monarchical faith. He was the FIRST to assail monarchy in America and in France."* (p.148)

Thomas Paine's eloquent defense of King Louis XVI on January 19, 1793, was brilliant. A clerk of the French National Convention read the translation of the speech: "Very sincerely do I regret the Convention's

---

*   caps mine

vote of yesterday for death. I have the advantage of some experience; it is near twenty years that I have been engaged in the cause of liberty, having contributed something to it in the revolution of the United States of America. My language has always been that of liberty and humanity…" (p.158)

A more worthy and more effective defender of the King did not exist. Yet, as is typical of Paine, he 'down-plays' his superb qualifications to speak as just a mere contributer of "something" to the complete success of the American Revolution. Also, Paine's claim of "some" experience is a gem of modified litotes as well as classic understatement.

Paine put his life on the line and as Conway wrote, "…toiled night and day to save the hapless King." Paine's aim was to kill the Monarchy, not the King. His logic and reasoning seemed invincible.

The execution of poor Louis would increase the enemies and decrease the friends of France; would cause war; would result in needless constraints on future assemblies; would offend Americans who regarded King Louis as their friend; and would give the "Tyrant of England the triumph of seeing the man perish on the scaffold who helped my much-loved America to break his chains."

These reasons along with the purest sentiments of gratitude were not to be compromised. Accordingly Paine remained ever grateful to Louis, the man. It was Louis XVI who "loaded Paine with favors." French troops, ships, arms, supplies, silver and generalship enabled the Americans to end the Revolutionary War and attain Independence with the glorious victory at Yorktown.

Paine persisted in his advocacy. Alas, blood vengeance and mob madness vanquished vision, virtue and rationality.

Regarding Thomas Paine's unjust imprisonment in France from (circa) December 28, 1793 to November 7, 1794, [according to M.D. Conway: 315 days. (p.221)] the following testimony is submitted. Upon learning of Paine's imprisonment, a group of Americans sent a long letter to the Committees of General Surety and Public Safety requesting Paine's release.

In this letter, the Americans referred to "...one of our country men most worthy of honor, namely, Thomas Paine, one of the political FOUNDERS of the independence and of the Republic of America."*

"Our experience of twenty years has taught America to know and esteem his public virtues and the invaluable services he rendered her." (The petition is): "to obtain the liberation of one of the most earnest and faithful apostles of liberty..." The letter of the Americans continues with additional descriptions of Paine: "this courageous and virtuous defender of Liberty" and "the man whose courageous and energetic pen did so much to free the Americans..." Finally, the petition by the Americans attests to "the purity of his (Paine's) principles in politics and morals." (p.199)

Thomas Paine left America in 1787 in order to secure British and French 'patents' for his iron bridge. His intention was to return in one year. He wrote "...but the French Revolution and the prospect it afforded of EXTENDING the principles of liberty and fraternity through the greater part of Europe..."* (p.177)

Moncure D. Conway wrote "Thus Thomas Paine, recognized by every American statesman and by Congress as a FOUNDER of their Republic, found himself a prisoner..."* (p.206)

"Mr. Thomas Paine is one of those men who have contributed the most to establish the liberty of America." (Abbe Sieyes, p.220)

In a letter to Gilbert Wakefield, A.B., Paine wrote, "When you have done as much service to the world by your writings, and suffered as much for them, as I have done, you will be better able to dictate..." (Pairs, November 19, 1795, p. 248)

"...founder of two great republics..." (p.276)

In 1806, Paine was barred from voting in a New Rochelle election. The refusal was based on the falsehood that Thomas Paine was not an American citizen. Conway's reply to this outrage was, "It was the

---

* caps mine

fate of this FOUNDER OF REPUBLICS to be a monument of their ingratitude."* (p.305)

"...on the soil which the generous services of Thomas Paine contributed to bless with freedom..." (*The Inskeep Letter*, p.305)

"Paine...the FIRST advocate of independence."* (p.317)

(Paine) "...the man who, as Jefferson wrote, 'steadily labored, and with as much effect as any man living, to secure American freedom'..." (p.318)

"...the man who unmade Thrones..." (p.321)

I believe that the History Scholars could find additional material in support of Paine's UNIQUE place in the origination and establishment of the United States.

MORE EVIDENCE

In his narrative about William Cobbett, Craig Nelson quoted from Cobbett, "...I saw Paine FIRST pointing the way and then LEADING a nation through perils and difficulties of all sorts, to independence and to lasting liberty, prosperity and greatness."* (p.5)

On page eighty, Nelson includes another important quote: "In October, 1775...I had then formed the outlines of *Common Sense* and finished nearly the first part..."(p.80) This shows that Paine was first in leading and pointing the way. Nelson also referenced what John Adams said about Thomas Paine's *Rights of Man*, "I detest that book and its tendency, from the bottom of my heart." (p.205) Then on page 206, Nelson records Jefferson's quote about Adams "apostasy to hereditary monarchy and nobility..."

John Adams stood in opposition to what Thomas Paine was creating. Adams was opposed to equal rights, universal suffrage, short terms and broad and equal representation. In short, Adams wanted the United States of Adams. But, Adams was too late. Yorktown secured

---

*   caps mine

the Independence and the result was the ESTABLISHMENT of an embryo Republic.

Paine was satisfied that he started the process. Remnant deficiencies such as voting rights, equal rights, and slavery could be corrected in time as enabled by an amendable constitution.

During the years after the Revolution, Paine devoted his time and energies – among other pursuits – to creating and promoting his iron bridge. He would suspend these activities when, in 1789, the events in France led to an opportunity that he could not resist. In a letter to George Washington, dated July 21, 1791(Foner II, p.1319), Paine referred to his part in the ESTABLISHMENT of the American Revolution. Now, he would work, "with the ardour of seventy-six" to ESTABLISH the Republic of France.

The above citations, along with those given in previous chapters provide a strong case that Paine was the originator of the United States. The astute scholar Nelson F. Adkins provided important additional evidence as we shall see.

"So far from taking any ideas from Locke or anybody else, it was the absurd expression of a mere John Bull, in England, about the year 1773 that first caused me to turn my mind to systems of government." In speaking of the then King of Prussia, called the Great Frederick, he said, "he is the right sort of man for a King, for he has a deal of the devil in him." This set me to think if a system of government could not exist that did not require the devil and I succeeded without any help from anybody."(Adkins, p.XIV)

I see this quote as strong evidence that Thomas Paine had decided to create a new independent country with a new governmental system; and also as a personal assertion that he was first and alone when he initiated the action to achieve his goal. Later Paine wrote, "I saw an opportunity in which I thought I could do some good, and I followed exactly what my heart dictated. I neither read books nor studied other people's opinions. I thought for myself...I was struck...and impressed with the idea that a little more than what society naturally performed, was all the government that was necessary, and that monarchy and aristocracy were frauds and impositions upon mankind. On these principles I published the pamphlet *Common Sense.*"(Adkins, p.XX)

Adkins interjected, "The principles here alluded to are obviously those summarized so eloquently by Locke and others who had preceded Paine. Besides John Locke, I suppose, Adkins would include James Burgh and his Political Disquisitions, Franklin, Thomas Hobbes, David Hume, Machiavelli, Rousseau, Montesquieu, Newton, Adam Smith, Voltaire and others who had preceded Thomas Paine. None of the great thinkers created an integration of ideas that resulted in the establishment of the United States.

That integration came from the mind of Thomas Paine. What was achieved took time and the work to make America truly governed by the people is on-going. Adkins recognized that *Common Sense* was a "blueprint for a colonial organization" with a constitution as soon as Independence was attained."(p.XXII) "Blueprint" is the proper word for *Common Sense* because Thomas Paine was the architect. Paine was also the builder, just as Adkins would quote: "I continued the subject" of American Independence "under the title of the 'Crisis', till the complete establishment of the Revolution." (p.XXIV) How do I see this? I see that Independence was Thomas Paine's design and goal. I see that Paine worked for six years to establish Independence and have it recognized. I see that Paine persevered in spite of the mean, envious, peevish, prejudiced animadversion of the Adams, Jay, Gouverneur Morris cabal. Thomas Jefferson did not assist Paine during those six frustrating years when Paine was writing the *Crisis Papers.* Jefferson stayed in Virginia. George Washington failed to achieve Independence by force of a military victory in the field until "Yorktown" on October 19,1781; and then only with the aid of French planning, troops, arms ships and money; all of which were provided, to a large extent by Thomas Paine. It is my opinion that the genius of Paine was the master-mind behind the overall Franco-American joint land and sea tactical campaign against the British at Yorktown. We recall that Paine and Laurens embarked for France on February 11, 1781. They arrived in France on March 9, 1781; and departed from France on June 1, 1781. After, I presume a tense and trying voyage of eighty-six days, they arrived at Boston, with a ship laden with two and a half million 'livers' in sliver, on August 25, 1781. A mere fifty-five days later, October 19, 1781 Washington accepted the surrender of Cornwallis and the British forces at Yorktown. Because of Paine's amazing feat which enabled the Yorktown victory, American Independence was secured. The world changed.

Of course, Paine gave the credit for the world-class military victory at Yorktown to Laurens, Franklin, Washington, Rochambeau, Louis XVI and the brave men who fought and died in the battle. However, Yorktown was the result of Thomas Paine's work. It was the final, war ending stroke of a strategic masterpiece. It all started with an improbable journey of a young officer and an unpaid civilian when they embarked on a cold winter's voyage to France. The journey ended with a glorious triumph. Later, Paine would recall the mission and write, "Perhaps two such travelers as Col. Laurens and myself on such national business is a novelty."(Nelson, p.155)

Although the entire Yorktown event is omitted by Nelson F. Adkins, he is to be commended for including key quotes which indicate Paine's authorship and innovations of principles such as: non-hereditary legislation, the sovereignty of the people and an amendable constitution, the founding (and defense) of the North American Bank, his thoughts on defensive war, equal rights, the problem of paper money – (sound money is a boon for all people including the poor) – I believe that all of these ideas can be summarized with Pain's famous quote, "The end of all political associations is the preservation of the natural and imprescriptible rights of man." (Adkins, p.XXXIX) Also, I applaud Adkins because he was brave enough to include an extract of an historically important letter from Paine to George Washington in his biography. This is the letter in which Paine described Washington as unprincipled, treacherous, and as a hypocrite. Adkins wrote that "Washington had been negligent in performing his duties." As president of the United States, a mere word from Washington would have effected Paine's release. Even the negative influence of G. Morris "does not excuse Washington."(p.XIV) Clearly Washington was derelict in his duty as president and as a man for not obtaining the release of a former comrade-in-arms. But Adkins labeled Paine's letter as the "product of indiscretion and tactlessness". It was also the product of truth. In this letter, Paine wrote, "And as to you, Sir, treacherous in private friendship (for so you have been to me, and that in the day of danger) and a hypocrite in public life, the world will be puzzled to decide whether you are an apostate or an imposter; whether you have abandoned good principles, or whether you ever had any." (Adkins, p. XLVI)

There is no question in my mind that one of the most important consequences of Thomas Paine's letter was that 'Czar' George did not seek a third term as president. After two terms Washington 'relinquished' the Presidency in 1797. Thus, providentially, the American electoral process was not crippled by the haunting specter of a pernicious precedent which might subject the voting public to endure a "president for life." Washington disgraced himself by failing to reclaim Paine from prison; and he dishonored America by signing the "Jay Treaty".

Nelson F. Adkins concluded that despite his "human frailties, Paine was one of those great humanitarian spirits who illuminate with rare intensity the age into which they are born." Adkins then asks us to remember Paine as the apostle of political liberty and the spokesman of the – common man in America – in England – and in France!"(p.XLIX) As to Paine's "frailties", they evaporate when compared to his brilliant accomplishments and his often stated creed of "Loving Mercy, Doing Justice and Helping his Fellow Man." Paine lived his creed and there is no biographical evidence to contradict the fact that Thomas Paine lived a life of heroic virtue and if he had lived longer, I believe that he would have continued in a life of heroic virtue.

As regards Thomas Paine being an "apostle of political liberty", he was much more that that. He engineered the greatest advance in political freedom and liberty since the Exodus.

A LITTLE MORE

Seventeen years after the ideological supernova, *Common Sense*, ushered in a new societal era, Thomas Paine reminisced about his famous creation.

"I saw an opportunity in which I thought I could do some good, and I followed exactly what my heart dictated. I neither read books, nor studied other people's opinions. I thought for myself. The case was this: During the suspension of the old governments in America, both prior to and at the breaking out of hostilities, I was struck with the order and decorum with which everything was conducted; and impressed with the idea, THAT A LITTLE MORE that what society naturally performed, was all the government that was necessary, and that monarchy and aristocracy were frauds and impositions upon mankind. On these principles I published the pamphlet *Common Sense*."* (Adkins intro, p.XX)

In a dozen or more Thomas Paine biographies that I have read, a number of complimentary adjectives were used to describe his heroic 'exertions' to achieve Independence. They include, among others, - admirable, genius, brilliant, inspired, eloquent, clear, enlightened, strong, moral, intellectual, rational, logical, ORIGINAL, decisive, most uncommon, uncompromising, and visionary. Yet, it is a rare exception to find, in print, a clear statement identifying Thomas Paine as the originator of America.

As regards Paine's tireless work to create the sovereign and United States of America, various biographers described Paine, using such words as advocate, promoter, crusader, proponent, champion, popularizer, firebrand, catalyst, and prophet. These authors generally admit that Thomas Paine was the spirit of the Revolution; and that he made great

---

*   caps mine

contributions; had a pivotal role; was a major player; and did so much to bring forth the doctrine, in the work of achieving Independence.

In spite of all the accolades and credits bestowed on Paine, most of his biographers stop short of recognizing him as being the original Founder of the United States. Many allusions to Thomas Paine as Founder can be found in History books and in Biographies of him. Most of these pointed references include Paine in a group of other Founders. Here are some examples: Paine has been called the moral Founder; one of the select members of Founders; the unofficial "Founding father". (Hitchens, p.31)[I think Paine is official enough] Paine ranked himself "among the founders of a new Independent World".(Kaye, p.40) "...he clearly spelled out both independence and republicanism."(Kaye, p.43) Jefferson never formally acknowledged Paine's *part in the creation** of the Republican movement. In his "Notes on Virginia" – 1784, Jefferson wrote, "It is well known that in July, 1775, a separation from Great Britain and the establishment of a *republican** government, had never yet entered into anyone's mind."(W. S. Randall, p.250) "Indeed, for some years it would seem that Paine and his role in the MAKING of the United States would forever be ignored..."** (Kaye, p.117)

Thomas Paine's role in the "making" (Kaye, p.117) of the United States was that of innovator. Paine originated the complete plan of cession, Independence, democratic Republicanism, and a non-hereditary government with a revolving – annually – presidency.

With all of the credits and compliments accorded to Paine by his biographers, including those discredited writers who ineluctably recorded some of Paine's achievements, I believe that with "A LITTLE MORE" than what has been admitted, Thomas Paine would be identified, acknowledged, appreciated, extolled, and celebrated as the first and true Founder of the United States of America.

It's about time.

---

*   italics mine

**   caps mine

CHAPTER 23
INDEPENDENCE AND PEACE

I n a letter to General Nathanael Greene, dated September 9, 1780, Thomas Paine provided three significant indications that he was the author of the Declaration of Independence. They are given in the following extracts:

"...as I had a considerable share in promoting the Declaration of Independence in this country..."

"It was in a great measure owing to my bringing a knowledge of England with me to America, that I was enabled to enter deeper into politics, and with more success than other people..."

"I do not suppose that the acknowledgment of Independence is at this time a more unpopular DOCTRINE* in England than the declaration of it was in America immediately before the publication of the pamphlet *Common Sense*..." These quotes provide strong testimony to support Thomas Paine's priority in initiating the idea of total Independence and the Declaration of it.

Paine was saying that the DOCTINE OF INDEPENDENCE was unpopular prior to *Common Sense*. After *Common Sense*, the DOCTRINE OF INDEPENDENCE became popular in America. This means that the DOCTRINE OF INDEPENDENCE was contained in *Common Sense*.

---

* caps mine

The first quote, "as I had a considerable share in promoting the Declaration of Independence" is a rare, self-crediting disclosure in a private letter. This letter was not intended to be made public. The second quote, "…and with more success than other people…" is as much of an understatement as the first.

Why was Paine complementing himself? It was not like Paine to do that, even in a thickly veiled manner. What was the matter? The problem was five-fold. First, Independence was declared, but not recognized by Great Britain. Second, America was still at war and although persistent resistance continued in the south, Washington was dormant. Third, Paine did not trust any peace offers from the British. Fourth, the thirteen states did not bond together and mount a unified effort in order to drive the British armies off of the continent. Fifth, Congress was out of funds.

In the face of these obstacles, Paine proposed that he would go to England and work for a Treaty of Peace. It was his intention to end the war and end the bloodshed. He would do it his way. His plan was to bring out a publication, "under the cover of an Englishman who had made the tour of America incog." (incognito) Paine's goal was to make the acknowledgment of Independence a popular subject. Can you imagine? Paine wanted to assume the role of a secret agent; a kind of a literary mole, in order to plant the seeds of a peaceful end to a cruel war. He was willing to try anything within reason to secure the complete establishment of the Free and Independent States of America. He kept working on it. That is what innovators do.

CHAPTER 24
THOMAS PAINE –
INNOVATOR

Should Thomas Paine be recognized as the original, the first Founder, the "creator in sole" of the United States of America? The answer is yes. Why? Because Thomas Paine invented the idea to separate from Great Britain and establish an Independent country with a governance mechanism specifically designed to operate as a Democratic Republic.

Thomas Paine was an innovator. He developed a plan for steamboat navigation, and worked on producing smokeless candles. He invented the first iron bridge. He originated the idea of a combustion engine fueled by gun powder. He invented a planning machine to plane boards, a new type of crane, and a new wheel "of concentric rim".

Paine was the first to propose both total Independence and a Republic with an elected chief executive. He was the first one to propose a Constitution in order to achieve a Federal union of the States; provide national security and above all, secure the natural and civil rights of all. He was one of the first to propose 'Abolition', and at the same time expose the "execrable" slave trade in which "pretended Christians" participated. Paine became a *founding* member of the *first* American Anti-Slavery Society. Paine advocated protection for animals and proposed an international association to achieve global peace. He was a leader in advocating women's rights, including woman's suffrage and an uncompromising proponent for the education of children of both sexes. He proposed a system for international copyright. Thomas Paine provided a strong proposal for the immediate acquisition of the Louisiana Territory and how to go about it. Paine's letter to Jefferson provided incontestable reasons for the purchase and the letter included a method of calculating an approximate offering price. Jefferson had been dragging his feet on this unprecedented move. Paine's counsel succeeded in overcoming Jefferson's indecision. Properly understood, the Louisiana Purchase ranks with the foremost political events in history; for it shows how to acquire land without war and killing.

Thomas Paine was among the first to expose dueling as a crime; and he was among the first to suggest more rational ideas concerning marriage and divorce. There is more. The heart of Thomas Paine shines forth through the original ideas contained in his famous *Agrarian Justice*. In this, as in all of his humanitarian works for freedom and equal rights, Paine never deviates from his creed of Loving Mercy, Doing Justice, and helping his fellow man. Although variations in types of "Social Security" systems, as derived from Paine's pioneering construct, might suffer from political contamination, Paine's intent and goal to provide 'blessings' and benefits to mankind was pure. Here is Paine's idea.

Upon the death of a land owner, a flat tax of ten percent of the assessed value of the property would be levied. The legal receiver of the property would be required to pay the tax in four quarterly payments. The tax money would then be deposited into a "National Fund", out of which disbursements would be made, as follows. Fifteen pounds sterling would be paid to every person, "when arrived at the age of twenty-one years" "…And also, the sum of ten pounds per annum, during life, (would be paid) to every person now living of the age of fifty years, and to all others as they shall arrive at that age." (Foner, p.613)

There are two discernable problems, among others, with Thomas Paine's "National Fund" proposal. In the first case, political experience shows that there is scant likelihood that Paine's plan would survive

THE REAL THOMAS PAINE

intact, over the years, without being transmogrified into something unrecognizable.

The second problem reveals a contradiction in Paine's reform plan designed to provide desirable benefits to both young and old. The disparity arises out of the intrinsic long term operational nature of the system. As a continuing plan, enacted into law by one generation, it would bind future generations who did not vote for it. Hereditary monarchy, as well as hereditary laws, usurp the voting authority of future generations. Paine pointed this out in both *Common Sense* and *The Crisis*. He railed against the King's claim to bind the people in all cases whatsoever. Thomas Paine was a champion for the rights of all generations. He wrote, "Every age and generation must be as free to act for itself, in all cases, as the ages and generation which preceded it." (Foner I, p.251) He also wrote, "We ought to remember that virtue is not hereditary."(*Common Sense*, p.51)

Paine's vision of what we generally call "Social Security" was a "win-win" model. If successful, it would provide benefits. If it failed, Paine had two remedies. One, it could be modified or scrapped and replaced by the voting power of the people because the United States has an amendable constitution, which was first proposed by Thomas Paine. The second remedy lay in Paine's interest and aim, "to elevate the SCIENCE OF GOVERNMENT* to a height of perfection of which we have now no conception." (Aldridge, p.150) He wrote, "We are a people upon experiments" and "From what we now see, nothing of reform on the political world ought to be held *improbable***. It is an age of revolutions, in which everything may be looked for." (Kay, p.261)

Although "looked for" reforms such as Emancipation and Women's Rights were achieved by constitutional amendments, there has been scant evidence in the elevation of the science of government. The lack of reform progress in political America can be traced, for the most part, to

---

*   caps mine

**   italics mine

three of the so-called Founding Fathers; namely, the first three presidents. They disregarded three key elements in Thomas Paine's Blueprint. These factors were: Broad and equal representation; Short terms, (one year); and Frugality in the cost of operating the government. These fundamental features are required to have government of, by, and for the people. Operational implementation of these safeguards would have made a huge difference, in my opinion. With some other "improbable" changes, perhaps they would have made "all the difference".

Washington, Adams and Jefferson had no intention other than governance from the 'top down'. Listen to what William E. Woodward said, "The country had become an oligarchy with wealth and land as the determining factors of leadership. Only a small fraction of the male population could qualify as voters. The men elected to all important offices were either men of wealth or they possessed a far-reaching influence among the wealthy. The poor – the farm hands, the mechanics of the towns and cities, the clerks in the shops – none of these had anything to say about the problems of the nation, the state, or the city." (Woodward, p.309)

Thomas Paine was an innovator and he invented America. His plan, first of all, was to put the power of governing in the hands of the people from whence it springs. Next he forged a method to allow for and promote reform and improvement through the progress of science of government. The social security idea, in this chapter was given as an example that, "nothing of reform in the political world ought to be held improbable."

Washington, Adams, and Jefferson did not originate the United States. They did not have Thomas Paine's vision. They should have thanked Paine for creating a country without which they could not have become its first three presidents. Furthermore they failed to insure that the United States would be a true Democracy; that is, government of, by, and for the people – all of the people. The case was just the opposite. Why? I trust William E. Woodward's assessment of the matter:

"In the first place, American society as it then existed was an aristocracy. It was not a democracy in any true sense and the founders of the nation hoped it would never become one, for they constituted a caste of well-bred, well-to-do gentlemen who proposed silently to retain the governing power in their own hands. Their distrust of the common people was profound, and they intended to keep the members of the so-called "mob" down and under, as a permanent lower class. Even Thomas Jefferson was socially ostracized in Philadelphia in the 1790's, despite the fact that he was Vice President of the United States. Yet Jefferson was an aristocrat himself and far superior in intellect and achievement to his critics. His social offense was that he had faith in democracy and in the common people." (Woodward, p.309)

In spite of Thomas Paine's innovative Blueprint for a country governed by the people, history reflects that the power of governing, at the political birth of the United States, was preempted and held by the landed elite

CHAPTER 25
FOUNDATION

W as Thomas Paine the first one to propose Independence. I do not think so. The topic of independence had been discussed by others here and abroad. In a footnote on page twenty-one of M. D. Conway's *Life of Thomas Paine*, Major Cartwright's *American Independence the Interest and Glory of Great Britain*, October 25, 1774, and also Josiah Tucker's *The Revolution* (1762) in favor of separation were referenced. I assume that the number of Colonists who publicly advocated secession orally or in print must have been very small because sedition was a capital offense. While I would agree with the History Scholars, if they provided the names of those who not only advocated but also urged that the Colonies separate from Great Britain, declare Independence, eliminate the King; and establish a new system of government, I would conclude that such a list would describe a very narrow field of men eligible to be called "Founding Fathers".

Thomas Paine did the things as described above. In addition he proposed the establishment of a constitutional Republic such that the people themselves are the government. He published his ideas in *Common Sense*. The scholarly and perceptive Nelson F. Adkins wrote, "And in *Common Sense* he lays before us his BLUEPRINT* for a colonial organization with a congress, president, and charter (i.e. Constitution).

---

*   caps mine

Most striking, indeed, is his call for a Declaration of Independence". (Adkins, Intro. P. XXII) I have used the word BLUEPRINT before in order to stress that Thomas Paine presented an integrated plan which included all of the elements necessary to create an Independent Democratic Republic. The BLUEPRINT was a Thomas Paine original and as such, he was first and stands alone.

Washington, Adams, Jefferson, Jay, Patrick Henry, Sam Adams, James Otis, Benjamin Franklin and George Mason, did not propose all of the components necessary to establish an Independent Republic. Accordingly, they should be referred to as Following Founders. The following paragraphs provide a few citations which are early indications of Paine's thinking and his intention to propose total Independence.

If it was Thomas Paine's intention to create a new country where slavery would be prohibited, he would include both emancipation and future non-importation of slaves in his design plan. His uncompromising essay condemning the execrable practice of *African Slavery in America*, (March 8, 1775) as carried on by "pretended Christians", shows where Paine stood on this issue and he proposed a plan of liberation and resettlement. As a rule, when Paine proposed something, he would present a plan of action to accomplish it.

Later in an article titled *A Serious Thought*, October 18, 1776, Paine reflected on "a thousand instances of British barbarity" and wrote, "I firmly believe that the Almighty, in compassion to mankind will curtail the power of Britain." A few lines later he continued, "I hesitate not for a moment to believe that the Almighty will finally separate America from Britain. Call it INDEPENDENCEY* or what you will…"

These citations provide a clear indication that Thomas Paine was in favor of a separate and independent America at least three months prior to the publication of *Common Sense* on January 10, 1776. Paine had been working on *Common Sense* during the Fall of 1775 and had the outline of it completed in October, 1775. Common Sense was much

---

*   caps mine

more than a mere indication of Paine's thinking about Independence, it was a decisive call for Separation and Independence, or face ruin. "We ought not now to be debating whether we shall be independent (sic) or not, but anxious to accomplish it on a firm, secure and honorable basis…" and "In short, Independence (sic) is the only Bond that can tye (sic) and keep us together."

George Washington, who was acting in open rebellion, was an early convert after he read *Common Sense* in January 1776. Washington adopted Paine's ideas of separation and independence, and in this regard Washington was a follower, not a leader. The frequently quoted phrase: "The great American cause owed as much to the pen of Paine as to the sword of Washington" has been attributed to Joel Barlow. This is not correct. It would be more accurate to say the great American cause owed as much to the pen of Thomas Paine as to the sword of Thomas Paine.

I do not have a clear understanding of what Washington's intentions or objectives prior to the publication of *Common Sense*, but, after six years of war, Washington had lost his sword. He was dormant and militarily impotent and in no condition to mount even a limited offensive. His army (if it could be called one) was beset by mutinies and desertions. Provisions were scarce and morale was low. Although it may be too much to say that Washington was defeated, he certainly was not victorious.

It was Thomas Paine who obtained French money, arms, supplies and troops which enabled the Allied Victory at Yorktown. Washington was acclaimed a hero, Paine was ignored.

Thomas Paine originated the idea and goal of immediate Independence. He explained how to accomplish it. He persuaded a number of influential patriots and a number of American colonists to eschew reconciliation, and embrace Independence. He devoted all of his energy and talent, through six arduous years, in order to achieve Independence. Paine was phenomenally successful when he made the voyage to France, in the spring of 1781, in order to intercede with King Louis XVI for aid. King Louis "loaded Paine with favors", and entrusted him with a prodigious amount of money and supplies and placed a large, well trained, well equipped army at his disposal. In effect, Thomas Paine provided the means for the allied victory at Yorktown. And finally Thomas Paine deserves credit for what he started; what he worked for; and what he secured, i.e., Independence of the United States of America "Whose peace and happiness may God preserve, Amen." (*Common Sense*, Anchor Books, 1973, p.40)

CHAPTER 26
FORMATION

Alfred Owen Aldridge wrote an excellent biography of Thomas Paine. It was published in 1960. The scope and detail of the work shows that Aldridge was an outstanding scholar and intellectual.

Aldridge wrote that Thomas Paine was a "constitution-maker", and "one of the foremost bridge engineers of his time". "He rose to fame as the literary-political guide of the American nation. His contribution to the propaganda of its Revolution equaled that of Franklin to its diplomacy and that of Washington to its military strategy". (*Man of Reason*, A.O. Aldridge, p.7) These compliments place Paine in the first rank of "Founders" and, I am convinced that Thomas Paine was superior to both Washington and Franklin in military tactics, strategy and planning.

Aldridge continued, "There are two types of revolutionary reformers – the idealist and the agitator."(p.8). There are more than just two types. I would add innovator and participant. Thomas Paine was all four; and I would substitute the word teacher for agitator. Aldridge seems to miss the point that Paine was much more than a reformer. Paine did not work to reform the monarchic system, he worked to do away with it. Paine was creating something new and he said so. He wrote, "a new aera (sic) for politics is struck; a NEW* method of thinking hath arisen". Also, "…

---

*   caps mine

the means of giving rise to something better."(*Common Sense*) The result was the FORMATION of the United States. Because Aldridge did not fully understand the importance and scope of Paine's achievement, he criticized Moncure Daniel Conway's biography of Paine as being prejudiced in Paine's favor. Anyone who is thoroughly acquainted with Paine's works would surely prefer the complimentary descriptions of Paine and his achievements over the crude and counter-productive invective of his detractors. Aldridge even faults Conway for portraying Gouverneur Morris as a "detestable villain". G. Morris was worse than that. Aldridge also wrote that "Paine was at times short sighted (and) at times vain..." (p.11) Aldridge did not give any examples as to how Paine was short sighted; and I am not aware of any such evidence. Paine was a "long-termer", and everything he did was for the benefit of future generations. As to Paine being vain, well, we all have egos. Washington had a big ego and he provided perseverance and little else. Results speak louder than egos. From Thomas Paine, we have an ageless *Declaration, The Crisis Papers, Yorktown, The Rights of Man* and a country. Aldridge wrote that, "Paine made many mistakes in his career – and some of his applications of principles were grotesque."(p.322)

Again, Aldridge failed to provide specific examples of this ostensible contention. No one is perfect; and I will leave, to some intrepid researcher, the task of ferreting out Paine's mistakes and "grotesque" applications for whatever value they may be worth. I remain totally confident that Paine's positive contributions far, far outweigh his mistakes.

Aldridge followed "Paine's influential career in the FORMATION* of the NEW* American nation..." and recorded "that he was INTIMATELY* concerned with the most important political events in the United States...", and wrote that "he made an imposing contribution to the FOUNDATION* of the United States."(p.11) However, Aldridge stops short of naming Thomas Paine as being the original founder of the United States. Later, on page one hundred and

---

*   caps mine

forty-five, Aldridge referred to, "a public appeal which Paine had made for the FORMATION* of a republic in France before anyone else had even hinted at the idea." Then, on page one hundred and forty-seven, Aldridge clearly stated, "Paine was literally the first to call publicly for the CREATION* of a republic in France as he had previously been the *first in America.*"** I was happy to see that Aldridge used the word FIRST*. This means firstness. This defines priority. It is true, as Philip S. Foner wrote in his introduction to the *Age of Reason* "Paine was not the first person to advocate independence in America; John Adams had done so, for example, even before *Common Sense* was published."(p.11) No doubt, there were many who spoke of a kind of Independence before Paine. Surely, the scholars and historical researchers could compile a list of names of men (women didn't count) who thought of Independence before *Common Sense*. T. Jefferson's name would not be found on such a list. But it was Thomas Paine who not only advocated Independence – "nothing can settle our affairs so expeditiously as an open and determined Declaration of Independence." – but went public with a concrete (*Common Sense*) step by step plan which included a Declaration, waging a defensive war, drafting a national constitution; and the creation of a Democratic Republic with large and equal representation; and short terms for elected government officers; women's rights and above all government of and by the people.

Philip Foner wrote, "It is clear that Paine was among the FIRST* to point out, even before the American Revolution was over, the need for a stronger central government to replace the weak Articles of Confederation." (Foner, Intro to *Age of Reason*, p.20) It is also clear that Thomas Paine was FIRST and alone when he proposed a continental convention in order to frame a Constitution. As Aldridge said, "Thomas Paine was a constitution maker", and the one "Drawn up by Paine and Franklin – the Pennsylvania Constitution – adopted late in 1776, provided for universal suffrage,

---

*   caps mine

**   italics mine

democratic representation, complete religious freedom, and a unicameral legislature, elected annually."(Foner, Intro to *Age of Reason*, p.13)

I do not hesitate to say that Paine himself thought that he was establishing a new country. He would allude to the part he took in 'so many words', but always indirectly. I can find no instance where Paine said – I alone created the United States of America. Some years later, he would write, "I had added my mite." He was referring to the raising of the American Colonies "to an independent Empire."(Foner, Intro to *Age of Reason*, p22) Some mite, some Empire. Philip Foner, in his Introduction to *Age of Reason* provided additional indirect evidence of Paine's accomplishment by including Jefferson's famous quote in praise of Thomas Paine:

> "I am in hopes you will find us returned generally to sentiments worthy of former times. In these it will be your glory steadily to have laboured, and with as much effect as any man living."(p.39)

Clearly, this compliment places Thomas Paine in the first rank of "founders". Of course, I believe that Thomas Paine's labours had more effect in the FORMATION OF THE United States of America than any other man living at that time. That is why I believe that future generations will honor the memory of Paine as the original Founder and creator in sole of the United States.

CHAPTER 27
FOUR FOLLOWERS

George Washington, John Adams, Thomas Jefferson and Alexander Hamilton were converts to Thomas Paine's original plan for American Independence. They deserve praise and credit commensurate with the merits of their contributions during the Revolution. However, none of these honored patriots were able to secure the declared Independence of July 4, 1776 for five years of a bloody, dismal, frustrating and destructive war. As Presidents, the first three enjoyed the fame and honors derived from Thomas Paine's creation. They accepted titled positions of authority and together with courts and congress, assumed the distinct powers of governing over the people. This was not Paine's idea. Paine's goal was government of the people and by the people. His design specification called for the people to be over the government, not subordinate to the government. (Thomas Paine used the terms PEOPLE, SOCIETY AND NATIONS interchangeably.)

The difference between government and 'the people' has caused a lot of confusion over the years. In the opening sentence of *Common Sense*, Paine wrote, "Some writers have confounded society with government..." I will clear this up now. People are the government. Society is the government. The nation is the government. "In republics, such as those established in America, the sovereign power, or the power over which there is no control, and which controls all others, remains where nature placed it – in the people; for the people in America are the foundation of power." (Paine, *Dissertations on Government*)

In the United States, representatives are selected out of the public. They are elected to perform the work of governing, for limited periods of time. Those elected to serve as officials and agents in the various governmental departments, are still members of the body of people. They remain members of society and members of the nation. Washington, Adams, Jefferson and Hamilton ignored Thomas Paine's proposals for equal and broad representation, yearly elections, and one year terms of office, and periodic review of the constitution in order to make such changes as voted by the people. Instead, they laid the groundwork for a powerful Federal government which would grow to require a budget over three trillion dollars.

I do not think that Washington, Adams, Jefferson or Hamilton had any intention of following Paine's lead in governing from bottom up. They wanted to be the governors, not the governed. They considered themselves to be part of the "upper class", the elite. According to Kaye "George Washington had referred to small holding farmers as the 'grazing multitude', (and) lawyer John Adams had spoken of working people as the common Herd of Mankind" (Kaye, p.31) Without broad and equal representation, even with women's suffrage, and without short terms for elected representatives, there was little chance for political democracy.

In addition to governmental control from the top down, there was, and always has been secrecy in the government of the United States. Secrecy in government is inimical to democracy. How can a government of the people keep secrets from the people?

George Washington was an elitist. He would not have enlisted in the Revolutionary army as a foot soldier as did Thomas Paine. He volunteered to serve, but it is doubtful that he would have accepted a commission with a rank less than general grade. His military record during the Revolutionary war was poor. Although Washington managed a few tactical successes, there is no evidence that he knew anything about military strategy. Trenton was Paine's idea. Washington wanted to defend Philadelphia. He was handed a proposal that he could not refuse; either move on Trenton or step aside and be replaced by another general. Paine got extra troops. Washington got the credit for the victories at Trenton and Princeton. These stunning victories were very important. Craig Nelson did not fail to recognize that, "the country for the first time was rallying to congress and its army, and the cause of liberty was saved from premature collapse."(Nelson, p.111)

Again, six years later, in the autumn of 1781, Washington had to be persuaded to engage Cornwallis at Yorktown. Up to this time he had not been victorious over the invading forces of Great Britain. Paine had had enough of our do nothing arm-chair general. Paine devised a new plan. He decided to side-step Washington and go to France with young – 26 years old – Major John Larens as his political consultant. The mission was to solicit additional money, arms and supplies in support of the war against the British. The mission was a phenomenal success. It was an extraordinary historical event. David Henley wrote, "...and he (Paine) secured finances from France for the decisive battle of Yorktown." (Colloquim, p.97) Paine must have been invincibly persuasive because, "French minister to America Lamartine reported that 'the King loaded Paine with favors.'" (Nelson, p.153) According to Nelson, the 'favors' amounted to 4.8 million livres in money and materiel. That is not the whole story.

King Louis XVI gave his royal sanction to General Jean Baptiste, Comte de Rochambeau and his five thousand trained soldiers to mount an offensive against the British. The King also ordered Admiral Francois Joseph Paul Comte De Grasse and the French fleet, carrying three thousand soldiers, to support Rochambeau's engagement. The battle plan was to have Washington's six thousand troops, encamped with the French, in Pennsylvania, join Rochambeau's army, proceed south, and mount a siege assault against Cornwallis and some five thousand, or more, British regulars at Yorktown, Virginia. The plans laid for the Yorktown campaign were concluded without Washington's participation or knowledge.

Craig Nelson informed us, "Washington's reaction was to have a tantrum that raged for half an hour." (Nelson, p.155) Washington had been planning an ego strike against fourteen thousand well armed British troops in well fortified and prepared New York, which was loaded with loyalists. Wiser heads prevailed. Washington would not be allowed to place the French troops in jeopardy; nor be permitted to squander millions in French aid in an ill-conceived quest for a victory in order to offset his questionable generalship during six years of war. Washington had no choice but to go along with the battle decisions which were already made. The Yorktown attack plan ranks as one of the most brilliant strategic assaults in military history. After General Nathanael Greene forced Cornwallis to retreat to Yorktown, the attack required the critical coordination of the 'allied' land and naval forces. Admiral DeGrasse cut off Cornwallis' escape route. It should be mentioned that important contributions to the Yorktown campaign were made by Lafayette, Baron Von Steuben, General Daniel Morgan, and General Anthony Wayne and many others. The most important factor was that unless, "a frigate loaded with money brought from France by Col. John Laurens and THOMAS PAINE*, (had) arrived at Boston the twenty-fifth of August, almost two months before Cornwallis surrendered", (Foner,II,p.959) there would not have been the glorious, war ending victory at Yorktown on October 19, 1781.

Years later (1804) Paine wrote, "This timely supply ENABLED* Congress to go on and the army to proceed to Yorktown. It took sixteen ox teams to remove the money brought by this frigate, the *Resolve* from Boston to Philadelphia. Thomas Willing, now president of the U.S. bank received it." (Foner,II, p.959)

---

*   caps mine

Washington was acclaimed as the hero of 'Yorktown'. He took credit as the victor when he should have been effusive in his praise and gratitude to Franklin, Rochambeau, the allied armies, Lafayette, Morgan, Wayne, especially General Nathanael Greene, and most of all Thomas Paine. More research is needed. Remember, Washington was making preparations to attack New York. He had to be persuaded to reverse his position and drive south to the Chesapeake Bay. "There he and his army embarked on a fleet of transports…" (Rise of the American Nation, Heritage Edition, p.116) Who arranged for the transports?

John Adams knew that Paine provided the means for the Yorktown triumph. Yet, he gave all the credit to young John Laurens. This was a mean, vile trick on the part of Adams; and a blind-side slap in the face to both Paine and Franklin. Craig Nelson was right when he said, "Adams will in time have many terrible things to say about Paine, just as he had many dreadful things to say about nearly everyone he ever knew save Abigail…"(Nelson, p.95) John Adams excelled in "bearing false witness'.

From the accounts that I have read, Alexander Hamilton fought bravely during the siege at Yorktown. Thomas Jefferson did not participate.

CHAPTER 28
NECESSITY

The words necessity and necessary were used by Thomas Paine in his timeless masterpiece *Common Sense*. Counting them together, the words necessity and necessary appear no less than ten times in that work. They also appear four times in the Declaration of Independence. They are given below for reference purposes. From the Declaration:

"When in the course of human events it becomes NECESSARY* for a people to advance from that Subordination…"

"…and Such is now the NECESSITY* which constrains them to expunge their former Systems of Government."

"He (King George III) has refused his Assent to Laws, the most wholesome and NECESSARY* for the public Good."

"…and acquiesce in the NECESSITY which denounces our eternal Separation."

The words necessity and necessary have been taken from the Anchor Press edition of *Common Sense*.

"Thus NECESSITY*, like a gravitating power…" (p.14)

"…the NECESSITY* of establishing some form of government…" (p.14)

"…it will become NECESSARY* to augment the number of representatives…" (p.15)

---

*   caps mine

"...a mode NECESSARY*..." (p 15)

"...I likewise mentioned the NECESSITY* of a large and equal representation..." (p.50)

"...we had been driven to the NECESSITY* of breaking off all connections with her (Britain)..." (p.52)

"Until an independence is declared, the continent will feel itself like a man who continues putting off some unpleasant business from day to day, yet knows it must be done, hates to set about it, wishes it over, and is continually haunted with the thoughts of its NECESSITY*." (p.52)

"But it is the independence...the main and only object...like all other truths discovered by NECESSITY*..." (P.55)

"And the instant, in which such a mode of defence becomes NECESSARY*..." (p.59)

"...in support of Independence...Every day convinces us of its NECESSITY." (p.60)

Finally, in his *Crisis III,* Thomas Paine wrote: "The NECESSITY* likewise, of being independent, even before it was declared, became so evident and important, that the continent ran the risk of being ruined every day she delayed it." (p.101)

It was Thomas Paine who came up with the innovative concept that the American Colonies should unite and form their own sovereign country. Paine arrived at this conclusion independently. Unless there is evidence to the contrary he was the first to do so. His method was pure reason. "The most formidable weapon against errors of every kind is Reason. I have never used any other, and I trust I never shall." (*Age of Reason*)

Paine's idea was that the American people should advance from that subordination in which they remained and assume among the powers of the earth, the equal and independent station to which they were entitled. I think that "advance from that subordination" is stronger and more explicit than "dissolve the political bands." Paine's thinking was

---

* caps mine

that there is a time when a Colonial entity, which is dependent on and subservient to a "mother country", should break away and institute their own new government. He said so, repeatedly, in *Common Sense*. Such a disconnection would be a grave event. Accordingly, it should not be attempted for "light and transient causes".

Thomas Paine thought that there were compelling reasons and causes for the American Colonies to separate from Great Britain and establish their own government. On the other hand his arguments against reconciliation were no less compelling. That is why he used the word NECESSARY: "When in the course of human Events it becomes NECESSARY*..." Looking back, Paine provided an autobiographical note three years after American Independence was declared. He wrote: "My first endeavor was to put the politics of the country right and to show the advantages as well as the NECESSITY* of independence, and until this was done, independence never could have succeeded. America did not at that time understand her own situation; and though the country was then full of writers, no one reached the mark..." (*Writings*, Vol.8, p.69)

It was Thomas Paine who recognized that to achieve the benefits, goals and blessings of freedom for people, Independence was absolutely necessary. He wrote, "If there is any true cause of fear respecting independence, it is because no plan is laid down." (*Common Sense*, p.39)

Paine was up to the "mark," and "to put the politics of the country right, he devised a step by step plan to create the United States. To this end, it was necessary for the Colonies to unite and separate from Great Britain and renounce all allegiance to the King. It was necessary to publish a manifesto to all of the countries of the world, declaring the cession and announcing that the United States is a sovereign and independent country and we are open for business.

It was necessary to reject the monarchic form or any other autocratic form of government. The essence, the purpose of the American Revolution

---

*   caps mine

was to create a new Country with a new system and governed from the bottom up, not from the top down. Paine wrote, "...for the people in America are the fountain of power." (*Dissertations on Government Writings*, Vol.8, p.289)

Paine's plan was to replace monarchic rule with a Democratic Republic. The sovereignty of the new country would be exercised by electing representatives who would act for all of the people because they are as Paine said, "...empowered by the people." (*Common Sense*, p.40)

Next, it was necessary to have a constitutional convention. Its duly elected members being met, "let their business be to frame a Continental Charter or Charter of the United Colonies..." "Securing freedom and property to all men, and above all things, the free exercise of religion, according to the dictates of conscience; with such other matter as is necessary for a charter to contain." (p.40)

Paine wrote that America was without a navy. He thought that America should build a fleet because "our methods of defence ought improve with our increase of property." He concluded, "These are circumstances which demand our attention, and point out the necessity of naval protection." (p.46)

LAW

While America remained dependent on Great Britain the powers of governing would remain in the hands of the King. Paine wrote that America "ought to have the legislative powers in her own hands." (p.55) Independence was necessary in order to enable America to pass its own laws.

TRADE

Once peace is achieved, national and international trade becomes paramount. Paine wrote, "Our plan is commerce" (p.31) and "peace with trade is preferable to war without it." (p.60) Paine concluded that

Independence was necessary for America to control her commercial affairs.

SUMMARY

By hindsight, it is easy to see the steps that had to be taken in order to create the United States. The American Colonies had to unite and separate from England and publish a formal declaration explaining the cession. They had to terminate both King and Monarchic rule and establish a Democratic Republic by means of a system of elected representatives as described in detail in Paine's *Common Sense*. A national constitution had to be written and ratified. As regards naval affairs, Paine devoted four pages in *Common Sense*, urging the construction of a fleet. He considered both an army and a navy necessary in order to "leave to posterity with a settled form of government (and) an independent Constitution."

It is sad to recall that the defensive war against the British invaders had to be carried through until the Americans were victorious. (See Paine's *Letter to the Quakers*. It is a timeless masterpiece of rhetorical persuasion and incontestable logic.)

Finally, unfettered control of both the legislative process and commercial affairs had to be secured by America as a sovereign nation.

Taken all together, the above listed steps formed an integrated plan to create the United States of America. Although some Colonists harbored some selected thoughts regarding Independence, most were loyalists, "and their single object was reconciliation." (Lewis, p.38)

Only one man had a complete plan. That integrated plan was a willful, independent and innovative construct produced by the prodigious mind of Thomas Paine.

[I decided to include the chapter on necessity because of a thought triggered by Alan Dershowitz in his book America Declares

Independence, page 2: "Finally it (the Declaration) invokes the claim of necessity." Whether the American Revolution was a necessity, or should have occurred at all, is debatable. What is not debatable, or rather is indisputable, is the fact that Thomas Paine thought that it was necessary for him to create a new country with a new system of governance without a King and without compulsory hereditary laws.]

CHAPTER 29
NEWFOUNDLAND
FISHERIES

F ishing Rights in the North Atlantic Ocean became an issue during the summer of 1779. Secret discussions were carried on in Congress, about the Newfoundland Fisheries in case peace negotiations with Britain were initiated.

The right for the United States to fish off the coast of Newfoundland was included in the terms of the Treaty of Paris, September 3, 1783.

Looking forward to a possible treaty of peace, one spineless writer published a letter in the Pennsylvania Gazette, June 23, 1779, about 'The Fisheries". In this letter article, its author presented some lame arguments that America should surrender its rights to fish off the coast of Newfoundland to the British.

Thomas Paine, in a series of articles in the Pennsylvania Gazette, totally refuted this pusillanimous idea by showing that the Newfoundland Fisheries are a source of wealth, food and jobs. They give rise to commercial enterprise and augment international trade and act as a catalyst for America's budding ship-building industry, and provide a training ground for future seamen.

The feckless wuss, who was willing to concede maritime rights to England was totally routed. Besides, the loss of these rights would result in a great injury to France, America's best ally. Finally, Paine wrote, "to leave the Fisheries wholly out, on any pretense whatever, is to sow the seeds of another war." (Conway, p.60)

From his excellent exposition on the "Fisheries", we learned that Paine was soon at work in the interest of America, in spite of being unjustly induced to resign from Congress, on January 8, 1779. There was no time for recriminations. In time his stand against Silas Deane would be proved to be correct. Deane became a traitor. Paine intensified his efforts not only in his unfailing support of the Revolution, but also, to protect his creation, his love, America , against future calamities. None of the so-called Founding Fathers exhibited such unalloyed zeal.

CHAPTER 30
INTENT

The following extracts are taken from Paine's *CRISIS* number seven. "It was my fate to come to America a few months before the breaking out of hostilities...their (the colonists) attachment to Britain was obstinate...and their single object was reconciliation...I had no thoughts of independence or of arms. But when the country, into which I had but just put my foot, was set on fire about my ears, it was time to stir. It was time for every man to stir." (*Crisis VII*, Anchor Press, p. 167) Thomas Paine stirred, all right. He became the author of *Common Sense*, which holds a place in the top rank of innovative, political composition. In it, he wrote, "No man was a warmer wisher for reconciliation than myself, before the fatal nineteenth of April 1775, (The Battles of Lexington and Concord) but the moment the event of that day was made known, I rejected the hardened, sullen tempered Pharaoh of England forever..." (*Common Sense*, Anchor Press, p. 36)

Thomas Paine repeated the thought quoted above in a very long letter, dated May 16, 1778, to Benjamin Franklin who was in Paris, France.

"The affairs of England are approaching either to ruin or redemption. If the latter, she may bless the resistance of America." For my own part, I thought it very hard to have the country set on fire about my ears almost the moment I got into it; and among other pleasures I feel in having uniformly done my duty, I feel that of not having discredited your friendship and patronage." (Conway, p. 46)

Paine did his duty, all right. His immortal *Common Sense* resulted in a declared independent and sovereign nation. I believe that Paine's acknowledgment in "having done my duty" supports the proposition that Thomas Paine intended to effect a separation from Great Britain and create a new country. Paine did his part. How should that part be identified and described?

COUNTERFEIT MONEY

It is generally accepted that an inventor or an innovator is keenly protective of his or her creation. Thomas Paine had 'hair trigger' sensitivity when it came to any act or expression which would militate against the authority of Congress or the successful completion of the American Revolution and the unassailable security and permanency of the United States of America.

As soon as Paine heard that the British were issuing counterfeit money – "continentals" – he wrote a letter dated, April 11, 1778, to Henry Laurens, president of Congress.

In this letter, Paine characterized these emissions as operating to the injustice and injury of the whole continent. He equated counterfeiting with forgery and called the practice a sin against all men (and women) alike; and as such, denounced by all civil nations. Paine concluded that all counterfeiting should be punishable as a felony. Who else recognized and acted on the cruel tactic of counterfeiting by the British? Independent of Washington, Adams, and Jefferson, Paine immediately grasped the danger of this subversive tactic and he moved to put an end to it.

SILAS DEANE

Volumes have been written about the Silas Deane affair. Thomas Paine, ever anxiously vigilant and poised to detect even the slightest event that would be hurtful to the Revolutionary Independence of America, exposed Silas Deane. Deane had schemed to embezzle money from arms procurement agreements with France. Congress was ignorant, both of all of the facts of this disgraceful matter and Thomas Paine's overall plan.

On one hand, the members of Congress did not know that Deane was guilty. On the other hand, Congress was not fully aware that Paine would not suffer an attempt, by any person, to abuse the Revolution, just to line his pockets with the blood money of those patriot soldiers who were sacrificing their lives to preserve the Independence.

A motion to fire Paine as acting Secretary of Foreign Affairs was never adopted but Paine resigned any way on January 8, 1779. Later, Paine was exonerated and he was now free to work tirelessly for the fulfillment of his plan to establish the United States of America, away from misguided commotions of Congress.

AN UNWRITTEN WARNING

"Tis an ill wind, indeed, that brings no good." After all the fuss about the Deane affair, the French Alliance was preserved and America did receive substantial aid from France in the form of arms, powder, uniforms, supplies, money, officers and troops. There was another large and important outcome from the Silas Deane debacle. It was this: Thomas Paine put the members of Congress on notice that they were never to engage in or countenance any act that would besmirch, debase, defame, stain, traduce or corrupt the honor of the American Revolution, which deserved to be protected from a single blot on her reputation; and a Revolution, "which to the end of time must be an honor to THE AGE that accomplished it." (*Crisis VIII* Anchor Press, p. 226) I believe that Thomas Paine used the expression, "THE AGE", as a modest and recondite way of referring to himself.

Moreover the Revolution is not to be exploited for money profits. Paine's goal was to establish the United States of America in a manner such that "everything about her wore the mark of honor." (*Crisis VIII*, Anchor Press, p. 225)

CHAPTER 31
ARCHITECT

"It was the cause of America that made me an AUTHOR."* (*Crisis* XIII, p.229) That's right. Thomas Paine was an author and the cause of America was total Independence. Thomas Paine took up the cause and authored a plan, a blueprint, with explicit specifications in order to establish an Independent, sovereign democratic Republic. The records of his works and writings show, without a doubt, that Paine worked without surcease, until he saw the basic elements of his prototype design become a reality at Yorktown in 1781; and ratified by the Treaty of Paris in 1783.

Paine knew that a union with Great Britain was impossible; and reconciliation with her was unnatural. He knew that the only line that could "cement and save America" was "a Declaration of Independence". These conditions "made it impossible for me, feeling as I did to be silent". I count this sentence to be a profession by Paine that he is the author of the Declaration of Independence. No one else could have been the author of the "Declaration", because no one else "reached the mark". (*Life and Writings*, book 8, p.69) Paine did not remain "silent". He spoke; He declared. It may not be unnecessary to recall that when Thomas Paine speaks, he does so with his pen.

---

* caps mine

Paine continued, "Independence always appeared to me practicable and probable; provided the sentiment of the country could be formed and held to the object"...How does one form the sentiments of a country? The task boggles the mind. Paine, alone, undaunted, took the job, and produced *Common Sense*. It was successful enough to result in a paper which declared Independence. Would the colonists hold to Paine's desired object of Independence? Paine went to work again in order to make Independence a reality. This time his immortal *Crisis Papers* held the object in view through five "soul-trying" years, until the beginning of 1781. At this time, the object was not attained, but would not be lost as long as Thomas Paine was alive.

At this time, early in 1781, Congress was bogged down with jealous wrangling and dissensions, and out of funds. (*Secret History*, p. 234) Washington, crippled with desertions, mutinies and food shortages was powerless. The paper currency was not "worth a continental". Unified support from the States did not materialize. Rampant inflation choked normal domestic and international trade. Spies and treachery were constant threats. "Sunshine patriots" could be enticed to aid and abet the British for a few silver coins. A number of Americans were tired of the war and more voices were heard suggesting that America should give up. British peace offers "made many honest Philadelphians wonder if it would not be wiser for America to return to its old place in the Empire on favorable terms than to go on fighting bloodily for independence". (*Secret History*, p. 181)

There is no evidence that would indicate that Paine would give up. During the last six years, from 1775 through the summer of 1781, Paine had expended his exertions "with unabated ardour" in order to achieve Independence. At the start of 1781, America was on the verge of collapse. Although the war was not lost, it was not won. A victory was needed and Paine would have to act alone to make it possible because Congress was in no position to help. Acting alone was nothing new to Paine. He had supported Washington in opposition to John Adams and his clique. He worked to eliminate counterfeiting. He exposed Silas Deane. He preserved the fishing rights in the Atlantic Ocean. He succeeded in abolishing slavery in Pennsylvania. He donated a significant sum of his own money to help the army, and this at a time when he had little to spare. In addition he helped raise funds for Washington's troops when they were short of food. He helped found the North American Bank in order to finance the war effort and, later defended it.

There is no historical evidence to contradict that Thomas Paine consumed his energies in order to cement the 'keystone' of his design in place. Independence was achieved, but four important "specs" were overlooked. Two of these fundamental specifications, i.e., Emancipation and Women's suffrage, were secured later by means of America's amendable Constitution. The two remaining items, unfortunately, are absent. In spite of this, America had a glorious and honorable birth. What other country "can boast so fair an origin"? (Crisis XIII) Thank you, Thomas Paine! God bless America.

CHAPTER 32
FOUNDER

This chapter is intended to supply irrefutable testimony in support of the proof that Thomas Paine is the original, stand alone, founder of the United States of America. To this end I now give the following quote:

"I am certain no man set out with a warmer heart or a better disposition to render public service than myself, in everything which laid in my power. My first endeavor was to put the politics of the country right, and to show the advantages as well as the necessity of independence; and until this was done, independence never could have succeeded. America did not at that time understand her own situation; and though the country was then full of writers, no one reached the mark;" (This quote will be continued)

At the end of December, 1775 no one was writing, for general publication, that Independence was a necessity. No one was writing a detailed exposition, in concrete language, advocating, nay, insisting on total amputation from England. What a turn around that would be. It would mean secession and Independence. In America there was talk, and only talk, of independence. Thoughts about this seditious subject were usually spoken in hushed voices. Independence was a "Hobgoblin" to Adams; repugnant and forbidden by the King; and fraught with fear by the Colonists.

Paine wrote, "...a new aera (sic) for politics is struck; a new method of thinking hath arisen." (*Common Sense*, p. 28) "If there is any true cause of fear respecting independence, it is because no plan is yet laid down." (p.39)

Paine developed the plan to create a new Nation as a Democratic Republic. He had to speak for the American people because "America did not at that time, understand her own situation". All of the elements of Paine's plan to create the Free and Independent states of America are contained in *Common Sense*. They are as follows:

Separate from Great Britain; Prepare a formal Declaration of Independence to the world; Replace the monarchic system with a Democratic Republic; No king; Selection of officials and representatives by vote of the people; Short terms of office; No hereditary offices; Broad and equal representation; Equal Rights for men and women, without distinctions; Build a navy; Wage a defensive war in order to secure the declared, sovereign Independence; Government operations should be conducted with simplicity, frugality and openly; No secrecy; Frame an amendable constitution to secure the Natural and civil rights of all, so that each individual can live and pursue his or her own means for their own happiness, so long as they do not interdict or interfere with the natural and civil rights of others.

Thomas Paine referred to his innovative construct as the "Free and Independent States of America". Later, in the second *Crisis Paper*, he named the new Nation, the United States of America.

There is no evidence that there ever existed a committee of "Founding Fathers" which met and agreed on all of the steps, as listed above, necessary to create the United States; and also agreed to publish their proposals to secede from Britain and declare independence. The plan to establish the United States of America was not the product of a committee. In the introduction to the second edition of *Common Sense* (February 14, 1776), Thomas Paine referred to his work as the "Doctrine of Independence". *Common Sense* was much more than mere doctrine. *Common Sense* set forth an integrated blueprint with explicit specifications along with a step by step procedure in order to create a new Independent country. No one else originated such a plan. No one else took the time, the fearful risk, and the expense in order to have such a determined design published for the general public. Thomas Paine produced *Common Sense* outside of, and totally independent of the Second Continental congress. Paine was never an elected member of Congress.

There is no evidence that Benjamin Franklin, George Washington, John Adams, Thomas Jefferson, James Madison, James Monroe, Patrick Henry, George Mason, Sam Adams or John Jay designed and composed an integrated plan in order to create and establish the Free and Independent United States of America, prior to the publication of *Common Sense.* No historian credits any one of the above listed Patriots as being the sole author of an integrated plan to originate and establish the United States as a sovereign, Independent Republic. Reasoning by a system of exclusion provides apodictic proof that Thomas Paine is the real Founder of the United States of America.

CHAPTER 33
SERVICE

The quote on the first page of the preceding chapter was taken from the *Life and Writings of Thomas Paine*, the Centenary Memorial Edition, Book 8, page 69. Paine had decided that Independence was a necessity. The quote shows, clearly, that Paine's intent was to have America separate from Great Britain, and his intent to form the colonies into a new Independent Nation.

In order to attain Independence, Paine had "to put the politics of the country right". He took the job on by himself because: "and though the country was then full of writers, no one reached the mark…" Paine continued: "neither did I abate in my service, when hundreds were afterwards deserting her interests and thousands afraid to speak, for the first number of the *Crisis* was published in the blackest stage of affairs, six days before the taking of the Hessions at Trenton".

Paine continued to write and work for Independence. He wrote thirteen *Crisis* papers and contributed other literary, military and advisory services to aid the Revolution. Paine persevered in his exertions in order to secure Independence up until, and even after, the amazing victory at Yorktown. It is my opinion that Thomas Paine deserves a great share of the credit for the war-ending defeat of the British at Yorktown. Paine provided the means. He was largely responsible for getting the money, the troops and the arms from France. I also think that the tactical battle plan came from Paine, because Paine had a masterful command of military tactics and strategy. Napoleon was of the same opinion.

My main point in this chapter is that innovators and inventors work on and improve their creations after they produce the initial model. There is a large body of evidence of this practice, especially in the domain of physical inventions; such as the airplane, the light bulb, the telephone, and countless other technological innovations. Innovation in the "Socio-Politico" domain is very different from material or tangible invention. The differences between the two are not part of this discussion. Never the less, I maintain that the enduring body of Paine's work provides strong support for the proof that Thomas Paine is the originator and sole founder of the United States.

CHAPTER 34
THE HENRY LAURENS
LETTER

In a letter to Henry Laurens dated September 14, 1779, Thomas Paine made a notable admission about his part in initiating the American Revolution with the goal of freedom and Independence. He wrote, "I need not repeat to you the part I have acted or the principle I have acted upon…it was neither the place nor the people but the cause itself that irresistibly engaged me in its support; for I should have acted the same part IN ANY COUNTRY* could the same circumstances have arisen there which happened here." (Conway, p.60)

The "cause" was originated by Thomas Paine. He did not join in. Others joined him. Paine started the cause in order to create a new country, a new nation. The, so called, Founding Fathers were participants after the fact. They followed Paine's lead. They joined him; they were converts; and as such they deserve great credit, as followers, but not as originators. Also, the clause, "it was neither the place nor the people, but the CAUSE itself, that irresistibly engaged me…" warrants special consideration because Paine had a habit of deflecting credit for his achievements, from himself and ascribing it to others. Here is an example. In the Letter to the Abbe Raynal, Paine wrote, "… the attachment of the Americans to these principles – the value and

---

* caps mine

quality of liberty, the nature of government, and the dignity of man –
PRODUCED* the Revolution." (Foner, p.219)

The CAUSE, which was the production and complete establishment
of a free, separate, independent and sovereign country as a broadly
represented Republic, governed by the people, by means of a system
of frequently elected agents, without a King, and administered with
minimum expense, was the integrated idea that came from the amazing
mind of Thomas Paine.

That the American Colonists held intuitive, if varied beliefs, in the
dignity of men and women could be conceded, in my view. However, I
question whether most Americans had anything above a fundamental
understanding of, and "attachment" to the value and quality of liberty
and the nature of government.

Of course, immigrant colonists from Spain, Germany, France,
Sweden, indeed, any country, knew about Kings. However, many
communicated in their native tongue. Diversity was the rule, not
the exception. Living in thirteen separate colonies, the colonists had
different customs and different religions. Where was the unity? Most
were opposed to ending monarchic tradition. Most did not understand
the inter-workings of a democratic republic. Many of the colonists
were moving westward and I suppose they had as much interest in
establishing a new form of government as they had in paying taxes. I do
not believe that the elastic mass of colonists had a basic understanding
of government of, by and for the people.

The colonists came around, in time, to embrace the Revolution and
Independence. Thomas Paine personified the integrated idea of it. The
Americans reaped the benefits of its effects. Paine's disclosure, "The
cause itself", lends support to the proposition that he is the "stand-
alone", originator of the United States.

---

*   caps mine

Note: Henry Lauren (1724-1792) was a Revolutionary statesman and patriot from Charleston, South Carolina. He was a member of the Second Continental Congress form 1777 to 1779; and President of Congress from November 1777 to December 1778. This letter is very important because it provides substantial biographic information about Thomas Paine and his leading part in the American Revolution.

CHAPTER 35
THE RAYNAL LETTER, 1782

D o you wish to learn about Thomas Paine? Read the "Raynal Letter". The correct title of the Raynal Letter is: *Letter to the Abbé Raynal, on the Affairs of North America: in which the Mistakes in the Abbé's Account of the Revolution of America are Corrected and Cleared up.* This "Letter" to Raynal was published in pamphlet form by Thomas Paine in 1782. Paine wrote this letter in answer to Raynal's article entitled *Révolution d'Amérique,* i.e. *The American Revolution.* The Abbè's account was full of mistakes.

The *Raynal Letter* reveals a great deal about Paine himself. At the same time, it provides an excellent condensation of the history of the American Revolution. It is a brilliant masterpiece; and undoubtedly, must rank with the best explanations of the Revolution. I believe that Thomas Edison would agree that the Raynal Letter would make an excellent class-room study.

In 1781, the Abbè Raynal, a distinguished French Historian and Philosopher wrote an article attacking the American Revolution giving his opinion as to the cause of the American Revolutionary War. The work was published in London and Philadelphia in September, 1782. In it, Raynal wrote: "none of those energetic causes, which have produced so many revolutions upon the globe, existed in North America." (Writings Vol. 8, p. 187)

"The whole question was reduced to the knowing whether the mother country had, or had not, a right to lay, directly or indirectly, a slight tax upon the colonies." (p.187)

Of course, Raynal's conclusion was absolutely wrong. Thomas Paine could not let Raynal's misrepresentation go unanswered.

Thomas Paine proceeded to show that Raynal was wrong when he wrote that a small tax was the original cause of the American Revolution. In order to prove his case, Paine quoted Raynal's position verbatim. Raynal's arguments in this paragraph (p. 187) are as follows:

Neither religion nor laws had there been outraged.
The blood of martyrs or patriots had not there streamed from scaffolds.
Morals had not there been insulted.
Manners, customs, habits, no object dear to nations, had there been the sport of ridicule.

Arbitrary power had not there torn any inhabitant from the arms of his family and friends to drag him to a dreary dungeon.

The principles of administration had not been changed there.
The maxims of government had there always remained the same.

Raynal was declaring that none of the usual causes, as listed above, existed in America. As said, he wrote that the whole question of the cause of the revolution was reduced to a slight tax on the colonies.

Raynal's statements, taken all together, had the effect of concluding that there was no REAL CAUSE for the American Revolution.

In the following ten pages, Thomas Paine deconstructed Raynal's thesis, point by point. He concluded that the Abbè's fallacious statements reduced his declaration to a nullity."

Paine continued: "Had the Abbè said that the causes which produced the Revolution in America were originally different from those which produced revolutions in other parts of the globe, he had been right."

Different? How were the causes which produced the American Revolution different? What was the difference? Listen to what Thomas Paine said: "Here the value and quality of liberty, the nature of government, and the dignity of man, were known and understood, and the attachment of the Americans to these principles produced the Revolution, as a natural and almost unavoidable consequence."

I have no wish to debate with Thomas Paine. But, I can't agree with his contention that the causes which produced the American Revolution were the attachments of Americans to the principles of Liberty, Government and Human Dignity.

No, it was not the colonists, but rather Thomas Paine's attachment to the principles of Liberty, Government and the Dignity of man, and his desire to create a new nation without a King that were the real causes.

Thomas Paine knew the value and quality of these principles. He wrote volumes on these subjects. There were others who embraced these ideas. But, until *Common Sense*, most Americans wanted reconciliation with Great Britain. The colonists resented British authority. They disliked taxation and British imposition. But it was Thomas Paine, acting in concert with no one, who was first to go public with an incontestable plea for total independence.

Independence was anathema to most of the Quakers. Likewise, independence was not an option for the Tories, who remained loyal to the King. Many of these Loyalists packed up and left the Colonies after the breaking out of hostilities. Reconciliation was considered practicable and desired by many prosperous business men; perhaps most of them in the first months of 1776. They did not want to 'rock the boat'. Surely, they did not want to cut off profits from trade with England. Prior to Thomas Pine's *Common Sense*, reconciliation was the order of the day.

In retrospect, Thomas Paine wrote on November 12, 1778: "I happened to come to America a few months before the breaking out of hostilities. I found the disposition of the people such that they might have been lead by a thread and governed by a reed. Their suspicion was quick and penetrating, but their attachment to Britain was obstinate, and it was at that time a kind of treason to speak against it. (Treason was punishable by death by hanging, or possibly a slower method.) They disliked the Ministry, but they esteemed the nation. Their idea of grievance operated without resentment, and their single object was RECONCILIATION."*
(J. Lewis, p. 38) (*Crisis #7*, Anchor Books, p. 167)

None of the so called Founding Fathers were advocating total Independence prior to *Common Sense*. It is no less true that none of the so called Founding Fathers provided a detailed plan to cashier the King and create a democratic Republic by a method of elected representatives prior to *Common Sense*. Moreover, Thomas Paine's concrete specifications explicitly excluded any autocratic form of government.

No one disputes the fact that Washington, Adams, Jefferson and Hamilton were converts to the idea of American Independence.

TRENTON

The Abbè Raynal wrote: "On the twenty-fifth of December they (the Americans) crossed the Delaware and fell accidentally upon Trenton..." (Vol 8, p. 201) HA!

Of course, Thomas Paine answered: "The Abbè is likewise wrong in saying that the American Army fell accidentally in Trenton." (Vol 8, p. 204)

Then, Paine, as is typical of him, gave total credit to Washington by saying: "It was the very object for which General Washington crossed the Delaware." (Vol 8, p. 204)

---

* caps mine

Yes, it was the object. However the IDEA and the PLAN to attack Trenton came from Thomas Paine. Thomas Paine not only presented the plan to Washington (probably through Joseph Reed), he had to urge, persuade him to do it. No easy task, this, because Paine had to overcome strong opposition from Washington's staff and Washington himself.

Washington did not even think of mounting an attack against anyone. He was on the edge of despair. George Washington's gloom and doom letter to Lund Washington says a book. "Our only (hope)… is upon the speedy enlistment of a new army, if this fails, I think the game is pretty near up." (*George Washington, Man & Monument* by Marcus Cunliffe)

Alexander Hamilton was sick and in bed. "He lay bedridden at a nearby farm…but he somehow gathered up the strength to leave his sickbed and fight." (*Alexander Hamilton* by Ron Chernow, Penguin Press, New York, 2004) In my opinion Alexander Hamilton was a fearless fighter and a Revolutionary War hero.

I believe a young Lieutenant, one James Monroe, knew that it was Thomas Paine who conceived the idea along with a detailed plan of battle, to surprise the Hessians at Trenton.

Arms were necessary, secrecy was requisite for a successful assault. These, alone are not enough. It is morale, that is the '*sine qua non*', that is needed to achieve victory.

Then, the First, "These are the times that try men's souls" Crisis paper burst forth from the pen of a genius, Thomas Paine. The 'Victory from the jaws of defeat' cliché applies here. Paine 'saved the day' and extended the life of the military part of the Revolution.

Military History, war History, is far down on my list of priorities. But, we should learn from these negative events for purposes of security and self-defense.

In the future, the History scholars will pay due credit to Thomas Paine for the marvelous victories at Trenton and Princeton.

REVOLUTIONARY MONEY

During five years of the Revolutionary War – 1776 to 1781 – Congress issued paper money called dollars.

At the end of five years the value of these dollars was worthless. On average, these dollars depreciated about 20% each year.

Thomas Paine estimated that the cost of the war was "ten or twelve millions". The public might have been taxed in order to pay the expenses of the war. But, as Paine stated, "there were none, or few valuable taxes paid." Consequently the public paid for the cost of the war indirectly. Instead of paying out 10 or 12 million by direct taxation, the public sustained a loss of 10 or 12 million in purchasing power when the value of each dollar depreciated to ZERO.

Whether by a system of taxation or by a method of inflation by issuing a stream of paper dollars, Paine wrote: "the event to the public was the same". [I don't know "money is money and paper is paper". (Anon)]

In effect, Thomas Paine reasoned that between taxation or depreciation, the public chose the latter.

I am not so sure about this. I have a gratuitous suspicion that fifty percent or more of the Americans, at that time would have rejected either option.

Yet, Thomas Paine, standing pat on his position, that the paper currency was issued for the express purpose of carrying on the war, insisted that it was the voluntary conduct of everyone that caused the value of the dollar to become worthless. "Every man depreciated his own money by his own consent, for such was the effect which the raising of the nominal value of goods (and services) produced. Thus, the amount of loss sustained by each person was equal to the amount of taxes he or she would have paid. {What a huge debt of gratitude we owe to our revolutionary patriots, by whose sacrifices we inherited a country.}

PEACE OFFERS
(Offers: also, proposals or "BILLS")

This part is about the "Peace Proposals" offered by the British on February 17, 1778.

In his *The Revolution in America*, the Abbè Raynal wrote that the British Ministry sent to the new world public agents, authorized to offer everything EXCEPT Independence, and "this plan of conciliation…was rejected with disdain."

Congress received these offers on April 21, 1778.

At this time, Thomas Paine was secretary in the Foreign Department of Congress (Vol. #8, p. 222)

Congress appointed a committee to examine and report on these propositions on the same day that they were received, i.e. April 21, 1778. The report was brought in the NEXT DAY, April 22, 1778. Of course the offers were immediately rejected out of hand, and unanimously so.

The report listing the reasons for rejecting the 'peace' proposals is a masterpiece. Thomas Paine wrote: "there is a vigor of determination and spirit of defiance in the language of the rejection." Here, Paine refers to the rejection report, coming from a committee, as a work authored by someone other than himself. We shall see about that.

The rejection of the British proposals takes up 4 1/2 pages of small print in volume #8 of *Writings*. (Centenary Memorial Edition p 225-230)

That the proposals were answered and rejected in just one day after receiving them is very interesting. Of course the length of the rejection report is noteworthy.

In the following précis, I will give the substance of the reply to the British offer of reconciliation.

1. The offers were not sent to Congress.
2. False thinking that a 'cease fire' would cause the U.S to be remiss in there preparations for war.

3. Because of a false belief that the Americans are tired of the war and will opt for peace on Britain's terms.
4. Because they expect that it will prevent foreign countries from giving aid to these states.
5. Because England might need her entire fleet in order to defend herself.
6. Because England cannot be victorious.

In addition to the above, the proposals show the weakness and the wickedness of the enemy.

Their weakness:

1. Because Britain would give up its right to bind these states in all cases whatsoever, and after resorting "by the sword", shows their inability to enforce it.
2. Because their Prince HATH rejected America's petitions for reconciliation and HATH waged a most cruel war against his own people, and employed the savages to butcher innocent women and children. But now, the same Prince pretends to grant to the arms of America what he refused to her prayers.
3. Because they have labored to conquer this continent
4. Because the constant position of Britain was not to negotiate with the Americans "while they have arms in their hands: Yet, now an offer is about to be made for treaty."

"The wickedness and insincerity of the enemy appear from the following consideration"

1. Either the bills contain a direct or indirect elimination of a part of their former claims, or they do not. If they do, then the (British) have sacrificed many brave men in an unjust quarrel. "If they – the proposals – do not, then they are calculated to

deceive America into terms, to which neither argument before the war, nor force since, could procure her assent.

2. The first of these bills – proposals – appears to assert the right of the British to levy taxes on these states. The states can't grant or concede a right which Britain is waging war to obtain.

3. The British right to tax is a pretended right. Things change, Parliament changes. Who knows how far parliament might go if America concedes to Britain the right to tax?

4. Taxing of the states would be suspended for now, but could be reinstated by future Parliaments.

5. The King can make a treaty, but Parliament can overturn it. (Silly business in my mind. JH)

6. The offer of Pardons is false because the American Patriots are not criminals.

7. The inhabitants of America are not subjects of England, as claimed. They are citizens of the United States.

8. Because the bill would allow the commissioners to negotiate with private individuals: a measure highly derogatory to the dignity of national character.

The last part, in four paragraphs is a powerful conclusion to the rejection of the British proposals. It merits attentive readings.

Thomas Paine says, as only he can do, that the BILLS (offers) are a part of a plan to cause division and effect defections. It is a divide and conquer scheme in order to achieve total domination of America.

The 2nd paragraph of the concluding part:

"Upon the whole matter, the committee (I think the committee is Thomas Paine) beg leave to report it as their opinion that the Americans united in this arduous contest upon principles of common interest for defense of common rights and privileges, which union HATH* been

---

* caps mine

cemented by common calamities, and by mutual good offices so the great cause in which all mankind are interested must derive its success from the continuance of that union. Wherefore, any man or body of men who should presume to make any separate or partial agreements with commissioners under the crown ought to be considered and treated as open and avowed enemies of the United States." (v. 8, p. 229)

The 3rd paragraph of the concluding part

"And further your committee beg leave to report it as their opinion, that these United States cannot with propriety, hold any conference or treaty with any British commissioners unless they shall as a preliminary either withdraw their fleets and armies or else, in positive and express terms acknowledge the independence of the said states." (v. 8, p. 229)

The 4th paragraph of the concluding part

"The design of the enemies of these states is to lull them into a fatal security. We may expect and we should be prepared for future contention and bloodshed. Accordingly, the states should "use the utmost strenuous exertions to have their respective quotas of Continental troops in the field as soon as possible, and that all the militia of the said states be held in readiness, to act as occasion may require." (v. 8, p. 229)

It is noted that in the above answer, i.e. rejection, the author of it uses the word HATH, instead of has, nine, 9 – count 'em – 9 times.

I pause here, to ask, why would Thomas Paine write a 103 page answer to the Abbè Raynal's attack on the American Revolution?

Of course, Paine desired to set the record straight and correct the errors and defects in the Abbè work.

But why 103 pages?

I ask, also, where are the refutations of Raynal's Reflections written by G. Washington, A Hamilton, T. Jefferson, B. Franklin, John Adams, or John Jay?

POST SCRIPT

In the last part of Paine's answer of the (Bogus) British peace offers, Paine saw that they were intended to create divisions and produce defections among the Americans.

In the <u>Declaration of Independence</u> Thomas Paine wrote: "He (the King) has incited treasonal Insurrections of our Fellow Citizens, with the Allurement of Forfeiture and Confiscation of our property."

Paine's answer – last part – to the British proposals.

The peace offers are a part of "the insidious plan, which...hath involved this country in contention and <u>bloodshed</u>."

From the <u>Declaration of Independence</u>: "to invade and deluge Us in <u>Blood.</u>"

In Thomas Paine's answer to the British offers: "The (British) lust for domination", and "the <u>design</u> of the enemies of these states to lull them into a fatal security –"

From the <u>Declaration of Independence</u> "...evinces of <u>Design</u> to reduce them under absolute Power..."

The bogus peace offers were an attempt to nullify the Declaration of Independence. Accordingly, they were promptly and politely – in four and a half pages – rejected out-of-hand.

RAYNAL – GUILLAUME – THOMAS - FRANCÓIS – DE ABBÈ
1713-1796

A French historian and philosopher. Regarded as a leader among the French freethinkers; educated for the priesthood. Wrote histories of Netherlands (1747) and of English Parliament (1748); edited literary periodical *Mercure de France* (1750-54). With Denis Diderot wrote *Histoire philosophique et politique des établissements et du commerce des Européens dans les deux Indes* (1770), which was publicly burned (1781) by order of the parliament because of its attacks on the clergy and on Europeans for their conduct and policies toward the natives in the Indies. (*Webster's New Biographical Dictionary*)

CHAPTER 36
INVECTIVE

In 1945 William Woodward wrote, "For about a hundred and fifty years Tom Paine has been a target for abuse." (Woodward, *America's Godfather*, p.5)

Each generation has produced a number of wrong-headed gossip mongers who have tried to ruin Thomas Paine's good reputation. Leading from ignorance, they have called Paine a falling down drunk, indolent, a heretic, an apostate, a devil, a whore monger, cruel, an adulterer, filthy, ill-tempered, loathsome, a hater of Jesus Christ, a man steeped in sin, a dirty infidel, a godless blasphemer, and an atheist. The invective could fill pages. However, much progress in eradicating the lies and slanders about Thomas Paine has been made in the last fifty years. Yet, examples of the falsehoods about Paine still surface and they are repeated as if they were true.

> "The tendency to falsify the facts about Paine is so well established and deep seated that it may be described as a literary disease. It was started by Paine's enemies while he was still living and its purpose was to destroy his influence upon the people by casting aspersions upon his character and his motives. To do that it was necessary to make Paine appear despicable. Today this tendency is still active, and one of its curious features is that it appears

frequently in the utterances of Paine's ardent admirers, as well as in the attitude of his enemies." (p.28)

The source of the abuse can be traced to two quarters. One was King George III; and the other was the elite Federalist faction. In the first case, the King wanted to suppress Thomas Paine's immortal *Rights of Man*. In the second case, the object was to clear the way for John Adams and "company" to "mount up the federal government."

"With independence won, and the Colonies free of the mother country, the great landowners, the aristocrats, and their henchmen applied themselves to the formation of a new nation. What they had in mind was a republic of aristocracy and wealth, with all the power in the hands of the upper class." (p.15)

The attacks on Paine were contrived in order to discredit him because of his strong views and arguments on the limits of government; his unyielding advocacy for human rights; his opposition to Negro slavery; and his dream that the New Republic would be governed with minimum expense by officials who had short terms and who would be elected through a system which provided broad and equal representation.

After the publication of *The Age of Reason*, the shameless assault on Thomas Paine became vicious and relentless. Two examples should suffice.

"How Tom gets a living, or what brothel he inhabits, I know not...Like Judas he will be remembered by posterity. Men will learn to express all that is base, malignant, treacherous, unnatural, and blasphemous, by one single monosyllable – Paine." (William Cobbett from Woodward, p.295)

"What! Invite to the United States that lying, drunken, brutal infidel, who rejoiced in the opportunity of basking and wallowing in the confusion, devastation, bloodshed, rapine, and murder, in which his soul delights?" (p.309)

After the publication of *The Age of Reason*, the attacks on Paine intensified. His reputation was smeared by a relentless two-pronged attack. The combination of the execrable calumnies against the man and the scurrilous distortions of his Godly creed went to extremes. Thomas Paine's good character was damaged almost beyond recognition and nearly beyond redemption.

The Federalists and the Churchmen did their work well. Paine fell into disfavor. He was ignored and almost forgotten. But with a population of five or six million people, fledgling America soldiered on into the nineteenth Century. The power elite conducted government operations from the top down in a manner similar to that of England. The Revolution had come full circle; but instead of binding hereditary laws imposed by King, parliament and ministry, we are having hereditary laws enacted by president, congress and bureaus.

Looking back to the year 1800, the acquired freedom, an advance which was "something better" ushered in a new era. Hopeful America embarked on a century of unprecedented progress. In spite of terrible acts where liberty was shamefully debased into license; and in spite of international war, civil war, genocide, exploitation, and episodes of lawlessness, nineteenth century America achieved one of the greatest industrial and cultural advances in recorded history.

Freedom is ineffably powerful.

CHAPTER 37
GLOOM AND DOOM AND DELIVERANCE

Moncure Daniel Conway made reference to two doom and gloom letters written by George Washington while he was encamped in Morristown, New Jersey. One was dated January 5, 1780; the other, May 28, 1780. The first letter conveyed the sorry condition, the extreme distress of the army. There was no bread and no meat. "Some of the troops were compelled to maraud and rob from the local inhabitants, to keep from starving. The second letter, addressed to Joseph Reed, President of the Pennsylvania Assembly was the "gloomiest letter Washington ever wrote". (Conway, p.64)

In this letter, Washington reported that his problems had reached crisis proportions; "and we see in every line of the army the most serious features of mutiny and sedition." (p.64) Some of the soldiers had already accepted the amnesty offered by the enemy, according to Conway. Washington was desperate.

Paine read the letter to the assembly. When he finished, one member arose and said, "We may as well give up first as last". (p.64)

It could be argued that the war was over. The colonies would surrender. Britain would be victorious, and the Independence would be lost. Of course, there would be some loose ends. What about General Nathanael Greene's successful operations in the south? Did England really have the military and economic resources to sustain a prolonged occupation of the Colonies? Those and other questions would remain unresolved. No matter. There was no chance that the United States would capitulate as long as Thomas Paine was alive. The defeatist, who said, "We may as well give up…" shows that he, along with the majority of the colonists did not have the foggiest notion of what Thomas Paine was trying to create. Paine knew that the British could not conquer America. Few colonists understood that.

Again, "it was time to stir" Thomas Paine acted immediately. The events that ensued recount one of the brightest episodes in American history.

THE MEANS FOR THE END

Here is what Thomas Paine did. In early June, 1780, he proposed a 'subscription', a "fund raiser", in order to provide immediate relief for Washington. To start if off, Paine put up $500.00 of his own money. He got Robert Morris and others to contribute. We learn from Conway that "the subscription spread like wildfire" (4) and 300,000 pounds were raised. This money was used to establish the Bank of Pennsylvania in order to support Washington's army. I believe that Thomas Paine took a leading part in creating the Bank of Pennsylvania, which would, later, become the Bank of North America.

The patriotic success of the subscription was a temporary solution, and by the end of 1780, America was in serious financial straits. Congress proposed a Mission to France in order to seek funds. Young, 26 year old, Colonel John Laurens, son of Henry Laurens was selected and assigned to head the mission. Laurens requested that Thomas Paine accompany him as his secretary. Excellent choice! Paine agreed, and he paid his own way.

They sailed from Boston in February, 1781, and arrived in France in March, 1781. They did not arrive back in Boston until August 25, 1781.

The six month mission was a stupendous success. Both Craig Nelson and Moncure Conway recorded that King Louis XVI, "loaded Paine with favors." Estimates vary, but Paine, well aided by the estimable groundwork accomplished by Benjamin Franklin, had procured between five and six million livres in silver and supplies for the American cause. In my opinion this was a monumental achievement, and both Paine and Franklin deserved great credit and gratitude for their services. Young Laurens was praised and given credit for the success of this amazing mission. Franklin was berated by John Adams and ignored, and Paine was neglected and broke. Regarding gratitude, Paine usually came up short on the receiving end and long on the giving end. Paine was so grateful to King Louis, that he put his life on the line defending him.

CHAPTER 38
YORKTOWN

As a result of King Louis' aid, Washington was able to go on the offensive. Armed with money, munitions and supplies, Washington drove south to Yorktown, Virginia. His army of 4,000 men was joined by the Veteran General, Jean Baptiste Rochambeau and about 8,000 French troops who knew all about siege warfare. Also, this force was increased by 2,000 states militia volunteers.

Washington used a fleet of transports to sail down Chesapeake Bay to set up operations north of Yorktown. Yorktown itself was now occupied by General Cornwallis' army of about 6,000 men. Cornwallis had selected this site between the York and James Rivers near the mouth of the Chesapeake Bay so that he could receive supplies from the British navy and also have means to escape by sea. He had abandoned his campaign in the south due to the heroic and unflagging resistance of General Nathanael Greene and other brave patriots such as Francis Marion, Andrew Pickens, Thomas Sumpter, General Daniel Morgan and Colonel George Rogers Clark. What a debt of gratitude we owe to these valiant and self-sacrificing men, along with others like them who fought and died to give us a new country.

During the summer of 1781, a French fleet under the command of Admiral Francois De Grasse was dispatched to the West Indies to protect French shipping and to provide naval support to the Americans, as needed. He was great! De Grasse engaged part of the British fleet, won a battle at sea against them and then – "Mirabile Dictu" – (wonderful to say) blockaded the mouth of Chesapeake Bay. So Cornwallis was trapped. He was cut off from reinforcements by sea, and he could not escape. In the meanwhile, Washington and General Rochambeau were busy deploying troops and cannon in preparation for the siege of the fort at Yorktown. The assault began on October 9, 1781. This was only forty-five days after Thomas Paine landed in Boston. He did not arrive empty handed. Paine disembarked with a million *livres* worth of supplies and two and a half million livers of silver, according to Craig Nelson (page 154). I understand that a silver *livre* was a French coin in use at that time. My guess is that two and a half million *livres*, translated into American currency may have been as much as ten million dollars. "The *livre* is a former money of account and a group of coins of France, issued in coin form, first in gold, then in silver, finally in copper and discontinued in 1794." (*Webster's Encyclopedic Dictionary*)

I return now, to the battle of Yorktown. The siege lasted eight days. On October 17, 1781, the British surrendered. I must say that I applaud Lord Charles Cornwallis' decision. In this battle he never had a chance. I credit him for bearing the temporary shame of defeat in order to save lives. Otherwise, thousands of his hapless soldiers would have been slaughtered. Besides, Cornwallis would live to fight another day.

The glorious victory at Yorktown marked the end of the war part of Paine's step by step plan to create the United States of America. George Washington would be acclaimed as the supreme hero of six years of a bloody, destructive and atrocious war. It was a war of defense. It was caused and willfully and maliciously pursued by a cruel and ignorant German crowned prince who is unhappily remembered as King George III.

CHAPTER 39
THE WASHINGTON LETTER

"And to you, Sir, treacherous in private friendship (for so you have been to me, and that in the day of danger) and a hypocrite in public life, the world will be puzzled to decide whether you are an apostate or an imposter; whether you have abandoned good principles or whether you ever had any."

This is the last sentence in Thomas Paine's scathing censure and denunciation of Washington and his administration. In this letter Paine called Washington a liar (Paine used the word deceitful), an ingrate, a double-dealer, and a cold and mean man. He accused Washington of unmilitary conduct: "You slept away your time in the field, till the finances of the country were completely exhausted, and you have but little share in the glory of the final event." – Yorktown – "I know also that had it not been for the aid received from France, in men, money and ships, that your cold and unmilitary conduct…would in all probability have lost America; at least she would not have been the independent nation she now is." Paine then scolded Washington for assuming "the merit for everything himself." People at home in America and in Europe credited Washington with winning the war and establishing Independence all by himself. Absurd! In both cases Washington played a minor part.

Next, Paine speaks of his imprisonment in France. Washington should have demanded Paine's release. Instead Washington did nothing. Paine wrote, "Your silence in not inquiring into the cause of my imprisonment, and reclaiming me against it, was tacitly giving me up (to be decapitated by the guillotine). I ought not to have suspected you of treachery; but whether I recover from the illness I now suffer or not, I shall continue to think you treacherous, till you give me cause to think otherwise." Paine laid the blame of his imprisonment and almost certain assassination squarely on the shoulders of Washington. Further on he portrayed Washington's silence as "ungenerous" and "dishonorable.

Paine continued, "Errors or caprices of the temper can be pardoned and forgotten; but a cold deliberate crime of the heart, such as Mr. Washington is capable of acting, is not to be washed away. The Jay Treaty was a crime of the heart, and much worse. The Jay Treaty stabbed France in the back. By signing it, Washington disgraced himself and the American Nation. Paine described Washington's conduct in the Jay's Treaty affair as lacking in integrity and as a poltroon (coward) and as a hypocrite; and that Washington "had been playing a double game." The Jay Treaty allowed England to high-jack American shipping on the high seas. I can't elaborate on this now. It is my opinion that Washington's ratification of the Jay Treaty ranks with the most immoral acts of any American President.

Following this, Paine proceeds to discuss and question Washington's part in the Revolutionary War and wrote, "A stranger might be led to suppose, from the egotism with which Mr. Washington speaks, that himself, and himself only, had <u>generated</u>, <u>conducted</u>, <u>completed</u> and <u>established</u> the Revolution: in fine, that it was all his own doing. In the first place, as to the political part, he had no share in it; and therefore the whole of that is out of the question with respect to him."

As to the military part, Paine wrote, "It would have been prudent in Mr. Washington not to have awakened inquiry upon that subject." Paine gave a detailed description of Washington as a nominal Commander-in-Chief who for the most part remained inactive during the war years from 1775 to 1780. Washington was goaded into attacking Trenton and Princeton. History will pay due credit to Thomas Paine for these crucial victories. Washington had nothing to do with the stunning American victory at Saratoga in 1777; and he was of no help to General Nathanael Greene in the south. "Nothing was done in the campaigns of 1778, 1779, 1780, in the part where General Washington commanded, except the taking of Stony Point by General Wayne."

Thomas Paine was right when he wrote, "The commencement of his command was the commencement of inactivity", and "No wonder we see so much pusillanimity in the President, when we see so little enterprise in the General!" Further on, Paine wrote, "Discontent began to prevail strongly against him (Washington), and a party was formed in Congress...for removing him from command of the army". The plot to sack Washington failed, in my opinion, mainly because Paine defended Washington in his fifth *Crisis Paper*.

At the beginning of 1781, the war was at a stalemate. Washington had not been victorious over the British for five years. His army was crippled with mutinies and desertions. Congress was bankrupt, and the Continental Treasury was empty. Paine lamented, "And yet the sole object, the establishment of the Revolution was a thing of remote distance." Paine by-passed Washington, formed a plan for victory and sprang into action.

He sailed to France on February 11, 1781, and obtained from the King six millions of livres and ten millions more as a loan, and the support of a fleet of not less than thirty sail of the line. "Colonel Laurens and myself returned from Brest the first of June following, taking with us two millions and a half of livres (upwards of one hundred thousand pounds sterling) of the money given, and convoying two ships with stores." After eighty-six (I presume anxious) days at sea, "We arrived at Boston (on) the twenty-fifth of August following." Admiral DeGrasse and the French Fleet arrived off Chesapeake Bay at the same time. "And it was by the aid of this money, and this fleet, and of Rochambeau's army, that Cornwallis was taken; the laurels of which have been unjustly give to Mr. Washington. His merit in that affair was no more that that of any other American officer."

I must pause here to quote Alfred Owen Aldridge's comment on Paine's magnificent feat. "Very little can be discovered about Paine's activities during this brief visit to France (March 9, 1781 to June 1, 1781) apart from a few references by members of Benjamin Franklin's entourage in Paris." (Aldridge, *Man of Reason*, p.88) The perceptive and erudite Craig Nelson said the same thing, in effect. "This episode is one of many where the lack of Paine documents is especially regrettable." (Nelson, p.154)

Thomas Paine gave full credit to "Venerable" Franklin for his years of ground-breaking service in France. However, it was Paine who brought Franklin's work to fruition. What an enlightening bonanza it would be to learn by new research discovery what transpired during Paine's 'audience' with young King Louis. What an outpouring! What alacrity! What largess! This included millions in 'hard money', ships, troops, arms and supplies. "Bis dat, cito dat." He who gives quickly, gives twice.

We can only imagine what was said when Paine met with the King.

We know that the King "loaded Paine with favors." No wonder why Paine put his own life on the line in order to save the King's life. "It is only by the aid of this money, and this fleet, and of Rochambeau's army, that Cornwallis (at Yorktown) was taken." In just fifty-three days after Paine returned to America, on August 25, 1781, the war-ending victory at Yorktown on October 17, 1781, achieved what Washington was unable to do in five years.

Yorktown transformed the Declaration of Independence from a promise to reality. I do not hesitate to say that History will show that it was Thomas Paine who "had generated, conducted, completed and established the Revolution". I trust Thomas Paine. Although I believe that Washington was treacherous, an ingrate, incompetent, and a hypocrite, I am grateful for the good things he did and I leave to others to decide for themselves whether he was an "apostate" or an "imposter".

Note: Except as indicated in the text, all of the quotes in this chapter have been taken from *Letter to George Washington* in Complete Writings by Philip S. Foner, Vol.2,p.691 to 793.

CHAPTER 40
JEFFERSON

Prior to June 10, 1776, there is no evidence, not a scrap, that Thomas Jefferson INTENDED to compose an American Declaration of Independence. Prior to June 28, 1776 there is no evidence that Thomas Jefferson had written anything advocating a total separation from Great Britain and total rejection and renouncement of all allegiance and subjection to the Kings of Great Britain, or advocating the utter dissolution and breaking off of all political connection with Great Britain.

The only evidence that Jefferson is the author of the Declaration is the copy of the original Declaration as composed by Thomas Paine, in Jefferson's handwriting and submitted to Congress on Friday, June 28, 1776. Jefferson made at least six other handwritten copies as follows:

1. To James Madison, June 1, 1783
2. To Philip Mazzei, September 16, 1825
3. To Richard Henry Lee, July 8, 1776
4. To John Page (not confirmed) July 8, 1776
5. John Pendleton, July 29, 1776
6. George Wyth, August 6, 1822

Jefferson wrote, "These rough drafts I sent to distant friends who were anxious to know what was passing – but how many and to whom, I do not recollect." (Hazelton, Appendix) We can form our own opinions as to why Jefferson went to so much trouble. Ironically, his copies went to the educated and propertied elite whereas Paine's ideas in the Declaration were expressed in plain, Common Sense, down-to-earth language designed for, or to be read to common men and women, many of whom could not read. A copy is a copy and an original is an original. Words on paper prove penmanship, not authorship. Jefferson copied his "rough draft" from Thomas Paine's original Declaration. Joseph Lewis believed "that Jefferson and Adams both copied the Declaration from the original manuscript". (Lewis, p.304) I trust Joseph Lewis and I believe that Thomas Paine is the author of the Declaration of Independence.

John Adams in a letter of 1822 to Timothy Pickering wrote, "I have long wondered that the original draft has not been published." (Hazelton, p. 180)

The esteemed John H. Hazelton's monumental opus, *The Declaration Of Independence-Its History*, is a treasure chest of information. I owe him a large debt of gratitude. Hazelton's work, along with Joseph Lewis' book, and the writings of many others on the Declaration over the last two centuries, oblige me to limit my comments to five points.

It is absurd to think that Jefferson believed that *all men are created equal, in the order of creation*, in 1776.

It is absurd to think that Jefferson would write, "It is their right, it is their duty, to throw off such government…"

Jefferson is not the author of the "Slave Clause", and I do not believe that he would describe slavery as an "execrable commerce" and "that this Assemblage of Horrors might Want no Fact of distinguished Die."

The Declaration was also a formal Declaration of the war which was already in progress. I do not believe that Jefferson would have undertaken to be the author of such a document as an original of his own composition. He was assigned as the fifth member of the Committee – including Franklin, Adams, R. Livingston and Roger

Sherman – quite probably because Richard Henry Lee was called home. He dutifully complied. I agree with Joseph Lewis who wrote "Thomas Jefferson turned to 'neither book nor pamphlet' in writing the Declaration because – and this is my firm conviction – he merely copied it from the manuscript prepared by Thomas Paine…"

I turn now to the celebrated work, *A Summary View of the Rights of British America*. By Jefferson's own admission, it is not exclusively his work. Jefferson wrote, "I prepared what I thought might be given, in instruction to the Delegates who should be appointed to attend the General Congress proposed. They were drawn in haste, with a number of BLANKS with some UNCERTAINTIES and INACCURACIES of HISTORICAL FACTS…"* (Padover, *Writings*, p.244) Jefferson's proposed instructions were neither adopted nor printed by the Virginia Assembly. The piece was edited and "shaped" by others and privately published; and "They gave it the title of *A Summary View of the Rights of British America*."

What comes down to us as *A Summary View* was not written in August 1774. The whole piece is a revision. Its most important message is that Jefferson was a Loyalist in 1774. We may assume that whoever made changes to Jefferson's original must have filled in the blanks and corrected the uncertainties and inaccuracies. In any case, there is nothing in the *Summary View* that would justly qualify Jefferson to be called a Founding Father of the United States of America. I am not aware that there exists any conclusive evidence that would contradict the truth that Jefferson was a reluctant, Johnny-come-lately, disinterested, "passive" and "silent", slave-owning participant in the establishment of the United States.

Thomas Jefferson was a 'Virginian'. Even David McCullough in his John Adams book said, "When Jefferson spoke of my country, he usually meant Virginia." (p. 114). "As soon as Jefferson learned that the Virginia Convention had declared independence from Great Britain and

---

*　caps mine

was creating a commonwealth, he set about writing the first of three drafts of a new constitution for his home country."(W. S. Randall, p. 267) During this time Jefferson was not composing the Declaration. He copied it from Thomas Paine's original. Jefferson did not defend the Declaration submitted to Congress. He sat as a silent witness during two and a half days of debate and brutal and hack and slash editing of the Declaration.

Prior to June 10, 1776, Jefferson had written nothing recommending Independence and establishing a Republic. Because Jefferson worked with Dickenson and joined with those to delay the vote for Independence, and let it be known that he did not want a second term in Congress (Randall, p.279); and made repeated pleas to be relieved; there were rumors that Jefferson was a Loyalist. To Jefferson, "The Continental Congress was but a temporary meeting in convention of delegates from the new states, of little importance in the long run. Even if there were a permanent confederacy of states, it would be of far less importance than the reshaping of the weak old English Colonies into strong independent countries. Jefferson wanted to join his friends in Virginia in an effort that mattered far more to him than writing of declarations and resolutions in Philadelphia." (p. 279)

Jefferson did not stay in Congress and contribute to the work to help nurture the infant Republic; nor did he assist in the war effort. Two months after Independence was declared, he went home to Monticello. Jefferson was a Virginian.

All credit to Jefferson for what he did accomplish. Sadly, he did not support Lafayette and the French Revolution; and he did not block the infamous Jay Treaty; and he did not rescue Thomas Paine from prison. However, I am grateful for his efforts as the United States third President. I only wish that Jefferson had written a "long and detailed expression of his appreciation and gratitude to honor the genius who made his presidency possible.

CHAPTER 41
FOUNDER IN SOLE

"Let any man look at the position America was in at the time I first took up the subject, (of Independence) and published Common Sense, which was but a few months before the Declaration of Independence; an army of thirty thousand men coming out against her, besides, those which were already here, and she without either an object or a system, fighting, she scarcely knew for what, and which, if she could have obtained, would have done her no good. She had not a day to spare in bringing about the only thing which could save her a REVOLUTION*, yet no one measure was taken to promote it, and many were used to prevent it; and had independence not been declared at the time it was, I cannot see any time in which it could have been declared, as the train of ill-successes which followed the affair of Long Island left no future opportunity." (*Writings*, Book 8, p. 61 & 62)

S o, Thomas Paine took it upon himself to *generate, conduct, complete* and *establish* the United States of America. These are the very words that Paine used to describe credits which were falsely ascribed to Washington. (Foner, II, p.718) Washington did not originate the idea to unite the thirteen colonies and separate from Britain and establish a

---

*   caps mine

new independent nation as a Democratic Republic. As to the political part, Paine wrote that Washington had "no share in it". (p.178)

As regards the military part of the Revolutionary War, Washington never achieved victory over the British for over six years; that is from July 1775 through September 1781. Yorktown was, for the most part, a French victory. Washington held the nominal rank of Commander-in-chief and as a figurehead participated in the Yorktown triumph mostly as a spectator, in my opinion.

It was Thomas Paine who GENERATED the Revolution. Neither Washington, nor Adams, nor Jefferson, nor Hamilton, nor Madison, nor Monroe had written anything for publication advocating the creation of an American Republic, waging war against the British, forging a constitution; and declaring Independence. In short these "Founding Fathers: did not compose and publish *Common Sense*. It is with profound respect and gratitude that we honor these men along with all of those patriotic men and women for their individual contributions. However, it was the principles of Thomas Paine that held Congress together with his nonpareil *Crisis Papers*. In my view, Congress operated as a minority junta. Thousands of Loyalists opposed Congress. Women could not vote. Men without property could not vote. Many did not know what was going on in Congress; and many did not care. This is why I do not believe that Congress had the voice and the sanction of the majority of the Colonists.

Congress itself could be, and was swayed by a small influential and determined group. John Adams took this opportunity to advance his Federalist designs as well as his own power ambitions. He was joined by Washington, Hamilton, Jay and others who needed no coaxing. The result was a strong Federal, Elitist government; not government by and for the people specified and insisted on by Thomas Paine. John Adams was a poison pill. He looked down on people. He was a power seeker and worked against Paine. John Adams did not GENERATE the American Revolution. He even admitted that History will ascribe the American Revolution to Thomas Paine.

In my view, John Adams failed in his mission as president of the War and Ordinance Board. Adams missed a great opportunity for praise and acclaim when he rejected the chance to go to France in 1781, in order to solicit more aid from King Louis XVI. Thomas Paine jumped at the chance. He sailed to France with Major John Laurens and he was phenomenally successful. French aid enabled Paine to COMPLETE what he GENERATED and the result was the ESTABLISHMENT of the United States of America.

During the Revolutionary years from 1774 to 1783, Thomas Jefferson, true to form, stayed in character as a "passive auditor", in the GENERATION and formation of the United States. Jefferson's contributions in the political part were small during the war; and he did not participate in the military operations of the war. No biographer of Jefferson could claim that he generated, conducted, completed and established the Revolution.

Jefferson did nothing about women's suffrage, Emancipation, Broad and Equal representation and short terms. Sadly, he did not work to free Paine from prison. The traditional image of Jefferson is, for the most part, mythical. Jefferson wrote, "I have sometimes asked myself, whether my country is better for my having lived at all? I do not know that it is. I have been the instrument of doing the following things; but they would have been done by others; some of them, perhaps, a little better." (See *The Writings of Thomas Jefferson*, Selected and Edited by Saul K. Padover, p.231)

I don't know either; and I am not sure that Jefferson meant the United States or Virginia when he wrote "my country".

We are thankful for what we receive. Thomas Paine had offered "something better" and he exerted himself in helping CONDUCT the work called for in the plan that he GENERATED until it was COMPLETED at Yorktown; and he continued working until the sovereign Independence of the United States was formally ESTABLISHED by the Treaty of Pairs in 1793.

CHAPTER 42
THE INSKEEP LETTER:
"TO JOHN INSKEEP, MAYOR OF THE CITY OF PHILADELPHIA"

"I saw in the *Aurora* on January the 30th a piece addressed to you and signed Isaac Hall. It contains a statement of your malevolent conduct in refusing to let him have Vine-st. Wharf after he had bid fifty dollars more rent for it than another person had offered, and had been unanimously approved of by the Commissioners appointed by law for that purpose. Among the reasons given by you for this refusal, one was, that '*Mr. Hall was one of Paine's disciples.*' If those whom you may chuse to call my disciples follow my example in doing good to mankind, they will pass the confines of this world with a happy mind, while the hope of the hypocrite shall perish and delusion sink into despair."

"I do not know who Mr. Inskeep is, for I do not remember the name of Inskeep at Philadelphia in '*the time that tried men's souls.*' He must be some mushroom of modern growth that has started up ON THE SOIL WHICH THE GENEROUS SERVICES OF THOMAS PAINE CONTRIBUTED TO BLESS WITH FREEDOM;[*] neither do I know what profession of religion he is of, nor do I care, for he is a man malevolent and unjust, it signifies not to what class or sectary he may hypocritically belong."

---

[*] caps mine

As I set too much value on my time to waste it on a man of so little consequences as yourself, I will close this short address with a declaration that puts hypocrisy and malevolence to defiance. Here it is: My motive and object in all my political works, beginning with *Common Sense*, the first work I ever published, have been to rescue man from tyranny and false systems and false principles of government for himself; and I have borne my share of danger in Europe and in America in every attempt I have made for this purpose. And my motive and object in all my publications on religious subjects, beginning with the first part of the *Age of Reason*, have been to bring man to a right reason that God has given him; to impress on him the great principles of divine morality, justice, mercy, and a benevolent disposition to all men and to all creatures; and to excite in him a spirit of trust, confidence and consolation in his creator, unshackled by the fable and fiction of books, by whatever invented name they may be called. I am happy in the continual contemplation of what I have done, and I thank God that he gave me talents for the purpose and fortitude to do it. It will make the continual consolation of my departing hours, whenever they finally arrive."[*]

THOMAS PAINE

---

[*] (Printed in the Philadelphia Commercial Advertizer on February 10, 1806, See Conway, p.304)

CHAPTER 43
RICKMAN AND FRANKLIN

In referring to the period after 1802, when Thomas Paine returned to America from France, Thomas Rickman wrote, "Thousands, who had formerly looked up to Mr. Paine as the *principal founder of the Republic** had imbibed a strong dislike to him on account of his religious principles…" (p.5)

On page ten, Rickman credited Paine as being "THE PRINCIPAL AGENT IN CREATING THE GOVERNMENT OF THE AMERICAN STATES…"**

Rickman also wrote, "Even Mr. Burke (Edmund, 1729-1797, member of Parliament in 1765; early advocate for British-American Reconciliation) writing on one of Mr. Paine's works *Common Sense*, said that celebrated pamphlet, which prepared the minds of the people for independence." (p.12)

On page thirty-four, Rickman wrote, "After the establishment of the independence of America, of the vigorous and successful exertions to attain which glorious object, HE HAD BEEN THE ANIMATING PRINCIPAL, SOUL AND SUPPORT…"**

Again, on page fifty-four, Thomas Clio Rickman refers to Thomas Paine as the "PRINCIPAL FOUNDER OF THE AMERICAN REPUBLIC** and the happiness of its citizens."

---

*   italics mine
**   caps mine

All of the quotations in this part have been taken from Thomas Clio Rickman's *Life of Thomas Paine* as printed in the Centenary Memorial Edition of the *Life and Writings of Thomas Paine*.

BENJAMIN FRANKLIN

Franklin wrote:

"You Thomas Paine are more responsible than any other living Person on this continent for the creation of what we call the United States Of America."

This Franklin quote was taken from the splendid article *September and Thomas Paine*, by Roy Meador; published by Book Source Magazine (now Book Source Monthly) in Volume 20, Number 1, November-December, 2003, page 31, through the courtesy of Mrs. Helen Meador.

CHAPTER 44
LOOSE ENDINGS

CONSTITUTION

I believe in the Constitution of the United States of America. It is a proven amendable document. "We live to improve or we live in vain." We have seen that historic corrections were achieved with Emancipation and Women's Rights. It appears that more work is "wanted".

According to Thomas Paine, good government requires broad and equal representation, short terms, simplicity, clarity, and should be conducted openly and with the least expense

> "I draw my idea of the form of government from a principle in nature, which no art can overturn, viz. that the more simple any thing is, the less liable it is to be disordered, and the easier repaired when disordered..." *Common Sense*

In the interest of saving time and space, I will comment on openness and expense only. As to openness – meaning full disclosure in the administration of government – it is compromised by secrecy. Government of and by the people is impossible if elected officials keep secrets from the people. As regards to the cost of running the government, the goal should be frugality.

"Wherefore, security being the true design and end of government, it unanswerably follows, that whatever form there of appears most likely to ensure it to us, with the least expense and greatest benefit, is preferable to all others." *Common Sense*

THE SCIENCE OF GOVERNMENT

Thomas Paine was signally interested in what he called "the science of government". He wrote, "In every land throughout the universe the tendency of the interest of the greatest number is in the direction of good rather than of evil, and the inevitable result must be to elevate the *science** of government to a height of perfection of which we have now no conception." (Aldridge, p.150) America can improve. We have the means, an amendable constitution, to do it.

HEREDITARY LAW

"Every age and generation is and must be (as a matter of right) as free to act for itself in all cases as the age and generation that preceded it. The vanity and presumption of governing beyond the grave is the most ridiculous and insolent of all tyrannies. Man has no property in man; neither has one generation a property in the generations that are to follow." (Adkins, p.161)

To paraphrase Thomas Paine, we act as tyrants when we legislate for, and bind, future generations, and we become slaves when we are bound by laws enacted in former generations. Serious unforeseen economic and social problems can arise in either of the cases, as described above, when such legislation mandates an increase in taxes. Hereditary monarchy and hereditary laws are closely related.

---

*   italics mine

ABUSE AND ATONE

The last sentence of Doctor Philip S. Foner's introduction to Volume II of his monumental *Complete Writings of Thomas Paine*, is, "Seeing all this (Paine's credits) the reader will readily agree that the time has come once and for all, to end the torrent of abuse that has been heaped upon Thomas Paine for about a hundred and fifty years." Because of the vile, libelous attacks on Paine, his writings have been hounded out of most sectarian and many non-sectarian classrooms longer than a hundred and fifty years.

That comprehensive studies about Thomas Paine's works and achievements have, in general, been excluded in Jewish, Roman Catholic, Protestant and other schools, is understandable. The combined negative effects of the persistent lies about Paine, along with the false interpretations of his timeless *Age of Reason*, have been stumbling blocks to the inclusion of Paine's writings in American history classes.

As Thomas Paine and his ideas become better known, I believe a way will be found to do justice to his productions in school rooms. Much progress continues to be made. More than a half dozen new books have been published about Paine since the year 2000. One example, among others is Mark Wilensky's ground breaking *The Elementary Common Sense of Thomas Paine. An Interactive Adaptation For All Ages.* Also, an outstanding article by Jennifer James entitled *Tom's Words* was published in June 28, 2009 edition of the Los Angeles Times. It was printed in large type in the Kids Reading Room section.

MORE WORK IS WANTED

I hope more research will be done on Paine's mission to France in the spring of 1781. What triggered King Louis' magnanimous and immediate response to Paine's appeal? What military plans were laid while Paine was in France for the combined land and sea assault on the British at Yorktown? Did Paine make any reciprocal promises in exchange for the millions receive in aid? We know that the King "loaded Paine with favors" which enabled the glorious war-ending triumph at Yorktown and the end of subordination to Great Britain. As noted before, Washington had no part in the planning for the Yorktown attack. He was excluded on purpose. Washington was opposed to the plan when he first learned about it; but he changed his mind. Also, it would be wonderful to learn the name of the author of the Franco-American Treaty of Alliance of February 6, 1778; and who were the members of the "Navy Board in 1777." Additional information on these and other questions would be most welcome. Let the research continue.

REVOLUTIONARY WOMEN

The stories of the women patriots during the Revolutionary war are amazing. They provide unique insights into the suffering and trials of that cruel contest. I gained a deeper understanding of the creation of the United States from *First Ladies* by Betty Boyde Caroli and *Founding Mothers* by Cokie Robers. I found Cokie Robert's production – well aided by Ann Charnley and many other contributing scholars and intellectuals – to be delightfully readable and historically accurate. I would happily recommend *Founding Mothers* to anyone.

The wives of the first three presidents did all they could in support of their husbands and the Revolution. Martha Washington and Abigail Adams were "stand-outs". I pause here to record my special recognition and gratitude to Elizabeth Kortwright Monroe. Elizabeth was only eight years old in 1776. Eighteen years later, as the wife of James Monroe – then Minister to France – Elizabeth welcomed the critically ill Thomas Paine into her Paris home, after James had rescued him from prison. It is my understanding that Elizabeth Monroe provided the tender nursing care which resulted in Thomas Paine's recovery at the time when it was thought that he would die in two or three months. Paine stayed in the Monroe's home for eighteen months. When I think about

Elizabeth and James Monroe, it is always with a heart full of gratitude and appreciation. I shall remember them. So should we all.

> "Mrs. Monroe showed him all possible kindness and attention. She provided him with an excellent nurse, who had for him all the anxiety and assiduity of a sister. She neglected nothing to afford him ease and comfort when he was totally unable to help himself." (Aldridge, p.238)

CRISIS

It is my firm opinion that the primary readership target of Paine's *Crisis Papers* was congress; so that all of its members would persevere until total Independence was won. Unfortunately Thomas Paine was unable to effect the unity of the Thirteen Colonies such that, in concert, they would provide the men, money, and material, sufficient to achieve final victory over the British. As president of the War and Ordnance Board, John Adams was a total failure; and John Jay and Gouverneur Morris were of little help, if any. Besides, all three of these men were working against Paine behind his back.

So, Paine went to France and secured the troops, arms, supplies, a bonanza of "hard money", the generalship, the naval support; and laid the battle plans for the final victory at Yorktown.

MONEY

Some of the biographer's of Thomas Paine seem to relish writing about his financial affairs. They attempt to show that Paine wrote for personal money profits. Here is an example:

Alfred Owen Aldridge wrote, "His (Paine's) fundamental honesty did not keep him from accepting clandestine rewards for his propaganda, particularly from both the American government and the French Ministry for his writings on the American Revolution. He never ceased alluding to the free bestowal of his services. Yet after the battle was won he set up an unending clamor for additional financial compensation. *His self-sacrificial pen is largely a myth.*" (*Man of Reason*, p.319)

Aldridge's remark is a distortion. To describe Paine's letters as "unending clamor" and his tireless exertions and achievements as "largely a myth", is an exercise in baseless embroidery on one hand, and disregard of the facts on the other. Paine created a new nation, a new Country born in freedom. What is that worth? By way of comparison, Louisiana cost fifteen million. What would have been a fair compensation for Thomas Paine? Paine persuaded some key men to assist him in order to achieve Independence. They followed his lead, became famous and reaped the laurels of honor and office. After the war, Paine was ignored and neglected. In his *Essential Thomas Paine*, John Dos Passos was more accurate than Aldridge when he described Thomas Paine as a person who had "reckless disregard for his personal interests" (p.12); and "who always lived from hand to mouth" (p.16): and who "when he had any money, he would subscribe it to some cause or other or give it away." (p.17); and who, at the end of the war, was "broke again." (p.18)

Thomas Paine was not interested in becoming money rich. To Paine money was only a means to survive; and to buy paper and ink; and to invent and innovate; and, above all, money was a means to promote humanitarian goals. Paine's letters about remuneration had two aims. The first was official recognition and credit for what he did. The second aim was to give to the elitists the chance to save face by paying for value received.

Later, Paine was awarded a farm in New York; and Pennsylvania provided a grant of three thousand dollars.

---

*   italics mine

Proper recognition and gratitude for Paine's accomplishments is yet to be forthcoming.

DISCLAIMER

Some years ago, I started to write letters to my children about Thomas Paine and his ideas. Later I decided to combine these compositions and have them bound as a memorial. Of course, I consider my efforts to be an "ego trip".

I am not a writer. I am not an author. I am not an historical scholar. Accordingly, corrections, objections, criticism and exceptions, of any kind, from anyone, are cordially invited and warmly welcomed. I would benefit from them.

I cherish every hour I spend studying the works of Thomas Paine. The reading provides its own reward. The idea content remains compellingly educational, and is, for me always delightful. Others may differ, but I find that Thomas Paine productions read like "mystery novel page turners".

What Thomas Paine accomplished, however, is no mystery. He created a new nation, designed to be governed by the people. The United States of America was Thomas Paine's innovation. Most of Thomas Paine's biographers fail to give to Paine the explicit recognition, the acknowledgement, and the unalloyed credit for being the creator-founder in sole of the United States. To me, that is a mystery.

CHAPTER 45
THOMAS PAINE'S *COMMON SENSE*
IS
THE SOURCE OF THE
DECLARATION OF INDEPENDENCE

Thomas Paine is the author of the Declaration of Independence, and the Declaration of Independence is *Common Sense* in brief outline form. *Common Sense* is the long form of the Declaration of Independence. No one disputes the fact that Thomas Paine is the author of *Common Sense*. The words and ideas in the Declaration of Independence come from the author of *Common Sense*, -- Thomas Paine. The citations in the following pages will prove that beyond a doubt.

Thomas Paine set out to create a new country, separate and independent from Great Britain. He originated the idea that the new country should be a Republic. There would be no need for a King.

"Of more worth is one honest man to society, and in the sight of God, than all the crowned ruffians that ever lived."

THOMAS PAINE'S design specification for his Republic called for a democratically controlled country through a system of elected representatives. The representatives, chosen by vote of the people would manage the legislative part of the government.

> "This will point out the convenience of their consenting to leave the legislative part to be managed by a select number chosen from the whole body..." "In this first parliament every man by natural right will have a seat."

In *Common Sense*, Thomas Paine produced a determined proposal that the American Colonies Unite and:

- ✓ Separate from Great Britain;
- ✓ Declare Independence;
- ✓ Unite to establish a Republic;
- ✓ Secure natural and Civil Rights for all;
- ✓ Frame a continental Constitution;
- ✓ Build a Navy: and
- ✓ Wage a defensive war in order to Secure Independence.

Thomas Paine deserves the credit for creating the United States of America. He invented the idea; and he did so, independently. The integration of the above listed principle components was done by Thomas Paine alone. He invented the plan to achieve independence. He convinced enough courageous people to follow his lead. He worked tirelessly to have the United Colonies declared to be the "FREE and INDEPENDENT STATES of AMERICA."

Thomas Paine's ideas were innovative and revolutionary. It is Thomas Paine who merits the title of Father of his Country. He is the real founder of the United States.

"If there is any true cause of fear respecting independence, it is because no plan is yet laid down. Men do not see their way out, wherefore, as an opening into that business, I offer the following hints; at the same time modestly affirming, that I have no other opinion of them myself., than that they may be the means of giving rise to something better."

Franklin, Washington, Adams, Jefferson, Madison, and Monroe were converts. They were following founders of the United States; and until after the unanimous Declaration of Independence, these, so-called founding fathers were rebels; and before *Common Sense*, their desires and aims went no further than redress and reconciliation with Great Britain.

Thank you, Thomas Paine, for giving us something better.

PART 1
IDEAS FROM THE PAGES
OF *COMMON SENSE*

Page No.	
15	Perpetual exclusion from voting.
	Hereditary monarchy is folly, absurd.
16.	Hereditary monarchy – custom then a right!?
	How did Kings come into existence?
	{by lot -} No precedent established for hereditary monarchy.
	{by election -} No precedent established for hereditary monarchy.
	by usurpation – coercive and immoral.
17.	Hereditary monarchy takes away the <u>right to vote of future generations.</u>
18.	Hereditary succession opens a door to the foolish, the wicked and the improper.
	The throne could be possessed by a minor; and heredity succession does NOT preserve a nation from civil wars.
19.	English History (BLOOD) York & Lancaster etc.
20.	What is the business of the King? – "make war and give away places …"
	"Of more worth is one honest man to society…"
21.	<u>The period of debate is closed.</u>
22.	"The sun never shone on a cause of greater worth"
	"'Tis not the concern of a day, a year or an age…"
	"<u>Now</u> is the seed time…"
	The question of union with GREAT BRITAIN is terminated.
23.	? <u>Separation</u> or dependence? – Examine.
	That America flourished under GREAT BRITAIN and That GREAT BRITAIN protected America are both fallacious – we produced, we protected. GREAT BRITAIN acted in her selfish interest.

Page
No.

24. Throw off dependence and America will be at peace with
France and Spain.
Objection: The Colonies have no relation to each other
except through England.
Objection: England is the PARENT – false! – Europe is.
Objection: A union with GREAT BRITAIN – we would be
the dominate super-power.

25. American inhabitants come from France, Germany, Sweden,
Holland plus other countries and don't forget Native Americans.

26. Reconciliation is truly farcical. Our plan is commerce.
I challenge the warmest advocate for reconciliation to
Renounce the alliance with GREAT BRITAIN

27. Dependence involves us in European Wars. Not
reconciliation, but separation.
"Everything that is right or natural pleads for separation."
"…'Tis time to part"
Distance is an argument for separation
America is a sanctuary for the persecuted.

28. English rule must end sooner or later.
"…We are running the next generation into DEBT,…"
Reconciliation is espoused by
Interested men – They have a profit interest.
Prejudiced men - who will not see.
Weak men – who cannot see.
Moderate men.
Renounce a power in whom we can have no trust.

29. (Consider) the doctrine of Reconciliation.
HATH your House been burnt, HATH your property been
destroyed.

Page
No.

30.	It is NOT in the power of GREAT BRITAIN to conquer America. The present winter is worth an age.
	It is repugnant to reason to remain subject.
	No plan short of <u>SEPARATION</u> will work
	<u>Reconciliation</u> <u>now</u> a fallacious dream.
	Every quiet method for peace <u>HATH</u> been ineffectual.
31.	"For Gods sake let us come to a final <u>SEPARATION;</u>"
	And NOT leave it to the next <u>generation</u>.
	It is absurd for an island to govern a continent.
32.	I espouse the doctrine of <u>SEPARATION &</u> <u>INDEPENDENCE.</u>
	<u>Independency</u>...sooner or later.
33.	After April 19, 1775, I rejected RECONCILIATION and the hardened, sullen-tempered Pharaoh of England...and disdain the wretch
	What would come from (Reconciliation)?
	The power of Government would remain with the King.
	"...No laws but what I please." George III.
34.	The King will keep America LOW & LESS.
	Differences: GREAT BRITAIN vs. America
35.	The King would use America for his purpose.
	"<u>Reconciliation</u> & ruin are nearly related".
	Nothing but Independence.
36.	I dread <u>Reconciliation</u>.
	GREAT BRITAIN could not preserve peace if civil war breaks out.
	I could never relish <u>Reconciliation</u>.
	A republican government, formed on more <u>natural</u> principles.

Page
No.

37. Rivalry between colonies? Where there are no distinctions, there can be no superiority; perfect <u>equality</u> affords no temptations.

Fear of <u>independence</u> – "because NO PLAN is yet laid down."

Let the assemblies (of the colonies) be annual, with a president only. Equal representation. There business wholly domestic and subject to a continental congress.

(National) Congress to elect a President, annually from each Colony (STATE) in turn and by lot.

38. Let a Continental Conference be held

39. Frame a Continental Charter, securing freedom and property to all men, and above all things, freedom or religion.

40. "A Government of our own is our Natural right:"

"…form a constitution of our own."

41. "Ye that appose independence now."

"…ye are opening the door to eternal tyranny."

42. "O! ye that love mankind…stand forth! Freedom – haunted. (hounded) warned to depart, "O! receive the fugitive, and prepare an asylum for mankind."

43. <u>Separation</u> and <u>Independence,</u>

"the time <u>hath</u> found us."

44. <u>Build a Navy</u>, we have an army, and a small population; no debts.

Form a Government and an <u>independent constitution.</u>

45. Cost of building a Navy.

46. We have all the raw materials {timer, tar, iron cordage}.

47. We ought to have a fleet.

48. We must protect ourselves; not another – Build a Navy.

This concludes Part 1, which includes the ideas from *Common Sense*. Taken as a whole these ideas provide the elements of a concrete plan for the formation and establishment of the United States of America.

PART 2

The words that appear in BOTH *Common Sense* and the Declaration are provided in this part.

HATH

In his immortal *Common Sense* Thomas Paine used the word <u>HATH</u> no less than <u>46</u> times.

Thomas Jefferson rarely used the word Hath. Author Joseph Lewis (*Thomas Paine Author of the Declaration of Independence*, p. 195) wrote "...in his (Jefferson's) ordinary correspondence and his individual State documents, Jefferson does not use the word once, despite the fact that (Jefferson's) voluminous writings aggregate more than 3 million (3,000,000) words. While in *Common Sense* and the Forester Letters alone, comprising less than 50 thousand words, Thomas Paine used the word <u>HATH</u> at least 125 times."

However, some of Jefferson's compositions, or rather, some compositions included in his works and papers, do contain the word <u>HATH</u>. In reference to such works, Joseph Lewis wrote: ", even his most ardent and admiring biographers admit that their composition is NOT in Jefferson's regular style of writing." (Regarding these exceptions, I wonder who was the real author?)

EQUAL

We hold these truths to be self-evident, that all men are created EQUAL.

On page #3 (*Common Sense*), Thomas Paine is calling for a new government. The legislative part would be managed by a select number chosen from the whole body of citizens. The select number of representatives would be chosen by means of free elections. "In this first 'parliament, every man (and woman) by natural right will have a seat."

Equality of voting rights is a concrete example of equality under the 'law'. This principle was not embraced by the framers of the U.S. Constitution. For example, women were not allowed to vote. (see Thomas Paine's Essay on Women's Rights)

"Mankind being originally EQUALS in the order of creation, the EQUALITY could only be destroyed by some subsequent circumstance..." – (page #9)

"As the exalting one man so greatly above the rest, cannot be justified on the equal rights of nature..." (page #10)

"For all men (and women) being originally EQUALS ..." (page #14)

"Where there are NO distinctions, there can be NO superiority; perfect EQUALITY affords no temptation." (page #37)

"Mankind being originally equals in the order of creation."
Common Sense

"Let the assemblies be annual, with a president only. The representation more equal."(page #37)

"He that will promote discord, under a government, so EQUALLY formed as this, would have joined Lucifer in his revolt."(page #38)

My understanding regarding Thomas Paine's assertion that all men are created EQUAL is as follows.

By equal, Paine meant that all men and women are subject to the natural "laws" of the physical world into which they were born. These 'natural' laws are hypotheses; they are given in generalizations as propositions in order to provide a description of the physical world. Human EQUALITY means that each person is affected due to the physical manifestations of the world such as: light, heat, weight, distance, time, weather, and so on. Human EQUALITY does NOT mean that each person is affected in the same way. Nor does it mean that all have <u>equal</u> abilities. We are all, <u>EQUAL</u> as subject to Natural Law, as we know it.

(The words Equal & Equality appear 14 times in *Common Sense*)

<u>RECONCILIATION</u>

In *COMMON SENSE*, Reconciliation appears <u>19</u> times.

"...to dissolve the political brands..."
"...to assume...the separate and equal station..."
– Declaration of Independence

Page	
22.	"Reconciliation...hath passed away..."
26.	"Reconciliation...is truly farcial..."
26.	"Reconciliation...(not) a single advantage"
27.	"...advocates for reconciliation..."
28.	"...the doctrine of reconciliation..."
30.	"Reconciliation is now a fallacious dream."
35.	"...reconciliation now is a dangerous doctrine..."
36.	"I dread the event of a reconciliation..."
36.	"...I could never relish...reconciliation,..."
41.	"... Harmony and reconciliation...?" and "Neither can ye reconcile Britain and America."
59.	"Which...reconciliation or independence?"
62.	"...reconciliation, perplexed and complicated..."
63.	"And if something is not done in time...neither Reconciliation nor, Independence will be practicable."
63.	"talking of reconciliation...how difficult the task...how dangerous."

<u>NATURE</u> (31 times)

<u>Nature</u> is defined as the essential character of a thing. The word NATURE refers to the quality or qualities that make something what it is. – (Webster's)

Page No.

(Introduction II)	"...declaring war against <u>natural rights</u>..."
(Introduction II)	"...whom <u>nature</u> hath given the power..."
2.	"In this state of <u>natural</u> liberty..."
3.	"...Every man by <u>natural</u> right..."
4.	"...the simple voice of <u>nature</u>..."
4.	"I draw my idea...from a principle in <u>nature</u>..."
5.	"Absolute Governments...the disgrace of human <u>nature</u>".
6.	"Absolute power is the <u>natural</u> disease of monarchy"
10.	"...on the equal rights of <u>nature</u>"
14.	"...<u>natural</u> proofs of the folly of hereditary right in Kings..."
14.	"is that <u>nature</u> disapproves it..."
23.	"...on the principles of <u>nature</u>..."
29.	"...to the touchstone of <u>nature</u>, ..."
41.	"...affection which <u>nature</u> cannot forgive..."
58.	Re: KINGS – "<u>nature</u> knows them not"
59.	"...the King...wickedly trampled <u>nature</u>"
62.	"He who takes <u>nature</u> for his guide..."

The words nature or natural appear in Thomas Paine's *Common Sense* no less than **31** times.

"...to which the Laws of Nature and of Nature's God entitle them..."
– <u>The Declaration of Independence.</u>

HAPPINESS (10 times)

References to <u>Happiness</u> appear no less than ten times (10) in Thomas Paine's immortal *Common Sense*.

Page
1.   "Society...promotes our <u>happiness</u>..."
4.   "...and the <u>happiness</u> of the governed..."
9.   "...Kings ...means of <u>happiness</u> or misery..."
23.   "...towards her future <u>happiness</u>, ..."
37.   "...to make every...person...<u>happy</u>..."
39.   "...Whose peace and <u>happiness</u> may God preserve"
40.   "...the greatest sum of individual <u>happiness</u>..."
46.   "...No country...is so <u>happily</u> situated..."
56.   "...to live <u>happily</u> or safely..."

"...that among these are, Life, liberty and the pursuit of <u>happiness</u>..."
– <u>Declaration of Independence</u>
In the handwriting of Thomas Jefferson, in the American Philosophical Society in Philadelphia.

"...among which are the Preservation of <u>Life</u> and the <u>Pursuit</u> of <u>Happiness</u>..."

John Adam's copy – <u>Declaration of Independence.</u>

"The road to <u>Happiness</u> and to Glory is open to us too;"
John Adam's copy – <u>Declaration of Independence.</u>

In referring to the Declaration of Independence, one, Mr. <u>Gilbert Chinard</u> said, "I do not believe that any other State paper in any nation had ever proclaimed so emphatically and with such finality that one of the essential functions of government is to make man <u>happy</u>, or one of his essential rights is the pursuit of <u>happiness</u>. This was more than a new principle of government, it was a new principle of life which was thus proposed and officially endorsed." (Lewis, p. 262)

Governments can't make people HAPPY. The function of a government is to allow men and women to pursue happiness. –J.H.5-18-7

"Gilbert Chinard was the Pyle Professor at Princeton University." – Joseph Lewis

SEPARATION (7 times)

"…The <u>separate</u> and equal station…"
- Declaration of Independence

Page	
23.	"….what we have to trust if <u>separated</u>…"
27.	"…will be wishing for <u>separation</u>…"
27.	"…Everything…pleads for separation…"
30.	"…a plan…of <u>separation</u>…"
31.	"…for God's sake let us come to a final <u>separation</u>…"
32.	"…the doctrine of <u>separation</u>…"
43.	"that a <u>separation</u>…would take place"

[The word <u>Separation</u> appears Seven [7] times in *Common Sense*.]

Also, from the "Declaration:" "…the necessity which denounces our eternal <u>separation</u>…"

DECLARATION (7 times)

"...we do assert and declare these Colonies to
be free and independent states..."
– Declaration of Independence*

From *Common Sense:*

Page

52.	"...and until an independence is declared..."
55.	"...nothing can settle our affairs so expeditiously as an open and determined declaration for independence..."
56.	"Should a manifesto be published, and dispatched to foreign courts, setting forth the miseries we have endured, and the peaceful methods which we have ineffectually used to redress; declaring at the same time, that not being able, any longer to live happily or safely under the cruel disposition of the British court, we had been driven to the necessity of breaking off all conexion with her;..."

INDEPENDENCE (26 TIMES)

"I have always considered the independence of this continent, as an event which sooner or later must take place..." – *Common Sense* pages 32-33

"; and finally we do assert and declare these Colonies to be free and independent states..." – (Declaration of Independent – John Adams copy.)

Page

35.	"...nothing but independence,..."
36.	"...many...dreaded an independence..."

---

* The John Adam's copy. Also, Jefferson's 'Rough Draft'

Page

37.	"…fear of respecting <u>independence</u>…"
40.	"A government of our own is our Natural right."
41.	"Ye that oppose <u>independence</u> now…"
43.	"…fitness of the continent for <u>independence</u>."
44.	"…An <u>independent</u> constitution of its own…"
50.	"…an argument in favor of independence."
55.	"…Nothing can settle our affairs so expeditiously as an open and determined <u>declaration for independence</u>."
56.	"…until by an <u>independence</u>, we take rank with other nations."
56.	"…until an <u>independence</u> is declared…"
57.	"-…and the (kings) speech…, prepared a way for the manly principles of <u>independence</u>."
59.	"…reconciliation or <u>independence</u>?"
60.	"But it is the <u>independence</u> of this country…"
62.	"…<u>independence</u> being a single simple line…"
65.	Independence appears once and independency appears twice on page #65.
65.	"There are three different ways by which an independency may hereafter be effected…" "By the legal voice of the people in congress; by a military power; or by a mob…"
66.	The word independence appears four times on page 66 of this the Barnes & Noble edition.
67.	"…and a virtuous supporter of the Rights of Mankind and of the Free and independent States of America.

The word <u>Independence</u> appears no less than 26 times in Thomas Paine's *Common Sense*.

"Tis Time to Part."

From: *COMMON SENSE*
[DO IT NOW]

TRADE AND COMMERCE (15 times)

"for cutting off our trade…"
-Declaration of Independence

(From *Common Sense*) [Trade appears 9 <u>times</u> Commerce appears 6 <u>times.</u>]

Page	
23.	"The articles of <u>commerce</u>…"
26.	"Our plan is <u>commerce</u>…"
26.	"…to have America a <u>free port</u>."
26.	"Her <u>trade</u> will always be a protection…"
27.	"As Europe is our market for <u>trade</u>…."
27.	"…(if) war, the trade of America goes to ruin;…"
32.	"A temporary stoppage of <u>trade</u>…."
44.	"the diminution of <u>trade</u>…."
46.	"…a fleet as an article of <u>commerce</u>,…"
49.	"To unite the sinews of <u>commerce</u> and defence…"
51.	"…an increase of <u>trade</u> and population;…"
56.	"…Our desire of entering into <u>trade</u> with them."
60.	"…limited in its <u>commerce</u>…"
60.	"It is the <u>commerce</u> and NOT the conquest…"
67.	"…offering to open the <u>trade</u>."
67.	", peace with <u>trade</u>, is preferable to war…"

"for cutting off our <u>Trade</u> with <u>All</u> <u>Parts</u> of the <u>World</u>;…"
- <u>Declaration of Independence.</u>

<u>Self Evident</u>
(From *Common Sense*)

Pages 59 and 60: "It is in reality a <u>SELF-EVIDENT</u> position…"

"We hold these truths to be self-evident…" –Declaration of Independence.

Note: Self-evident was crossed out in Thomas Jefferson's "Rough draught, and –"sacred and undeniable was written above it. Then self-evident was put back. The original wording - self-evident - was reinserted at the behest of Ben. Franklin or John Adams in my opinion; or possibly by Jefferson himself…

Also, from *Common Sense* - Page #7

"That the crown is this overbearing part in the English constitution needs not to be mentioned, and that it derives its whole consequence merely from being the giver of places and pensions is <u>self-evident</u>."

<u>From Common Sense</u>
<u>The "Slavery Clause"</u>

From the ORIGINAL '<u>Declaration of Independence</u>': He has waged cruel war against human nature itself, violating its most Sacred RIGHT of Life and Liberty in the Persons of a distant People who never offended him, captivating and carrying them into Slavery in another Hemisphere, or to incur miserable Death, in their Transportation thither. This piratical Warfare…is the warfare of the Christian King of Great Britain.

He has prostituted his Negative (veto) for Suppressing every legislative Attempt to prohibit or restrain an execrable Commerce, determined to keep open a Market where Men Should be bought and

Sold. Of course Thomas Paine meant men, women and children. He was well aware of what was going on in this execrable commerce.

Intro

I.   "...As the good people of this country are grievously oppressed..."

"The cause of America is, ...,the cause of all mankind

II.   "...declaring war against the natural rights of all mankind..."

Page No.

9.   "Mankind being originally equals in the order of creation..."

10.   "As the exalting one man so greatly above the rest, cannot be justified on the equal rights of nature..."

39.   "...frame a Continental Charter (Constitution)... ...securing freedom and property to all men..."

41.   "...(Britain) hath stirred up the Indians and negroes to destroy us-..."
(If slavery were abolished at the same time as the Declaration of Independence, the slaves would not HAVE BEEN tempted to join the British.)

43.   "...in order to remove mistakes..."

59.   "-Ye, whose office it is to watch over the morals of a nation..."

65.   "...We have every opportunity...to form the noblest, purest constitution on the face of the earth."

65.   ", and a race of men...are to receive their portion of freedom..."

67.   "and unite in drawing a line, which, like an act of oblivion, shall bury in forgetfulness every former dissention."

<u>Slavery</u>
[from: *Common Sense*]

Page no.

67.   "...and a virtuous supporter of the RIGHTS of MANKIND, and of the FREE and INDEPENDENT STATES of AMERICA."

"The slavery clause in the Declaration of Independence could Not have been written by an owner of slaves, nor could an owner of slaves have written the Declaration of Independence."
- Joseph Lewis, author of "Thomas Paine, Author of the Declaration of Independence."
(Pages 150 to 169 are very informative)

Thomas Jefferson was not interested in abolition; and he was not interested in abolition in 1776

- ✓ Thomas Jefferson did not think that slaves should be freed as a matter of principle.
- ✓ Thomas Jefferson did not believe that negroes had a fundamental right to be free.
- ✓ Thomas Jefferson did not believe that negroes could live under the same government as 'white' people.
- ✓ Thomas Jefferson did not think that the 'Bill of Rights' applied to negroes
- ✓ Thomas Jefferson considered blacks inferior.
- ✓ He did nothing to effect emancipation for – 50 – year after 1776; and nothing for – 46 – years after the Pennsylvania Act Abolishing Slavery, March 1st, 1780.

Thomas Jefferson was content "to leave to future efforts, its (slavery) final eradication..." (note: eradication, not emancipation) Thomas

Jefferson did not fight for or even defend the "Slavery Clause" in Congress and did not prevent its elimination. The sentiments in the Slavery Clause were not Jefferson's. A strong case could be made that the continuation of Slavery provided a political and an economic benefit to Jefferson.

I am not aware of any evidence that the OTHER members of the committee APPOINTED to write the 'Declaration', were opposed to the 'Slavery Clause'. (B. Franklin, John Adams, R. Livingston, Roger Sherman.)

Consider Thomas Paine's position. In 1798, Paine wrote: "I despair of seeing an abolition of the infernal traffic in negroes. We must push the (nefarious) matter..." Paine meant to continue the work for emancipation and abolition.

Joseph Lewis placed the responsibility for the elimination of the Slavery Clause squarely on Jefferson's shoulders. Joseph Lewis also wrote: "What a confession of weakness on the part of Jefferson..."

The Slavery Clause is a blistering condemnation of African slavery in America. The words come from the pen of Thomas Paine. The ideas are Thomas Paine's. They present an impassioned picture of King George's cruelty and Christian infidelity.

Would Jefferson compose such a piece and then change his mind and strike it out? I don't think so. Jefferson would not write an anti-slavery clause because he could not.

When Thomas Paine wrote: "Securing freedom and property to all men", he meant all men and women and no exclusions due to race, color or creed. In his essay condemning "African Slavery in America", March 8, 1775, Thomas Paine uses some strong words that do not appear in *Common Sense*; E.g. "...desperate wretches...willing to steal and enslave men by violence and murder..."; "savage practice', by "Christianized people; "By such wicked and inhuman ways"; "execrable commerce"; outrage against humanity and justice"; "practiced by pretend Christians", "the barbarous practice"...

No, Thomas Jefferson is not the author of the "Slavery Clause", and he is not the author of the Declaration of Independence.

Usurpation

"But when a long Train of Abuses and Usurpations…"
– (Declaration of Independence)

"…to disavow these Usurpations,…"
– (Declaration of Independence)

[from: *Common Sense*]

Page No.

Intro I.   "…to reject the usurpations…"

16.   (RE: Origin of Kings)
       "…viz., either by lot, by election, or by usurpation.…"

17.   "As to usurpation, no man will be so hardy as to defend it;…"

17.   "…and that William the Conqueror was an usurper is a fact Not to be contradicted."

Also, from the Declaration of Independence:

"We have appealed to their Native Justice…to disavow these usurpations…"

Usurpation appears four times in *Common Sense.*

Oppressions

"In every stage of these Oppressions…"
From the <u>Declaration of Independence.</u>

[from: *Common Sense*]

Page no.

I.   "…and as the good people of this country are
          grievously oppressed…"

8.   "…it is wholly owing to the constitution of the people,
          and not the constitution of the government that the
          crown is not as oppressive in England as in Turkey."

9.   "Oppression is often the consequence, but seldom or
          never means of riches."

11.   "The children of Israel being oppressed by the
          Midianites, Gideon marched against them…"

42.   "Every spot of the old world is overrun with
          oppression."

<u>Tyranny</u>

"A prince whose Character is thus marked by every Act which may define a Tyrant..."
<u>-Declaration of Independence</u>

"for tyranny over a people..."
<u>-Declaration of Independence in Thomas Jefferson's handwriting</u>
"on <u>S</u>o many Acts of Tyranny without a Mask..."
<u>-from the John Adams copy of the original Declaration of Independence.</u>

[from: *Common Sense*]

Page no.

5.	"When the world was overrun with tyranny..."
5.	"...tyranny in the person of the king."
5.	"...tyranny in the persons of the peers."
24.	"...the same tyranny which drove the first emigrants from home..."
41.	"Ye that oppose independence... Ye are opening a door to eternal tyranny..."
57.	"...offering up human sacrifices to the pride of tyrants.
58.	(RE: King George III speech, January 1776) "Brutality and tyranny appear on the face of it."

Tyranny appears six times in *Common Sense*.

DEBT

"...have full power to...establish commerce, and do all other acts and things which Independent States may of right do."
-From the Declaration of Independence:

Page

28.   "...As we are running the next generation into DEBT,..."

44.   "DEBTS we have none..."

44.   ..."...Leaving...a DEBT upon their backs..."

44.   "the DEBT we may contract..."

44.   "No nation ought to be without a DEBT."

44.   "A DEBT is a national bond..."

45.   ...for a part of English DEBT, (we) "could have a Navy."

45.   "America is without DEBT."

50.   Land sales could pay off DEBT.

61.   "It is by the sale of those lands, that the DEBT may be sunk..."

64.   "...our public DEBTS (...for defense) discharged..."

Note: the word DEBT does NOT appear in the Declaration of Independence.

Debt appears thirteen times in *Common Sense*.

Thomas Paine's treatment of the subject of DEBT (debts in caps on this page are mine) was done in order to overcome a possible objection to his "Manifesto" declaring total independence from Britain.

<u>British (Royal) Rule</u>:

The following – in brief outline form – is a list (not verbatim) of complaints given in the <u>Declaration of Independence</u>:

The present King of Great Britain has refused to pass Laws for the public good.

He has forbidden Laws of immediate and pressing importance.

He has refused to pass Laws that affect large districts of people.

He has called together legislative bodies at distant and inappropriate places.

He has dissolved Representative Houses.

He has exposed the States to dangers of invasion from without and…within.

He has refused to pass Laws to encourage emigration.

He has raised the conditions for Land acquisition.

He has obstructed the administration of Justice.

He controls the tenure and pay of Judges.

He has kept standing Armies among us.

He keeps the military over the civil authority.

He quarters armed troops among us. These troops are not held liable to capital punishment.

He has given his assent:
- ✓ for cutting off trade
- ✓ for imposing taxes
- ✓ for depriving us of Trial by Jury
- ✓ for transporting us to England to be tried
- ✓ for the expansion of Canada.

From the Declaration of Independence -
<u>Complaints of British Rule</u>

(The King) has given his assent. For taking away our Charters. For abolishing our most valuable laws. For altering our forms of Government.

For suspending our legislatures, (and) "declaring themselves invested with Power to legislate for us in all Cases Whatsoever –"

["America…ought to have the legislative powers in her own hands." –Common Sense]

"He has abdicated Government here, withdrawing his Governors, and declaring us, out of his Allegiance and Protection.

"He has plundered our Seas, ravaged our Coasts, burnt our Towns, and destroyed the Lives of our People.

"He is at this time transporting large Armies of foreign Mercenaries to compleat the Works of death, Desolation, and Tyranny, already begun with Circumstances of Cruelty and Perfidy unworthy the Head of a civilized nation.

"He has endeavoured to bring on the Inhabitants of our Frontiers, the merciless Indian Savages, whose known Rule of Warfare is an undistinguished Destruction of all Ages, Sexes and Conditions of Existence.

"He has incited treasonable insurrections of our fellow Citizens, and Allurements of Forfeiture and Confiscation of our Property."

"He has waged cruel War against human nature itself, violating its most Sacred Right of Life and Liberty in the persons of a distant People who never offended him, captivating and carrying them into slavery in another Hemisphere, or to incur miserable Death in their transportation thither. This piratical Warfare, the opprobrium of infidel Powers, is the Warfare of the Christian King of Great Britain.

"He has prostituted his Negative (veto) for Suppressing every legislative Attempt to prohibit or to restrain an execrable Commerce, determined to keep open a market where men should be bought and sold, and this Assemblage of Horrors might Want no Fact of distinguished Die."*

---

* Reference is made to the following extract: "…and this Assemblage of Horrors might Want no fact of distinguished Die." I do not believe that Thomas Jefferson is the author of this line. – J.H.

"...our repeated Petitions have been answered by repeated Injury. A Prince, whose Character is thus marked by every Act which may define a Tyrant, is unfit to be the Ruler of a People who mean to be free, -"

From the Declaration of Independence (not verbatim)
RE: British Rule

We have warned our British Brethren about their attempts to extend a Jurisdiction over these States.

We have reminded them of our emigration here and settlement at the expense of our own Blood and Treasure.

Submission to the British Parliament is not acceptable and never was.

We have appealed to their Native Justice to disavow these usurpations.

We must renounce these unfeeling Brethren; enemies in War, in Peace, friends.

The road to happiness is open to us.

We renounce all Allegiance.

We utterly dissolve and break off.

We declare these Colonies to be free and independent states.

We mutually pledge...our Lives our Fortunes and our Sacred Honor.

This concludes Part 2. It provides incontrovertible evidence that all of the ideas in the Declaration of Independence are contained in Thomas Paine's *Common Sense*.

PART 3
IDEAS FROM THE DECLARATION OF INDEPENDENCE AND CORRESPONDING IDEAS FROM *COMMON SENSE*[*]

---

[*]   (D. = Declaration of Independence)   (C. = Common Sense)

D.   to secure these ends, Governments are
        instituted.

    C.   the design and end of Government, viz.,   4
        freedom and security

D.   Whenever any form of Government becomes
        destructive of these ends

    C.   The <u>destruction</u> our property by an armed   65
        force.

D.   the Right to alter or abolish it.

    C.   "The doctrine of Separation."

D.   and to institute new government.

    C.   A government of our own is our natural right.   40

The numbers in the right margin refer to pages in the Barnes & Nobel
edition of *Common Sense.*

Corresponding Ideas

D.   likely to effect...Safety and <u>Happiness.</u>

    C.   strength of government and the <u>happiness</u> of   4
        the government.

D.   and usurpations.

    C.   "to reject the usurpations."

D.   the necessity to expunge their former systems
        of government.

    C.   the necessity of breaking off all connexion   56
        with her:

D.   establishment of an absolute Tyranny

    C.   "tyranny in the person of the King."

D.	He has refused Laws for the public good of immediate and pressing importance for the accommodation of large districts of people.	
C.	the king will have a 'negative' (veto) over the legislation of this continent.	33
C.	(King George III): "There shall be no laws but such as I like."	34
C.	the legislative powers in her own hands.	60
C.	Legislation without law.	62
D.	He has dissolved Representative houses repeatedly. He has (blocked) elections the State remaining in the mean time exposed to all the dangers of invasion from without and convulsions from within.	
C.	It is now the interest of America to provide for herself.	59
D.	He has obstructed the Laws for Naturalization in order to prevent population of these States.	
C.	…our newly arrived emigrants. Emigrants will not come…	3 35
D.	and raising the conditions of new Appropriations of Lands	
C.	The more land there is yet unoccupied, may be applied to discharge debt.	50
D.	He has made our Judges dependent on his will alone for their tenure and salaries.	
C.	In America the law is King.	40
C.	America…ought to have the legislative powers in her own hands.	60

D. He (the King) has sent swarms of officers to harass us and eat out our substance.

D. He has kept among us, in times of peace, Standing Armies and ships of war.

D. He has affected to render the Military superior to the Civil power.

D. For quartering large bodies of armed troops among us;

D. For protecting them from punishment for any murders, by a mock trial.

C. Is he, or is he not, a proper person to say, "You shall make no laws but what I please!"

D. For cutting off our trade.

C. Our plan is commerce. 26

C. "Peace with trade."

D. For imposing Taxes.

D. For depriving us of Trial by Jury.

D. For transporting us overseas to be tried.

D. For taking away our Charters.

D. For abolishing our most valuable Laws.

D. For altering the forms of our Government.

D. For suspending our Legislatures and

D. Declaring themselves to legislate for us in all cases whatsoever.

C. It is now the interest of America to provide for herself. 59

C. It is repugnant to reason to suppose that this continent can longer remain subject to any external power. 30

C. In free countries the law ought to be the king. 40

D.   He is waging War against us. He has plundered our seas; ravaged our coasts; burnt our towns; destroyed the lives of our people. He has transported armies of Mercenaries to compleat works of death and destruction, and tyranny and totally unworthy the head of a civilized nation.

C.   He (the king) hath wickedly broken through every moral and human obligation, trampled nature and conscience beneath his feet.   59

C.   America ought to have the legislative powers in her own hands.   60

C.   "The Rubicon is passed."   64

D.   He has excited insurrections and has endeavored to bring on the inhabitants of our frontiers the merciless Indian Savages.

C.   There are thousands…who would think it glorious to expel from the continent. That barbarous and hellish power, which <u>hath</u> stirred up the Indians and negroes and destroyed us.   41

D.   (The Slavery Clause)

C.   "Securing freedom and property to all men.

D.   He is now exciting those very people to rise in arms among us, and to purchase that liberty of which he has deprived them, by murdering the people upon whom he also obtruded them; thus paying off former <u>Crimes</u> against one people, with <u>Crimes</u> he urges them to commit against the lives of another.

C.   He hath stirred up the Indians and negroes   41
     to destroy us- the cruelty hath a double guilt.
     It is dealing brutally by us; and treacherously
     by them.

D.   Our repeated petitions have been answered
     by repeated injury.

C.   Every quiet method for peace hath been   31
     ineffectual. Our prayers have been rejected
     with disdain.

C.   As we have, without any good effect,   67
     withheld our trade to obtain redress, let us
     now try the alternative...

D.   A Prince whose character is thus marked by
     every act which may define a tyrant.

C.   Tyranny in the person of the King.   5

D.   is unfit to be the Ruler of a People who
     mean to be free.

C.   is he, or is he not a proper person to say to 33
     these colonies "you shall make no LAW but
     what I please"?

C.   is the power, who is jealous of our prosperity, 34
     a proper power to govern us?

C.   he hath wickedly broken through ever moral   59
     and human obligation..

D.   Attempts by their Legislature to extend
     jurisdiction OVER us.

C.   America...ought to have the legislative   60
     power in her own hands.

C.   "The blood of the slain, the weeping voice of 27
     nature cries, 'Tis time to part."

D.   We have reminded them of...our emigration and settlement here.

    C.   This new world hath been the asylum for the   24
persecuted lovers of civil and religious liberty from every part of Europe.
Hither have they fled, not from the tender embraces of the mother, but from the cruelty of the monster; and it is so far true of England, that the same tyranny which drove the first emigrants from home, pursues their descendants still.

D.   At the expense of our own Blood and Treasure.

    C.   ...no terms can be obtained ...equal to the   32
expense of Blood and Treasure we have been already put to.

D.   ...to send over not only soldiers...
and foreign mercenaries to <u>invade</u>...us.

    C.   the <u>invasion</u> of our country by fire and   65
sword.

D.   These facts have given the <u>last stab</u> of agonizing affection...

    C.   The <u>last cord</u> is now broken.   41

    C.   not being able...to live happily.   56

    C.   "The Rubicon is passed."   64

D.   To <u>renounce</u> forever these unfeeling brethren.

    C.   to <u>renounce</u> a power in whom we can have   28
no trust.

D.   reject and <u>renounce</u> all Allegiance and subjection to the Kings of Great Britain.

C. instructs us to <u>renounce</u> the alliance…	26
D. the road to <u>happiness</u> and glory is open to us too.	
C. …that not being able, any longer to live <u>happily</u> or safely. "Toward her future happiness."	56
D. We utterly dissolve and <u>break off</u> all political Connections…	
C. We had been driven to the necessity of <u>breaking off all</u> connexion with her.	56
D. That these United Colonies are, and of Right ought to be <u>free and independent states.</u>	
C. Natural rights of all mankind.	Authors Intro. II
C. and a virtuous supporter of the Rights of Mankind, and of the <u>Free and Independent</u> States of America.	67

REPUBLIC

C. "The word <u>republican</u> appears two times in *Common Sense* on page #5 Barnes and Noble edition 1995.

"….if we will suffer ourselves to examine the component parts of the English constitution, we shall find them to be the base remains of two ancient tyrannies compounded with some new republican materials."

First-…monarchical tyranny…

Secondly-…aristocratical tyranny…

"Thirdly- the new <u>republican</u> materials, in the persons of the commons, on whose virtue depends the freedom of England." (p. 5)

C. "The nearer any government approaches to a <u>republic</u>, the less business there for a king. (p. 20)

C. "Sir William Meredith calls (England) a <u>republic</u>...but it is unworthy of the name..." (p. 20)

C. "For it is the <u>Republican</u> and not the monarchical part of the constitution...which Englishmen glory in..." (p. 20)

C. "- and it is easy to see that when <u>republican</u> virtue fails, slavery ensues." (p. 20)

C. "Why is the constitution of England sickly, but because monarchy hath poisoned the <u>republic</u>, the crown hath engrossed the commons." (p. 20)

(the words Republic and Republican appear six times on page #20)

C. "...regal authority swells into a rupture with foreign powers, in instances where a <u>republican</u> government, by being formed on more natural principles would negotiate the mistake. (p.37)

The word REPUBLIC does not appear in the Declaration of Independence.

Paine, Thomas. *Common Sense*

CONSTITUTION
From the Declaration of Independence (not verbatim)

D. "Whenever any form of Gov't becomes destructive…

D. "…Right of the people to alter or abolish…

D. "…and to institute new Government

D. "…right…duty, to throw off such Government

D. and to provide new guards

D. "…to subject us to a jurisdiction foreign to our constitution

D. (the King, George III is responsible)

For:		
	Quartering troops	Plundering our seas
	Cutting off trade	Burning our town
	Imposing taxes	Permitting slavery
	Abolishing laws	Using foreign mercenaries
	Waging war against us	Rejecting our petitions for peace

D. "…but that Submission to their Parliament was no part of our constitution, nor ever in idea,…"

From Common Sense

"Let a continental conference be held…" (p.38)

"Let their business be to frame a Continental Charter…" (p.39)

Also, in a Letter to George Washington, July 30, 1796, reference is made to a Constitutional Convention.

"But as to the point of consolidating the states into a Federal Government, it so happens, that the proposition for that purpose came originally from myself. I proposed it in a letter to Chancellor Livingston in the spring of 1782, while that gentleman was Minister for Foreign Affairs". (*Life & Writings*, p. 178-179)

"But I can go to a date and to a fact beyond this; for the proposition for electing a Continental convention to form the Continental Government is one of the subjects treated in the pamphlet" (*Common Sense*)

PART 4

Thomas Paine knew that he was the creator, the inventor of the United States of America. No where, in all of Thomas Paine's writings, does he credit anyone else as the sole and independent innovator of the United States. Paine was quick and generous in his expressions of praise and gratitude to anyone who supported or contributed, even in the least way, to American Independence. He was just as quick to rebuke and censure anyone who attempted to subvert or traduce his revolutionary innovation.

All due credit and thanks should be given to George Washington, John Adams, Thomas Jefferson, Benjamin Franklin, Richard Henry Lee, Patrick Henry, George Mason, James Madison, James Monroe, James Otis, Nathaniel Greene; and many other Patriots including and especially those who suffered and died in order that we could enjoy the benefits of a new country born in freedom, for their contributions and the parts that they acted. But it was Thomas Paine and Thomas Paine alone who integrated all of the components necessary to achieve the republic of the United States as a government of and by the people.

These necessary components were: separation from England, unite to declare independence, eliminate a King, establish a representative Republic, mobilize and wage a defensive war against England until America is victorious, have each Colony write and ratify a state constitution, build a navy, convene a national convention in order to frame a continental constitution which would secure and guarantee natural and civil rights for all of the people without distinction; and would allow for change and correction by future amendments.

Not everything was accomplished by the Declaration of Independence. The American Revolution eliminated a monarchic system with one man or one woman, a king or a queen, or any autocrat, ruling over all of the people, and replaced it with a representative republic. The business of government would be conducted by the people and for the benefit of the people, and not, I repeat, not by career politicians. This was a world class innovation. This is not to say that the ideological revolution was perfect. What 'new invention', what successful invention, does not change as a result of improvements? Residual problems, among others, such as: 'Slavery, Individual Rights including women's rights, "and above all Freedom of Religion, and a ratified constitution, had to be addressed and resolved. Thomas Paine had all of these advances in his mind and in his heart.

It would be hard to believe that George Washington, although never shy about advancing in his own interests, and advancing his own station, could have devised a plan to secede from Great Britain, and formulate the design specifications in order to construct a democratic Republic. He never claimed that he did so. He did not have to, because the work was already done and published in *Common Sense* by Thomas Paine.

As regards Washington's record on Abolition, or even the importation of slaves, it may be best that the American History scholars tackle that job. They are welcome to it. I choose neither to join in their researches, nor question their findings. But, if it is insisted that Washington "is the father of his country", then he was the father of a slave country.

John Adams and Thomas Paine

John Adams hated Thomas Paine.

According to Harvey J. Kaye, Thomas Paine's egalitarian and democratic spirit troubled John Adams (p. 52) also Adams distrusted "the people" "and in years to come, he would grow to despise and envy Paine". Regarding *Common Sense*, Adams admitted that he could not have written any thing in so manly and striking a style and then berated Paine's abilities as a constitution writer.

But Kaye wrote, (p. 53) "Through the rest of his life, John Adams would never stop railing against Paine that "profligate and impious star of Disaster" and referred to Paine as a "poor, ignorant, malicious, short-sighted Crapulous Mass. Yet, John Adams wrote that "History is to ascribe the American Revolution to Thomas Paine". Whatever recondite meaning that Adams attached to it, Adams wrote that "History is to ascribe the American Revolution to Thomas Paine."

"Adams was no democrat" "...Adams feared Paine's plan for government" (Kaye, p. 53) Thomas Paine's plan was government of the people. This means that all governmental authority rests in the hands of the nations people, its citizens. John Adams didn't get it. Neither did the rest of the so-called Founding Fathers. None of the "following" founding fathers understood the concept of individualism and democracy. (Demo=the people, crat=rule). Democracy means that the government is run by the people. An annual election of a President by congress, selected from each state, by lot, on a rotating basis, as noted by Kaye on page 47, would have prevented many of the "necessary evils" of our government during the last 220 years, in my opinion. Incidentally, I am not aware of any natural law that says that a government must be a necessary evil.

Getting back to John Adams, a 'one-term' president, who lost to Jefferson in 1800, Kaye wrote: "Ever envious of Paine's talents and presumed place in history, outraged by his democratic ideals and appeal, and still bitter about the election, John Adams hated Paine."(Kaye, p. 94)

In 1805 Adams wrote to a friend: "I know not whether any man in the world has had more influence on its inhabitants or affairs for the last thirty years than Tom Paine. There can be no severer satyr on the age. For such a mongrel between pigs and puppy, begotten by a wild boar on a bitch wolf; never before in any age of the world was suffered by the poltroonery* of mankind to run through such a career of mischief". (p. 94) Future generations will call Thomas Paine HEROIC.

I am trying to be brief, but I must mention Abigail Adams who was Adams' "better half". One of Abigail's most famous quotes is given here: "I long to hear that you - John Adams - have declared independency. And, by the way, in the new code of laws which I suppose it will be necessary for you to make, I desire you would remember the ladies and be more generous and favorable to them than your ancestors. Do not put such unlimited power into the hands of the husbands. Remember, all men would be tyrants if they could. If particular care and attention is not paid to the ladies, we are determined to foment a rebellion and (we) will not hold ourselves bound by any laws in which we have no voice or representation."(*Letters*, p. 148)

John Adams rejected Abigail's protestations. He wrote: "Depend upon it, we know better than to repeal our masculine systems ...which would completely subject us to the despotism of the petticoat..." He was opposed to women's rights. He did not understand what Thomas Paine meant by equality. John Adams (1735-1826) died when he was 91.

Abigail Adams (1744-1818) died when she was 74. Abigail Adams was a remarkable woman and mother; admirable in every way.

In March of 1775, John Adams considered Independence such a colossal venture that he wrote: "(it) is an Hobgoblin of so frightful mein, that it would throw a delicate Person into fits to look it in the face."(Lewis, p. 36) On April 29, 1776, Adams wrote to Abigail, despite his personal jealousy and antagonism: "*Common Sense*, like a ray of revelation, has come in Seasonably to clear our doubts, and to fix our choice."(p. 51)

I believe John Adams' jealousy turned into envy. Perhaps, it might not be saying too much, that Adams harbored sentiments of disappointment when, in a letter to Jefferson, on June 22, 1776 he wrote, "...yet History is to ascribe the American Revolution to Thomas Paine."(p. 51) Yet that enigmatic character that was John Adams had a spark of integrity in its make-up. That light manifested itself when he copied out, word for word, Thomas Paine's, the original, Declaration of

Independence. It included all of the "HATHS", the capitalized words, the 'Slavery Clause', identifying expressions such as, "...the Warfare of the Christian King of Great Britain" and "He has prostituted his negative" (failed to veto wrongful and cruel pieces of legislation.), "execrable Commerce", "determined to keep open a market (sic) where men should be bought and sold", and (what I believe is a strange and unfamiliar, but autobiographical phrase, viz.): "and that this assemblage of Horrors might want no fact of distinguished Die".

John Adams ought to be remembered for his verbatim copy of Thomas Paine's Declaration of Independence because Jefferson made a hand drawn copy of Paine's original and then expunged the 'Slavery Clause'. Neither John Adams nor the other so-called Founding Fathers understood "Government of the people".

As a last note on John Adams and before some thoughts about Thomas Jefferson, some comments about David McCullough's biography of John Adams might not be out of order. In McCullough's book there are at least twelve references to Thomas Paine and his works. Of the twelve, three citations say the same thing, viz.: "Thomas Paine has a better hand at pulling down than building." These are derogatory statements and they are not true. The other nine references are merely innocuous citations from Paine's writings.

Thomas Paine was a builder, an inventor, the author of the Declaration of Independence and the creator and sole Founder of the United States of America. I took time to re-search carefully McCullough's 751 page book on John Adams. He did not include in it, a photo copy or a printed copy of John Adams hand-written copy of the original Declaration of Independence. How convenient. Tsk.

Thomas Jefferson

Thomas Jefferson deserves all of the credit due to him as one of the traditional "Founding Fathers". He was one of a group of illustrious men who followed Thomas Paine's lead. He was a convert to Thomas Paine's idea of creating a continental Republic out of the thirteen British Colonies in America. "In late 1774, no one, not even Jefferson, was ready to sever allegiance to the King or to separate the American colonies from the British Empire." (Randall, p. 215)

In his "A Summary View of the Rights of British America", Jefferson wrote, "It is neither our wish nor our interest to separate from her."(Randall, p. 250) (Britain) And in a letter to John Randolph, on November 29, 1775, he wrote, "Believe me, dear sir, there is not in the British Empire a man who more cordially loves a union with Great Britain than I do." (Lewis, p. 36) In this "Summary View of the Rights of British America", Jefferson was writing as a British subject who was loyal to the King. He did not give any indication of compromising or breaking his allegiance to the crown. He distained the British parliament. He wanted the colonies to make their own laws. At this time Jefferson was an advocate for redress and reconciliation. Each colony would be autonomous and control its own affairs, while staying loyal to the king and remaining part of the British imperial empire.

Jefferson was not a delegate to the first Continental Congress which met on September 5, 1774 and voted to reconvene in May, 1775. He was chosen to be a 'deputy' delegate to the second continental congress, just in case the ailing Peyton Randolph could not attend. (Randall, p. 228) Jefferson took two weeks to travel to Philadelphia in June, 1775. He stopped along the way to buy a racehorse (p. 239). In my opinion Jefferson was not thinking about total secession at that time. According to John Adams, Jefferson was a silent member of congress. Jefferson returned to Virginia in August 1775. During this month he expressed a wish to John Randolph that he could withdraw "totally from the public stage: and live in "domestic ease and tranquility". (p. 247)

In a letter dated November 29, 1775, to John Randolph, Jefferson wrote: "Believe me, dear sir, there is not in the British Empire who more cordially loves a union with Great Britain than I do". (p. 247) But he implied that any such union would have to be on American and not parliamentarian terms. Nine years later, Jefferson reflected in his "Notes on Virginia": "It is well known that in July, 1775, a separation from Great Britain and establishment of [a] republican government had never entered any ones mind." (Randall, p. 250) This is not true. It entered the mind of Thomas Paine.

The battles of Lexington and Concord took place on April 19, 1775. Thomas Paine wrote, "All plans [and] proposals prior to the nineteenth of April [1775] ...are superseded and useless now."(*Common Sense*, p. 22) "No man was a warmer wisher for a reconciliation than myself, before the fatal nineteenth of April, 1775, (Battle of Lexington) but the moment the event of that day was made known, I rejected the hardened, sullen-tempered Pharaoh of England forever, and disdain the wretch..." (p. 33) "...the independency of America should have been considered as dating its era from, and published by, the first musket that was fired against her." (p. 65)

At the end of 1775, Jefferson had many concerns. In addition to the lingering sorrow of the death of his little daughter, Jane, he was worried about the health of his wife, Patty. He was burdened with serious responsibilities involving his family, the cause of Virginia, his plantations and his reported eighty-three slaves, and of course, the war.

Then on March 31, 1776 his mother died. Her death, along with his other anxieties, "triggered a five week bout of migraine headaches that left him bedridden and unable to write about her death or anything else", according to Randall. During this period, "while Jefferson was convalescing at Monticello, his fellow congressman, Thomas Nelson, sent him, from Philadelphia, a copy of *Common Sense*. (Randall, p. 257) Randall wrote that Jefferson "agreed with most of it."

On May 6, 1776, Jefferson left Virginia and traveled north to Philadelphia and Congress. On May 14, 1776, according to Randall, Jefferson arrived in Philadelphia. "Here in late May and early June he finished writing a series of bleak reports and recommendations that resulted from the failed American invasion of Canada." (p. 263) On May 15, 1776, the resolution that Virginia's delegate to the Continental Congress be instructed to propose that Congress "declare the United Colonies free and independent states absolved from all allegiance to or dependence upon the Crown or parliament of Great Britain" (p.262) was passed unanimously by the Virginia Convention. On May 27, 1776, the instructions arrived in Philadelphia and they were presented to John Hancock (p. 262) Jefferson was 'in the dark' about Virginia's 'declare independence' resolution of May 15, 1776. It was twelve days before he learned of it on May 27, 1776.

But Jefferson wanted to be recalled to Virginia. Randall says he "brooded about being in Philadelphia" (p. 263) It was only two or three days after he arrived in Philadelphia, that Jefferson wrote a letter to Thomas Nelson [dated May 16, 1776 by Randall and dated May 17, 1776 by Joseph Lewis](Lewis, p. 37) expressing his wish to be recalled. "Should our convention propose to establish a new form of government, perhaps it might be agreeable to recall for a short time their delegates... for should a bad government be instituted for us..." Clearly, Jefferson was open to a form of reconciliation at this time.

In the same letter, Jefferson wrote: "I suppose they will tell us what to say on the subject of Independence."(p. 38) Jefferson was not leading anything. He was not writing about Independence. He wrote nothing about establishing a Republic. Far from being a passionate patriot, he seemed indifferent to the proceedings of Congress. He was not interested in the creation of the United States at that time. He wanted to go home.

On June 7, 1776, Richard Henry Lee proposed the resolution that "these colonies are, and of right ought to be, free and independent states." On June 9, 1776, congress voted to postpone the vote on Independence to July 1, 1776. (Randall, p. 266)

Jefferson welcomed the delay. In my opinion, Jefferson had a proclivity for procrastination. On June 11, 1776, Congress appointed a committee to prepare a Declaration of Independence. (p. 266) The committee members were: Benjamin Franklin, John Adams, Roger Sherman, Robert Livingston and Thomas Jefferson.

Was Jefferson writing a Declaration of Independence? No, he was not. What was he doing? According to Randall: "As soon as Jefferson learned that the Virginia Convention had declared independence from Great Britain, (May 15, 1776) and was creating a commonwealth, he set about writing the first of three drafts of a new constitution for Virginia, his home country." (p. 267)

Around this time, Jefferson wrote to Thomas Nelson, hinting that the Virginia Convention should recall him and use his writing skills. "He urged Nelson to have him recalled if even for a short time…" To Thomas Nelson, Jefferson wrote: "Should our (Virginia) convention propose to establish a new form of government, perhaps it might be agreeable to recall for a short time their delegates. It is a work of the most interesting nature and such as every individual would wish to have a voice in. In truth, it is the whole object of the present controversy, for should a bad government be instituted for us, in future it had been as well to have accepted at first the bad one offered us from beyond the water without the risk and expense of contest." Randall made the assumption: "He had little doubt that Congress would vote independence. The outcome in his native Virginia was far more important to him." (p. 267)

Jefferson was a Virginian and thirty-three years old and a lawyer. There is no question that Jefferson was a strong unyielding advocate for 'States' Rights'. But what on earth was he thinking? Congress was about to declare the United States a free and independent nation. Yet, Jefferson's beloved Virginia held top priority and instead of waiting for a vote to adopt the Declaration, Jefferson desired to leave Congress. But he stayed and signed.

Why was Jefferson so anxious to get back to Virginia? The "congressional resolution" passed on May 15, 1776, suppressing all royal governments in the individual colonies, meant that each colony had to frame its own constitution. There would be time for this after American independence was declared. Also, constitutions could be amended. Did Jefferson want to protect the 'country' of Virginia against the new United States Government? Did he want to guard against 'Emancipation'? Was Jefferson confused when he wrote, "should a bad government be instituted for us...beyond the water." Who would do the instituting, England? Jefferson knew that the passage of Richard Henry Lee's Resolution (June 7, 1776) was a forgone conclusion. Also, he had a copy of Thomas Paine's original Declaration of Independence in hand. The last clause in Jefferson's letter as given above is: "without the risk and expense of a contest." This was a strange idea in view of the fact that the colonies were already at war with England.

As noted above, Jefferson wrote three drafts of his proposed Virginia Constitution. He sent his third draft - a blueprint for a new nation – Virginia – to George Wythe on June 13, 1776. But Jefferson's proposed constitution was too late and George Mason's constitution was accepted. It is noted that Jefferson's plan was sent on June 13, 1776; six days after R.H. Lee's resolution was proposed. So, during this portion of time Jefferson was not writing the Declaration of Independence, he was writing Virginia Constitutions.

Thomas Jefferson wanted to return to Monticello. After the adoption of the Declaration of Independence, "his strongest reaction was to let it be known that he did not want a second term in Congress."(Randall, p. 279) "Disappointed that he played no important role in writing the new Virginia constitution, Jefferson was determined to quit congress and return to Virginia politics. He could not see into the future." (p. 279) (I take this to mean that we can eliminate the word visionary in the apotheosis of Thomas Jefferson, assuming that it has not been ruled out, already, by his record on Slavery.)

"To him the Continental Congress was a temporary meeting in convention of delegates from the new states, of little importance in the long run. Even if there were a permanent confederacy of states, it would be of far less importance than the reshaping of the weak old English colonies into strong independent countries." (p. 279) "Jefferson wanted to join his friends in Virginia in an effort that mattered far more to him than writing of declarations and resolutions in Philadelphia. He wanted to carry out a revolution that would last, a revolution in the laws of his native country."(p. 280)

The preceding quotes do not describe a man who desired to unite the new states and strengthen and further develop the embryo Republic of the United States. Rather, they describe a person who does not get the big picture. Lawyer Jefferson wanted "a sweeping legislative reform movement that would transform the old tidewater aristocracy into a democratic Republic."(p. 286) Jefferson begged to get out of Congress. His one-year term in Congress was due to expire in August of 1776. He wrote letters to Edmund Pendleton, George Gilmer and Edmund Randolph imploring to be relieved. "Despite his pleas, he was reelected." (p. 280) It appears that Jefferson was a reluctant "founding father". The following information, as provided by Randall lends support to this assumption.

Randall, then, recalls that Jefferson, in his 'Summary View' [of British Rights in America (the second part of the title was conveniently omitted)] "had not gone so far as to recommend independence; nothing he had written since then for public consumption had gone any further. In Congress, he had coauthored key documents with the conservative John Dickinson. (Dickinson was a reluctant, last minute patriot; but he finally came 'round.) (p. 280)

"When instructions from Virginia, to vote for independence, arrived in Philadelphia on May 26, 1776, Jefferson had been among those OPPOSED to introducing them for a vote until there was stronger support from the more timid states." (p. 280) It may not be unnecessary to recall Virginia's unanimous instructions to their delegates that they "propose that Congress declare the United Colonies free and independent states, and to give Virginia's assent "to whatever measures may be thought proper and necessary by the Congress for forming foreign alliances and a confederation of the Colonies." (p. 262) I am not aware that Virginia's instructions to their delegates authorized them to oppose and delay, for any reason, Virginia's assent to the Declaration. Jefferson had his reasons for the hesitation, I'm sure. However, it seems to be another example of procrastination. But a bigger question comes to mind. What was Jefferson doing to encourage and support those 'timid' states which were unready for independence but were 'fast ripening'? Where was the "passion"?

Contrast Thomas Paine's passion for independence against Jefferson's lack of interest and procrastination. Paine wrote: "Throw off dependence"; "the weeping voice of nature cries, 'tis time to part", "Everything that is right or natural pleads for separation": "The present time is the true time". (*Common Sense*, p. 51)

On the other hand, Jefferson was pleading to go home. He was "mounting a virtual campaign against his reelection" to Congress. Jefferson had a subordinate and reluctant role in the creation of America. He referred to himself as a PASSIVE AUDITOR of the proceedings of Congress. Did Jefferson's reticence engender some whisperings about his fealty to the Revolution? I don't know. Randall speaks of rumors of Jefferson's disloyalty to the revolution. Because it was known that he no longer wished to serve in Congress, he polled fourth out of the five new delegates. "Delegates had swung their votes to more willing candidates. But Jefferson still worried that he was suspected of being less than staunch in the cause of independence, that his desire to resign had marked him as a Loyalist."(Randall, p. 281) Whether Jefferson was an unwilling or a less than willing delegate, he felt it necessary to express his position to one of his friends. On July 1, 1776 in a letter to Will Fleming, he wrote: "If any doubt has arisen as to me, my country will have my political creed in the form of a "Declaration, etc" (sic) which I was lately directed to draw. This will give decisive proof that my own sentiment concurred with the [May 15] vote [for independence] they [the Virginia convention] instructed us to give. (p. 280)

In the above quote, "...my country will have my political creed...", I believe Jefferson was referring to Virginia. The part of the quote, "which I was lately directed to draw: shows that drafting the Declaration of Independence was an assigned duty. Jefferson did not originate the idea. He did not write a declaration before he was appointed to the committee on June 10, 1776 to draft the "Declaration". According to Jefferson: "The committee of 5 met, no such thing as a subcommittee was proposed, but they unanimously pressed on myself alone to undertake the draught. I consented; I drew it."(p. 261) Jefferson did not say I was the author or the 'Declaration' was an original composition of mine. In fact, Jefferson never claimed that he was the author of the Declaration of Independence. Besides, Richard Henry Lee's resolution that "these united colonies are..., free and independent states"(4) was proposed on June 7, 1776. We shall see that this resolution was approved unanimously by Congress on July 2, 1776.

In the same quote, as written above, the extract from the letter to Will Fleming which begins, "This will give decisive proof", Jefferson avowed that his sentiment concurred with Virginia's May 15, 1776 vote to declare Independence, that "they instructed us to give.

Clearly, Jefferson intended to follow the explicit instructions given by the Virginia convention on May 15, 1776. In this role he was a follower. Jefferson was not present in the Virginia convention when their vote to declare independence was unanimously adopted. He was not the originator of the Virginia motion to declare independence because he was en-route to Philadelphia at the time and did not learn of the instructions until May 26, 1776.

After July 4, 1776, Jefferson's emotionally charged efforts to be relieved continued. "By July 29, his pleas to go home were shrill." In a letter to Richard Henry Lee, he wrote, "For God's sake, for your country's sake and for my sake, come." Jefferson left Congress in September, 1776.

Jefferson could reflect that Richard Henry Lee's Resolution that "These United Colonies are...free and independent states..." was adopted, voted on, and passed unanimously by Congress on July 2, 1776. As of this date, England and the United States were separate countries.

In a letter to Abigail dated July 3, 1776, John Adams wrote, "yesterday, the greatest question was decided which ever was debated in America, and a greater, perhaps, never was not will be decided among men. A Resolution was passed without one dissenting colony "that these United Colonies are, and of right ought to be, free and independent States, and as such they have, and of right ought to have, full power to make war, conclude peace, establish commerce, and to do all other acts and things which other states may rightfully do."(*Letters of John and Abigail Adams*)

Look at the language. This was Richard Henry Lee's resolution of June 7, 1776.

These are the same words of the ending paragraph of the John Adams' copy of Thomas Paine's original Declaration of Independence.

"…and finally we do assert and declare these colonies to be free and independent states and that as free and independent states they have full power to levy war, conclude peace, contract alliances, establish commerce, and to do all other acts, and things which independent states may of right do." (Declaration of Independence)

Richard Henry Lee took these words from Thomas Paine's Declaration. Of course these ideas are all explicitly expressed in *Common Sense*.

When Jefferson was 77 years old, he wrote that he "turned to neither book or pamphlet while writing the Declaration". (Randall, p. 272) I don't think so. I think he copied it from Thomas Paine's original.

The Declaration was a universal notification document. It was an announcement, a publication proclaiming that the United States of America was its own sovereign country and 'we are open for business'. It was a "manifesto to all of the courts of the world", that our object was trade not war. It was a statement promulgating the innovative idea that America's government would be conducted by the people, all of the people without distinction and without a king. The actual act of secession and total independence was approved and passed unanimously by Congress on July 2, 1776.

Jefferson wrote that his task was "not to find out new principles or new arguments". He succeeded. The innovative principles and arguments were all contained in Thomas Paine's *Common Sense*, and Jefferson said that his task was, "to place before mankind the *Common Sense* of the subject." (p. 273)

As to new principles we find: equality of people as subject to the laws of nature; the powers of government come from consent of the people; the purpose of the government is to provide safety and security; a government that guarantees the rights of all so that each person can pursue his or her own happiness so long as the exercise of one's individual rights does not interfere with the rights of another; and the right to alter or abolish a destructive government.

As to the principle, the right to ALTER or ABOLISH a government, Jefferson never wrote anything like it. Moreover, he could not have authored such an idea. He would advocate changes in the laws, but until July of 1776, he would neither champion nor sanction the overthrow of an existing government and replace it with an entirely new system. No way! As mentioned before, two days after Jefferson arrived in Philadelphia, in the May 16, 1776 letter to Thomas Nelson, he wrote, "I suppose they will tell us what to say on the subject of Independence."

Thomas Paine had written: "A new area for politics is struck; a new method of thinking hath arisen."(*Common Sense*, p. 22) It should be noted that up to this time (May-June 1776), there is no evidence that Jefferson wrote anything about creating a Representative Republic or about Paine's *Common Sense*.

Jefferson's irresolute (none dare say wimpish) statement: "I suppose they will tell us what to say on the subject of Independence," indicates that he was not yet 'ripe' for 'falling off the stem' of Great Britain.

Referring again to Jefferson's famous paragraph in which he wrote that he "turned neither to book nor pamphlet", he also wrote, "Neither aiming at originality of principles or sentiment…" (Randall, p. 273) Nothing original? One would wonder if Jefferson was reading what he was copying. If the creation of the United States of America is not an original production, what is? The new country established on the North American continent was an original. The free and independent States of America was in innovation. The representative republic of America was original.

Jefferson did not have to aim at originality. That part was already accomplished. The wellspring of the innovative, the original ideas to create the United States of America came from the luminous mind of Thomas Paine. A key part of the originality was the principle of government of the people and by the people. This was not understood by Jefferson; nor was it understood by Washington, Adams and Hamilton. Government of, by and for the people was not understood in 1776 and it is not understood today, 2009.

After the "neither aiming at originality" clause, Jefferson wrote, "nor yet copied from any particular and previous writing …" Jefferson should have added OF MINE after the words "any particular and previous writing." Jefferson then wrote "it was intended to be an expression of the American mind." (p. 273) This is meaningless. The diversity of thought and opinion precluded the idea of a single American mind. Besides, there was no unity for Independence at that time.

- ✓ Loyalists were adamantly opposed to Independence.
- ✓ Many still held out hopes for reconciliation.
- ✓ Women could not vote.
- ✓ Slaves would fight for the side that promised them freedom.

In the interest of producing "something better", one man took upon himself the responsibility of speaking for all Americans. That man was Thomas Paine. What he said is contained in *Common Sense*, and his original Declaration of Independence is a distillation of *Common Sense* in cogent outline form.

During the deliberations on the Declaration, many cuts and changes were made. Throughout, Jefferson remained in character as a silent, passive auditor. Randall wrote that he was humiliated and disappointed by Congress's cuts. I don't know. Jefferson was not the real author of the Declaration. Besides, "he was determined to quit congress." (p. 279) He had no interest and no intention of staying in congress in order to assist with the war effort. Adams stayed and was elected as president of the 'Board of War and Ordinance'. (Adam's *Letters*, p. 188) Jefferson was relieved by Richard Henry Lee on September 3, 1776, according to Randall, and he arrived home on September 9, 1776.

As to the adopted version of the Declaration of Independence, Abigail Adams wrote: "I cannot but feel sorry that some of the most manly sentiments in the Declaration are expunged from the printed copy." The same quote of Abigail Adams appears on page 163 of Joseph Lewis' timeless opus. "Thomas Paine, Author of the Declaration of Independence." It's truly a book for all seasons and all ages. Thank you, 'Doctor Lewis'.

Jefferson sent a copy of the adopted Declaration to Richard Henry Lee. Lee's comment follows: "I sincerely wish, as well as for the honor of Congress, as for that of the States, that the manuscript had not been mangled as it is. It is wonderful and passing pitiful, that the rage of change should be so unhappily applied. However the thing is in its nature so good, that no cookery can spoil the Dish for the palate of Freemen."(Lewis, p. 157) Included in the mangling, was the elimination of the 'Slavery Clause'. Jefferson did not think that all men are born free and equal. Jefferson "never thought that women, Indians and freed slaves should be admitted to the same rights and privileges as other citizens." Gilbert Chinard (Lewis, p. 157)

-From The John Adams copy of the Declaration of Independence:

"We hold these truths to be self-evident, that all men are created equal and independent; that from that equal Creation they derive Rights inherent and unalienable; among which are the Preservation of Life and Liberty and the Pursuit of Happiness." Thomas Paine is the author of this sentence and the author of the United States of America.

-From the Preamble to the Constitution of Pennsylvania Declaration of Rights:

"That all men are born equally free and independent and have certain natural, inherent and unalienable rights, among which are, the enjoying and defending life and liberty, acquiring, possessing and protecting property and pursuing and obtaining happiness and safety." Thomas Jefferson was NOT the author of this sentence, and he is NOT the author of the Declaration of Independence.

I agree with all of the praise and credits bestowed on Thomas Jefferson that he deserves. But I do not believe he was a 'founding father'. He was a reluctant delegate to congress in 1776. He was assigned the task of drafting the Declaration of Independence from an original Declaration authored by and in the hand-writing of Thomas Paine.

Jefferson began his determined pleas to be relieved from congress a few days after he arrived in Philadelphia. On July 29, 1776, he wrote to Richard Henry Lee, "For God's sake, for your country's sake and for my sake, come...I pray you to come. I am under a sacred obligation to go home."(Randall, p. 282)

During his first four weeks (May 14th to June 13, 1776) Jefferson spent most of his time writing constitutions for Virginia. Thomas Paine's interest was continental while he was creating a representative Republic out of the United States.

Jefferson's main interest was the country of Virginia. In contrast, Thomas Paine wrote: "The sun never shone on a cause of greater worth. 'Tis not the affair of a city, a country, a province or a kingdom, but of a continent - of at least one eighth part of the habitable globe. 'Tis not the concern of a day, a year, or an age; posterity are virtually involved in the contest, and will be more or less affected even to the end of time, by the proceedings now." - *Common Sense*

Continent, posterity, to the end of time - pretty heady stuff. Thinking big seems to have come easy to Thomas Paine. After July 4th, 1776, Paine joined the revolutionary army. After September 3rd, Jefferson went home and I find little evidence that he did anything to advance the war effort. On the other hand, Thomas Paine started to write "The Crisis" after the sad retreat from New York. He then was the master-mind of the daring plan to attack TRENTON. In the face of heated opposition Paine persuaded Washington to carry the plan through to a glorious victory. Combined with the follow on success at Princeton, these victories gave the military operations component of the American Revolution an extended life.

Jefferson did not participate. Nor did he provide supplies from his plantations, from what I have read. During the last year of the war (circa June 1781), Jefferson was warned that Colonel Banastre Tarlton with 250 British dragoons was advancing on Monticello. Before fleeing, Jefferson took time to instruct his slaves what "silverware and other valuables to hide". The slaves "hid sacks of silver under the planks of the front porch floor."(p. 338)

Also, Cornwallis looted 'Elk Hill' Jefferson's best income producing plantation.

Jefferson described the event. "He destroyed all my growing crops of corn and tobacco. He burned all my barns containing the same articles from the last year, having first taken what corn he wanted. He used, as was to be expected, all my stock of cattle, sheep and hogs for the sustenance of his army", [Those sorely needed supplies and provisions would have been a godsend for General Washington's men, or better yet, a veritable blessing for the hard pressed troops of General Nathanael Greene who was the commander of the southern Continental Army] "and carried off all the horses capable of service. Of those "horses" too young for service, he cut the throat (sic); and he burned all the fences on the plantation, so as to leave it an absolute waste." (p. 339)

Randall recorded that Jefferson's losses amounted to $350,000, in 1993 dollars. Half of that amount would have made a splendid contribution to the Revolutionary war effort. The incident is a doleful piece of war-time irony. The result was a triple net loss.

One, an opportunity to render material aide to Washington was lost. Two, Jefferson sustained a large loss. Three, American provisions and supplies ended up aiding and abetting the enemy.

Jefferson rose through 'The chairs' (Governor, Ambassador, Secretary of State, Vice President) to become the third president of a new country, an established Representative Republic created by Thomas Paine. The high-point of Jefferson's presidency was the Louisiana Purchase. Thomas Paine was the first one to urge Jefferson to buy Louisiana. On Christmas Day (1802) Paine sent a letter, "a present" to Jefferson, recommending the purchase. He gave explicit advice as to how, when, why to do so, and even provided a formula to calculate an estimated offering price... American History books generally record the event but overlook the ideology. The message of the Louisiana Purchase is: Don't wage war to acquire land; get it the old fashioned way, buy it.

Later in life, Thomas Paine wrote, "The mere independence of America were it to have been followed by a system of government modeled after the corrupt system of English government, would not have interested me with the unabated ardour that it did."

"It was the cause of America that made me the author...The country appeared [to be] courting an impossible and an unnatural reconciliation... the only line that could cement and save her, a DECLARATION OF INDEPENDENCE, made it impossible for me, feeling as I did, to be silent.."(Lewis, p. 184)

In a letter to John W. Campbell, September 3, 1809, Jefferson, by his own admission, said that he could not claim authorship of the Declaration of Independence.

Regarding the Declaration of Independence, [the] report on the money unit of the United States, the Act of Religious Freedom, etc,

Jefferson wrote: "These having become the acts of public bodies, there an be no personal claim to them." (p. 288)

Thomas Paine gave many veiled indications that he was the creator of the United States and the true author of the Declaration. One example follows: In a letter dated February 10, 1806, to John Inskeep, the mayor of Philadelphia, Paine sharply criticized Inskeep for his "malevolent conduct' and "hypocrisy". Paine wrote, "he (Inskeep) must be some mushroom of modern growth that has started up on the soil which the generous services of Thomas Paine contributed to bless with freedom."(Conway, p. 305)

The Declaration of Independence was the first step in the creation of the United States of America. Thomas Paine was the independent innovator of the idea. He took on the task in the face of enormous opposition because no one else was up to the mark.

"My first endeavor was to put the politics right, and to show the advantages as well as the necessity of independence; and until this was done, independence never could have succeeded. America did not at that time understand her own situation; and though the country was then full of writers, no one reached the mark." (Foner, p. 186)

Thomas Jefferson did not and could not have written the "Declaration".

He never said I am the author of the Declaration of Independence. To my knowledge, none of the other four members - B Franklin, J. Adams, R. Livingston and R. Sherman - appointed by Congress to prepare a Declaration of Independence - ever wrote or claimed that Jefferson was the original and independent author of the 'Declaration of Independence.'

On Friday, June 28, 1776 the Declaration was submitted to Congress. According to Joseph Lewis, John Adams wrote that "the instrument was reported, I believe, in Jefferson's hand writing…"

No matter how it was submitted to Congress, the Declaration was the product of the mind and heart of Thomas Paine. To Thomas Paine alone belongs the honor and credit as the true author of the Declaration of Independence.

APPENDIX A

John Adams' Copy of Thomas Paine's Original
Declaration of Independence:
A Declaration by the Representatives of the
United States of America
in General Congress assembled

[ante 28 June 1776]

W hen in the Course of human Events it becomes necessary for a People to advance from that Subordination, in which they have hitherto remained and to assume among the Powers of the Earth, the equal and independent Station to which the Laws of Nature and of Natures God entitle them, a decent Respect to the Opinions of Mankind requires that they Should declare the Causes, which impell them to the Change.

We hold these Truths to be self evident; that all Men are created equal and independent; that from that equal Creation they derive Rights inherent and unalienable; among which are the Preservation of Life, and Liberty, and the Pursuit of Happiness; that to Secure these Ends, Governments are instituted among Men, deriving their just Powers from the Consent of the governed; that whenever, any form of Government, Shall become destructive of these Ends, it is the Right of the People to alter, or to abolish it, and to institute new Government, laying its Foundation on such Principles, and organizing its Powers in Such Form, as to them Shall Seem most likely to effect their Safety and Happiness. Prudence indeed will dictate that Governments long established Should not be changed for light and transient Causes:

and accordingly all Experience hath Shewn, that Mankind are more disposed to Suffer, while Evils are Sufferable, than to right themselves, by abolishing the Forms to which they are accustomed. But when a long Train of Abuses and Usurpations, begun at a distinguish'd Period, and pursuing invariably, the Same Object, evinces a Design to reduce them under absolute Power, it is their Right, it is their Duty, to throw off Such Government, and to provide new Guards for their future Security. Such has been the patient Sufferance of these Colonies; and Such is now the Necessity, which constrains them to expunge their former Systems of Government. The History of his present Majesty, is a History, of unremitting Injuries and Usurpations, among which no one Fact Stands Single or Solitary to contradict the Uniform Tenor of the rest, all of which have in direct Object, the Establishment of an absolute Tyranny over these States. To prove this, let Facts be Submitted to a candid World, for the Truth of which We pledge a Faith, as yet unsullied by Falshood.

He has refused his Assent to Laws, the most wholesome and necessary for the public Good.

He has forbidden his Governors to pass Laws of immediate and pressing Importance, unless suspended in their Operation, till his Assent Should be obtained; and when So suspended he has neglected utterly to attend to them.

He has refused to pass other Laws for the Accommodation of large Districts of People, unless those People would relinquish the Right of Representation in the Legislature, a Right inestimable to them, and formidable to Tyrants only.

He has dissolved Representative Houses, repeatedly, and continually, for opposing with manly Firmness his Invasions, on the Rights of the People.

He has refused, for a long Space of Time after Such Dissolutions, to cause others to be elected, whereby the legislative Powers, incapable of Annihilation, have returned to the People at large for their Exercise, the State remaining in the mean Time, exposed to all the Dangers of Invasion, from without, and Convulsions within-

He has endeavoured to prevent the Population of these States; for that purpose obstructing the Laws for naturalization of foreigners; refusing to pass others to encourage their Migrations hither; and raising the Conditions of new Appropriations of Lands.

He has Suffered the Administration of Justice totally to cease in some of these Colonies, refusing his Assent to Laws for establishing judiciary Powers.

He has made our Judges dependent on his Will alone, for the Tenure of their Offices, and amount of their Salaries:

He has created a Multitude of new Offices by a Self-assumed Power, and sent hither swarms of Officers to harrass our People and eat out their Substance.

He has kept among us, in Times of Peace, Standing Armies and Ships of War. He has affected to render the military, independent of, and Superiour to, the Civil Power:

He has combined with others to subject Us to a Jurisdiction foreign to our Constitution and unacknowledged by our Laws; giving his Assent to their pretended Act of Legislation; for quartering large Bodies of armed Troops among Us; for protecting them by a Mock Tryal from Punishment for any Murders they should commit on the Inhabitants of these States; for cutting off our Trade with all Parts of the World; for imposing Taxes on us without our Consent; for depriving us of the Benefits of Trial by Jury; for transporting us beyond Seas to be tried for pretended Offences: for taking away our Charters, and altering fundamentally the Forms of our Governments; for suspending our own Legislatures and declaring themselves invested with Power to legislate for US in all Cases Whatsoever.

He has abdicated Government here, withdrawing his Governors, and declaring us, out of his Allegiance and Protection.

He has plundered our Seas, ravaged our Coasts, burnt our Towns, and destroyed the Lives of our People.

He is at this Time transporting large Armies of foreign Mercenaries to compleat the Works of death, Desolation, and Tyranny, already begun with Circumstances of Cruelty and Perfidy unworthy the Head of a civilized Nation.

He has endeavoured to bring on the Inhabitants of our Frontiers, the merciless Indian Savages, whose known Rule of Warfare is an undistinguished Destruction of all Ages, Sexes, and Conditions of Existence.

He has incited treasonable Insurrections of our Fellow Citizens, with the Allurement of Forfeiture and Confiscation of our Property.

He has waged cruel War against human Nature itself, violating its most Sacred Rights of Life and Liberty in the Persons of a distant People who never offended him, captivating and carrying them into Slavery in another Hemisphere, or to incur miserable Death, in their Transportation thither. This piratical Warfare, the opprobrium of infidel Powers, is the Warfare of the Christian King of Great Britain.

He has prostituted his Negative for Suppressing every legislative Attempt to prohibit or to restrain an execrable Commerce, determined to keep open a Markett where Men Should be bought and Sold, and that this Assemblage of Horrors might Want no Fact of distinguished Die

He is now exciting those very People to rise in Arms among US, and to purchase that Liberty of which he has deprived them, by murdering the People upon whom he also obtruded them: thus paying off, former Crimes committed against the Liberties of one People, with Crimes which he urges them to commit against the Lives of another.

In every Stage of these Oppressions we have petitioned for redress, in the most humble Terms; our repeated Petitions have been answered by repeated Injury. A Prince, whose Character is thus marked by every Act which may define a Tyrant, is unfit to be the Ruler of a People who mean to be free. Future Ages will Scarce believe, that the Hardiness of one Man, adventured, within the Short Compass of twelve years only, on So many Acts of Tyranny, without a Mask, over a People, fostered and fixed in the Principles of Liberty.

Nor have we been wanting in Attentions to our British Brethren. We have warned them from Time to Time of attempts of their Legislature, to extend a Jurisdiction over these our States. We have reminded them of the Circumstances of our Emigration and Settlement here, no one of which could warrant So Strange a Pretension. That these were effected at the Expence of our own Blood and Treasure, unassisted by the Wealth or the Strength of Great Britain: that in constituting indeed, our Several Forms of Government, We had adopted one common King, thereby laying a Foundation for perpetual League and Amity with them: but that Submission to their Parliament, was no Part of our Constitution, nor ever in Idea, if History may be credited: and We appealed to their Native Justice and Magnanimity, as well as to the Ties of our common Kindred to disavow these Usurpations, which were likely to interrupt our Correspondence and Connection. They too have been deaf to the Voice of Justice and of Consanguinity, and when Occasions have been given them by the regular Course of their Laws of removing from their Councils, the Disturbers of our Harmony, they have by their free Election, reestablished them in Power. A[t] this very Time too, they are permitting their Chief Magistrate to send over not only Soldiers of our common Blood, but Scotch and foreign Mercenaries, to invade and deluge Us in Blood. These Facts have given the last Stab to agonizing Affection, and manly Spirit bids us to renounce forever these unfeeling Brethren. We must endeavour to forget our former Love for them, and to hold them, as we hold the rest of Mankind Enemies in War, in Peace Friends. We might have been a free and a great People together; but a Communication of Grandeur and of Freedom it seems is below their Dignity. Be it So, Since they will have it: The Road to Happiness and to Glory is open to Us too; We will climb it, apart from them, and acquiesce in the Necessity which denounces our eternal Seperation!

We therefore the Representatives of the united States of America in General Congress assembled, do, in the Name, and by the Authority of the good People of these States, reject and renounce all Allegiance and subjection to the Kings of Great Britain, and all others, who may hereafter claim by, through, or under them; We utterly dissolve and break off all political Connection which may have heretofore Subsisted between Us and the People or [Parliament] of Great Britain, and finally We do assert and declare these Colonies to be free and independent States, and that as free and independant States they shall hereafter have Power to levy War, conclude Peace, contract Alliances, establish Commerce, and to do all other Acts and Things which independent States may of Right do. And for the Support of this Declaration, We mutually pledge to each other our Lives, our Fortunes, and our Sacred Honour.

The unanimous Declaration of the thirteen united States of America,

When in the Course of human events, it becomes necessary for one people to dissolve the political bands which have connected them with another, and to assume among the powers of the earth, the separate and equal station to which the Laws of Nature and of Nature's God entitle them, a decent respect to the opinions of mankind requires that they should declare the causes which impel them to the separation.

We hold these truths to be self-evident, that all men are created equal, that they are endowed by their Creator with certain unalienable Rights, that among these are Life, Liberty and the pursuit of Happiness.--That to secure these rights, Governments are instituted among Men, deriving their just powers from the consent of the governed, --That whenever any Form of Government becomes destructive of these ends, it is the Right of the People to alter or to abolish it, and to institute new Government, laying its foundation on such principles and organizing its powers in such form, as to them shall seem most likely to effect their Safety and Happiness. Prudence, indeed, will dictate that Governments long established should not be changed for light and transient causes; and accordingly all experience hath shewn, that mankind are more disposed to suffer, while evils are sufferable, than to right themselves by abolishing the forms to which they are accustomed. But when a long train of abuses and usurpations, pursuing invariably the same Object evinces a design to reduce them under absolute Despotism, it is their right, it is their duty, to throw off such Government, and to provide new

Guards for their future security.--Such has been the patient sufferance of these Colonies; and such is now the necessity which constrains them to alter their former Systems of Government. The history of the present King of Great Britain is a history of repeated injuries and usurpations, all having in direct object the establishment of an absolute Tyranny over these States. To prove this, let Facts be submitted to a candid world.

He has refused his Assent to Laws, the most wholesome and necessary for the public good.

He has forbidden his Governors to pass Laws of immediate and pressing importance, unless suspended in their operation till his Assent should be obtained; and when so suspended, he has utterly neglected to attend to them. He has refused to pass other Laws for the accommodation of large districts of people, unless those people would relinquish the right of Representation in the Legislature, a right inestimable to them and formidable to tyrants only. He has called together legislative bodies at places unusual, uncomfortable, and distant from the depository of their public Records, for the sole purpose of fatiguing them into compliance with his measures. He has dissolved Representative Houses repeatedly, for opposing with manly firmness his invasions on the rights of the people. He has refused for a long time, after such dissolutions, to cause others to be elected; whereby the Legislative powers, incapable of Annihilation, have returned to the People at large for their exercise; the State remaining in the mean time exposed to all the dangers of invasion from without, and convulsions within.

He has endeavoured to prevent the population of these States; for that purpose obstructing the Laws for Naturalization of Foreigners; refusing to pass others to encourage their migrations hither, and raising the conditions of new Appropriations of Lands.

He has obstructed the Administration of Justice, by refusing his Assent to Laws for establishing Judiciary powers.

He has made Judges dependent on his Will alone, for the tenure of their offices, and the amount and payment of their salaries.

He has erected a multitude of New Offices, and sent hither swarms of Officers to harrass our people, and eat out their substance.

He has kept among us, in times of peace, Standing Armies without the Consent of our legislatures.

He has affected to render the Military independent of and superior to the Civil power.

He has combined with others to subject us to a jurisdiction foreign to our constitution, and unacknowledged by our laws; giving his Assent to their Acts of pretended Legislation:

For Quartering large bodies of armed troops among us:

For protecting them, by a mock Trial, from punishment for any Murders which they should commit on the Inhabitants of these States:

For cutting off our Trade with all parts of the world:

For imposing Taxes on us without our Consent:

For depriving us in many cases, of the benefits of Trial by Jury:

For transporting us beyond Seas to be tried for pretended offences

For abolishing the free System of English Laws in a neighbouring Province, establishing therein an Arbitrary government, and enlarging its Boundaries so as to render it at once an example and fit instrument for introducing the same absolute rule into these Colonies:

For taking away our Charters, abolishing our most valuable Laws, and altering fundamentally the Forms of our Governments:

For suspending our own Legislatures, and declaring themselves invested with power to legislate for us in all cases whatsoever.

He has abdicated Government here, by declaring us out of his Protection and waging War against us.

He has plundered our seas, ravaged our Coasts, burnt our towns, and destroyed the lives of our people.

He is at this time transporting large Armies of foreign Mercenaries to compleat the works of death, desolation and tyranny, already begun with circumstances of Cruelty & perfidy scarcely paralleled in the most barbarous ages, and totally unworthy the Head of a civilized nation.

He has constrained our fellow Citizens taken Captive on the high Seas to bear Arms against their Country, to become the executioners of their friends and Brethren, or to fall themselves by their Hands.

He has excited domestic insurrections amongst us, and has endeavoured to bring on the inhabitants of our frontiers, the merciless Indian Savages, whose known rule of warfare, is an undistinguished destruction of all ages, sexes and conditions.

In every stage of these Oppressions We have Petitioned for Redress in the most humble terms: Our repeated Petitions have been answered only by repeated injury. A Prince whose character is thus marked by every act which may define a Tyrant, is unfit to be the ruler of a free people.

Nor have We been wanting in attentions to our Brittish brethren. We have warned them from time to time of attempts by their legislature to extend an unwarrantable jurisdiction over us. We have reminded them of the circumstances of our emigration and settlement here. We have appealed to their native justice and magnanimity, and we have conjured them by the ties of our common kindred to disavow these usurpations, which, would inevitably interrupt our connections and correspondence. They too have been deaf to the voice of justice and of consanguinity. We must, therefore, acquiesce in the necessity, which denounces our Separation, and hold them, as we hold the rest of mankind, Enemies in War, in Peace Friends.

We, therefore, the Representatives of the united States of America, in General Congress, Assembled, appealing to the Supreme Judge of the world for the rectitude of our intentions, do, in the Name, and by Authority of the good People of these Colonies, solemnly publish and declare, That these United Colonies are, and of Right ought to be Free and Independent States; that they are Absolved from all Allegiance to the British Crown, and that all political connection between them and the State of Great Britain, is and ought to be totally dissolved; and that as Free and Independent States, they have full Power to levy

War, conclude Peace, contract Alliances, establish Commerce, and to do all other Acts and Things which Independent States may of right do. And for the support of this Declaration, with a firm reliance on the protection of divine Providence, we mutually pledge to each other our Lives, our Fortunes and our sacred Honor.

BIBLIOGRAPHY

Adams, John and Abigail. <u>The letters of John and Abigail Adams.</u> Introduction and notes by Frank Shuffelton. New York: Penguin Books, 2004.

Adkins, Nelson F. <u>Thomas Paine, Common Sense and Other Political Writings</u>. New York: The Liberal Arts Press, Oskar Piest, General Editor, 1953.

Aldridge, Alfred Owen. <u>Man of Reason</u>. London: The Cresset Press. 1960.

Best, Mary Agnes. <u>Thomas Paine, Prophet and Martyr of Democracy</u>. New York: Harcourt, Brace and Company, 1927.

Caroli, Betty Boyd. <u>First Ladies</u>. New York: Oxford University Press, Inc., 1987.

Chervow, Ron. <u>Alexander Hamilton</u>. New York: Penguin Press, 2004.

Collins, Paul. <u>The Trouble with Tom</u>. New York: Bloomsbury Publishing, 2006.

Conway, Moncure Daniel. <u>The Life Of Thomas Paine</u>. New York: Benjamin Blom, Inc. 1976 ed. (Published specially for the Free Enterprise Institute, 1976)

Cunliffe, Marcus. <u>George Washington, Man and Monument</u>. New York: The New American Library, Inc., 1958.

Dershowitz, Alan. <u>America Declares Independence</u>. New Jersey: John Wiley & Sons, Inc, 2003.

Fast, Howard. <u>Citizen Tom Paine</u>. New York: The Blue Heron Press, 1953.

Foner, Phillip S., PhD. <u>The Complete Writings of Thomas Paine</u>. New York: Citadel Press, 1969.

Galambos, Andrew J. Thrust for Freedom. Peter N. Sisco, Editor. San
    Diego: The Universal Scientific Publications Company, Inc., 1999.
Garraty, John A. The American Nation, Volume I. 5th edition. New
    York: Harper & Row, 1983.
Grafton, John. The American Revolution. New York: Dover
    Publications, Inc., 1975.
Hazelton, John H. The Declaration of Independence, Its History.
    A Da Capo Press Reprint Edition. New York: Dodd, Mead and
    Company, 1906.
Hitchens, Christopher. Thomas Paine's Rights of Man. New York:
    Atlantic Monthly Press, 2006.
Kaye, Harvey J. Thomas Paine and the Promise of America. New
    York: Hill and Wang, 2005.
Keane, John. Tom Paine, A Political Life. New York, Toronto and
    London: Little, Brown and Company, 1995.
Levin, Benjamin H. To Spit Against the Wind, A Novel. New York:
    The Citadel Press, 1970.
Lewis, Joseph. Thomas Paine, Author of the Declaration of
    Independence. New York: Freethought Press Association, 1947.
Liell, Scott. 46 Pages. Philadelphia: Running Press Book Publishers,
    2003.
McCullough, David, John Adams. New York: Simon & Schuster, 2001.
McCullough, David. 1776. New York: Simon & Schuster paperback
    ed, 2006.
Nash, Gary. Jeffrey, Julie Roy. Howe, John. Davis, Allen. The
    American People, Volume I. third ed. New York: Harper Collins
    College Publishers, 1994.
Nelson, Craig. Thomas Paine, Enlightenment, Revolution, and the
    Birth of Modern Nations. New York: Viking Penguin, 2006.
Paine, Thomas. The Age of Reason. Biographical Introduction
    by Philip S. Foner. New York: Citadel Press, Kensington
    Publishington Corp., 1988 ed.

Paine, Thomas. <u>Common Sense</u>. New York: Barnes & Noble Books, 1995.

Paine, Thomas. <u>Common Sense and The Crisis</u>. Garden City: Anchor Books,

Anchor Press-Doubleday, 1973.

Paine, Thomas. <u>The Centenary Memorial Edition of the Life and Writings of Thomas Paine</u>. Edited and Annotated by Daniel Edwin Wheeler. New York: Vincent Parke and Company, 1915.

Paine, Thomas. <u>In Search of the Common Good; Proceedings of a Colloquium* Held at the United Nations on December 10, 1987 in New York</u>. Edited by Joyce Chumbley and Leo Zonneveld. Nottingham, England: Spokesman Books, Rusell House, 2009. (*References in the text to this powerful work will be indicated by the single word, "Colloquium")

Passos, John Dos. <u>The Essential Thomas Paine</u>. Mineola, N.Y: Dover Publication, Inc, 2008.

Randall, Willard Sterne. <u>Thomas Jefferson, A Life</u>. Henry Holt & Co, 1993.

Roberts, Cokie. <u>Founding Mothers</u>. New York: Harper Collins Publishers, Inc, 2004.

Todd, Lewis Paul. Curti, Merle. <u>Rise of the American Nation</u>. Heritage Edition. New York: Harcourt Brace Jovanovick, 1977.

Van der Weyde, William. <u>The Life and Works of Thomas Paine</u>. Patriot Edition, Edited by William M. Van der Weyde, Introduction by Thomas Edison. New Rochelle, N.Y.: Thomas Paine National Historical Association, 1925.

Van Doren, Carl. <u>Secret History of the American Revolution</u>. New York: The Viking Press, 1941.

Woodward, William. <u>Tom Paine: America's Godfather</u>. New York: E. P.Dutton & Co., 1945. Reprint: Westport, CT, Greenwood Press, 1972.